WORLD WARSHIPS IN REVIEW 1860-1906

OSCAR II, SWEDISH ARMOURED COAST DEFENCE SHIP, 1907

WORLD WARSHIPS IN REVIEW 1860/1906

John Leather

With photographs by Beken of Cowes

MACDONALD AND JANE'S · LONDON

First published in 1976
by Macdonald and Jane's
(Macdonald & Co. (Publishers) Ltd)
Paulton House, 8 Shepherdess Walk
London N1 7LW
Printed in Great Britain by
REDWOOD BURN LIMITED
Trowbridge & Esher

ISBN 0 356 08076 5

CONTENTS

INTRODUCTION

The half-century spanned by the ships in this book saw the beginning of an ever quickening tempo in the design, construction, propulsion, armament and protection of fighting ships, which continues today in this age of gas turbines and rocket missiles. Now navies are accustomed to radical change, but it was only in 1860 that the ironclad, steam-propelled seagoing warship became reality, first emerging in France after centuries of wooden-hulled sailing predecessors. Although armoured, these new ships retained broadside-mounted guns firing through ports, and most were fully rigged, whether they could sail or not – a safeguard considered necessary when ocean-going marine engines were still regarded as unreliable, coal consumption was high and bunkering facilities far apart or non-existent in distant seas.

During the following thirty years wild experiments were made in warship design; instead of the size, armament and rig of warships being subject to gradual development, many were outclassed almost before the keel was laid. Improvements in guns, armour, size, engines and speed went forward so quickly, with each development interacting on the rest of the design, and all navies equally ignorant of the best design for a warship with particular duties, that major fleets became a curious collection of widely differing types. Eventually definite types emerged, but the rapid development continued.

Fascinating photographs of this period of greatest naval change were caught by the camera of Beken of Cowes, the internationally renowned family of marine photographers, and from their treasury of warship negatives I have selected one hundred and thirty-three of the best, illustrating ships of typical or special interest. Each ship portrait is hitherto unpublished and most have great clarity of detail. Ships of contemporary types in different navies are contrasted: battleships, armoured cruisers, protected cruisers, unarmoured ships, shallow-draught coast defence ships, sloops, torpedo boats, destroyers, torpedo gunboats, training ships and other craft. In a work of this size the general text serves only as an outline of a very complex period but the characteristics and careers of the selected ships are examined in detail.

My thanks are due to Tony Sutherland, a fellow ship surveyor, and to John Freestone, another colleague at Lloyd's Register of Shipping, who both helped with some difficult research, and to Kenneth Beken and his staff for willing help when selecting the photographs.

John Leather
Cowes, 1975

BATTLESHIPS I

The steam-propelled battleship succeeded the wooden sailing ship of the line as the principal force determining command of the sea. During the period 1860-1906, covered by this book, they underwent enormous changes and development, not only to counter improved guns and armour in ships of other fleets, but to overcome the increasing menace of torpedoes, torpedo boats and then the submarine. The principal powers owning battleships during this time were first France and Britain, with Russia, Italy and Austria closely following; then Germany, and finally America and Japan. Some other smaller nations could also boast of a battleship or two, sometimes of considerable power and sophistication, but never in quantity.

The era of heavily armoured warships dated from 1860 until 1945, and their dominance was effectively determined by the evolution of the "great gun", until aircraft and rocket power eclipsed them. But at the time the nations which owned the most of these sea mammoths ruled the seas, and throughout this period it was unquestionably Britain.

The gun-armed sailing warship had been developing since the fifteenth century, and had reached near perfection by the mid-nineteenth, when ships of the line were slightly larger and more heavily armed than those at Trafalgar *(Plate 1)* but still carried smooth-bore guns on one, two or three decks of wooden hulls. Warships of different nations varied little in construction, form, rig or armament, so that superiority of seamanship was all-important. Steam marine engines and the rifled shell gun were to change all that, but it was the screw propeller which really started the naval revolution.

Although steam paddle frigates were built for many navies, this system of propulsion was too cumbersome and vulnerable to be used in battleships. Trials with screw-propelled craft against paddle finally convinced the British Admiralty, and the screw frigate *Dauntless* was laid down in 1844 after the frigate *Amphion* had been converted with an auxiliary steam engine and propeller.

In 1850 the French 92-gun, wooden ship of the line *Napoléon* was completed as an auxiliary screw steamer, capable of 13¾ knots. The following year the British *Sanspareil* was similarly converted and in 1852 the two-decker *Agamemnon* was designed and built as an auxiliary. By 1858 thirty-two British wooden ships of the line had been built or converted with auxiliary steam engines and single screws and the French had the same number. The long-standing superiority of numbers of Britain's battle fleet had gone.

During 1858 four frigates were commenced for the French Navy. These were wooden ships but were designed with shell-resisting iron plates bolted on to the hull planking. These were the first ironclad seagoing battleships, intended to outclass the huge British fleet of auxiliary ships of the line and be capable of resisting the rifled shell-firing guns which were mounted in the major ships of most sizeable fleets. The effectiveness of these shells had been proved in 1853 when a squadron of six Russian ships of the line attacked ten Turkish frigates and corvettes in the Bay of Sinope. The Russian ships approached to within 500 yards through a storm of round shot from the Turkish ships and shore batteries and sank the whole fleet with shells.

During the bombardment of Kinburn, in the Crimean war, French floating batteries armoured with 4-inch iron plates were surprisingly successful in close bombardment of shore batteries, which failed to pierce their armour.

By 1857 French experiments with rifled shell-guns convinced them that only ships with thick iron armour outside their wood hulls would withstand these weapons. The large programme of wooden warship building was suspended while a design for a single screw, wooden-hulled armoured steam frigate was prepared by the leading French naval architect Dupuy de Lôme. He produced a 252ft ship with thirty-four broadside-mounted guns and the sides sheathed with 4½-inch thick iron armour from just below the waterline to the sheer. In March 1858 work on the *Gloire* and her sister ships *Invincible*, *Normandie* and the iron-hulled *Couronne* commenced. The speed was to be 13 knots and a three-masted barquentine rig was carried. Use of wooden hulls enabled them to be built quickly from available materials and labour.

In Britain, gun development and testing of armour had produced similar results and conclusions, but the Admiralty did not wish to start construction of any radical ships that might prejudice the country's immense lead in highly developed wooden sailing and auxiliary warships.

In May 1858 the Admiralty heard of the building of the new French armoured frigates and it became imperative to match them. However, in 1859 wooden-hulled steam battleships were still building in Britain, armed with 68-pounder shell guns having an effective range of about 1,200 yards. These ships were inferior to the first class steam frigates built during the previous five years for the British, American and French navies, which were heavily armed with long-range guns, and in addition had the speed and manoeuvrability of attack to suit the armament. If such ships could be armoured it would be decisive in a short-range action.

Thus the steam frigate carrying a broadside armament on one deck was the logical type for the first British "ironclad", which was commenced to Admiralty design in May 1859: 380ft long by 58ft beam, 8,600 tons displacement and capable of 14 knots with 5,000 IHP on one screw. The best feature of the design was the all-iron hull, far superior to the French ironclads, and armoured with 4½-inch thick iron amidships. She had a full ship rig and two stumpy funnels, was launched as the *Warrior* in December 1860 and commissioned in October 1861 as Britain's first seagoing armoured warship, followed in 1862 by the sister ship *Black Prince*. Both mounted twenty-six 68-pounders, ten 110-pounders and four 70-pounders – the two latter being breech loading. All guns were on one deck. 850 tons of coal were carried and a crew of 707 men. The ships were graceful in appearance, with a clipper bow, and were the pride of the Channel fleet for several years.

The *Gloire* was launched in November 1859 but did not complete until November 1860. Her successful trials caused ten more ironclads to be ordered for the French fleet, and the battleship race had begun. Other battleships, quickly termed "ironclads," followed, and the rival nations of Austria and Italy laid down similar ships in 1861. Russia ordered a 3,300-ton ironclad from the *Warrior*'s builders on the Thames and Turkey ordered three 6,400-tonners in England; while Spain commenced a 6,200-ton battleship.

The Admiralty quickly ordered more of the new ship type. The 280ft long *Defence* and *Resistance* were completed in 1861-2, then the similar *Hector* and *Valiant* in 1864 and 1868. They were barque-rigged ships with the guns on two decks, and had reverted to muzzle loading, which was preferred by the gunmakers at Woolwich Arsenal.

The 380ft long ironclad *Achilles* of 1864 was distinctive in having four masts and setting the greatest sail area of any British warship: 30,100sq ft. By then a squadron of ironclads maneouvring in the Channel was a common sight, though most were clumsy under canvas.

All these ships carried the guns as a broadside battery behind a belt of armour which varied in length. The idea of mounting one or two large guns in a revolving turret on a ship's deck was not new, and in the mid-nineteenth century was advocated energetically in Britain by a Captain Coles, among others. It was successfully demonstrated in the design of the American shoal draught iron steamer *Monitor*, and her many successors, during the civil war of 1861-5. Most of these ships were designed by John Ericsson, a Swede, though the Danish turret ship *Rolf Krake* and the Italian *Affondatore* were both designed and built in England before 1863, and other turret ironclads were building for Russia, Spain, Turkey and elsewhere. In the ironclad era which France had initiated, Britain was to have a tremendous advantage with her great and developing sources of industry which France could not match, so the British battle fleet increased from equal numbers in 1861 to superiority in numbers and construction after a decade, and thereafter maintained an increasing lead on France – regarded as her closest and likeliest enemy at the time.

In the early 1860's pressure of ironclad building was so great that Britain commenced several wooden-hulled armoured ships in the Royal dockyards: the *Royal Oak* of 1863 and the *Prince Consort, Caledonia* and *Ocean* of 1864-6.

In 1861 three large iron-built ironclads were ordered, the *Minotaur (Plate 2)*, *Agincourt* and *Northumberland* – 400ft long, single-screw ships displacing 10,700 tons. 9- and 7-inch muzzle-loading rifled guns were carried broadside on two decks and the most striking feature was a five-masted rig.

Until the 1880's, designers of warships for ocean-going fleets were compelled to create steam-driven armoured ships with full sailing rigs to placate naval officers and administrations who were suspicious of machinery breakdown. Britain was particularly conscious of her world role as patroller and peacekeeper, which meant that most major warships had to be capable of operating anywhere in the world, often well away from coal supplies. Therefore sail lingered on in ships of the 1860's and 70's and sail drill was at least as important as gun drill, while the engineering branch of the fleet was regarded by many officers, as a very secondary part of the service grown complacent with tradition and lack of major action.

So the broadside muzzle-loading guns and elaborate rig of the *Minotaur* must be seen against the prevailing strong prejudices and sense of radical change in naval ways which was as confusing to the British Navy as to most others. For thirty years major fleets were to be motley collections of specimens or experimental types of individual ships, often inefficient and always increasingly expensive, making the operation of battle fleets difficult because of differing ship characteristics – speeds and gunpower varying in particular. Naval estimates became a nightmare to many governments and politicians constantly sought to limit spending on new ships, but until 1914 the British fleet usually got what it needed, however grudgingly, as the government knew it was the best assurance of future peace of many countries.

The proving of seagoing ironclads occurred in the Adriatic where, in the war of 1866, the fleets of Italy and Austria met off the island of Lissa. Each side had ironclads directly derived from the *Gloire*, several almost new, and the Italians had the new turret ship *Affondatore*. As this was the first full fleet action to occur with the new type of warship it attracted considerable interest and some wrong conclusions which affected battleship design for some years. It was as much a clash of leadership and training as of material strength, with the Austrians under Admiral Tegetthoff having the best of it although the Italians, under Admiral Count Persano had two hundred rifled guns against the Austrian's seventy-four smaller pieces. During the action Tegetthoff's flagship, the ironclad *Ferdinand Max*, rammed and sank the Italian ironclad *Re d'Italia*. The small warship *Palestro* was also sunk but although the Austrian ironclads fired 1,386 shots, besides extensive firing by their unarmoured ships, Italian casualties, apart from those lost in the ships sunk, were only eight killed and forty wounded. The Italian fleet fired at least 1,400 shells but the Austrians had only three killed and thirty wounded in the ironclad ships. This vindicated iron armour as seagoing protection, and the successful ramming of the *Re d'Italia* confirmed a branch of naval thought convinced that future sea battles would be decided by the ram bow reinforced by heavy gunfire.

For a few years the armoured ship remained proof against gunfire until gun development caught up, and a leapfrogging contest began between gun designers and armour makers, which continued until the 1940's when battleship building ended.

Amongst the many British armoured ships ordered in the flurry of battleship building in 1861 was the ironclad *Research*, first to carry a few large guns in an amidship armoured "box battery" or "central battery" across the ship, arranged with ports to allow her 100-pounders to fire broadside, ahead or astern by recesses in the topsides. The *Research* was only 195ft long but was quickly followed by the similar and larger ships *Enterprise*, *Favorite*, *Pallas*, *Penelope* and *Hercules*, all fully rigged. Broadside ironclads such as the *Lord Warden*, *Lord Clyde*, *Bellerophon*, *Zealous*, *Royal Alfred* and *Repulse* continued to be built until 1870, and advocates of the turret principle pressed for a trial in a first class British battleship. However the Admiralty would only agree to turrets being fitted in low freeboard, unrigged coast defence ships and the first, the iron-hulled, armoured *Prince Albert*, was started in 1862 to carry four guns in single centreline turrets with low freeboard to maintain the centre of gravity as low as possible, a minimum of deck erections with a flying bridge over, and a short funnel – features common to many other ships of the coast defence type built for the British and other fleets.

Before the *Prince Albert* was completed the 131-gun, three-decked wooden ship of the line *Royal Sovereign* was cut down to a low freeboard ship with side armour and four circular turrets; the forward one having two 10½-inch guns and the three others single guns. Three light masts and a huge funnel made her the ugliest battleship ever built.

Many other small British turret ships followed: the *Scorpion* and *Wivern* of 1865, the mastless *Cerberus*, *Magdala* and *Abyssinia* for colonial service in India and Australia, the *Glatton*, the turret coast defence ram ships *Rupert* and *Hotspur* and the later *Cyclops*, *Gorgon*, *Hecate* and *Hydra*.

Persistent turret enthusiasts persuaded the Admiralty to order the seagoing turret ship *Monarch* in 1866, and this 330-footer was launched three years later with two turrets mounting four 12-inch muzzle-loading guns placed amidships above a low freeboard hull with a full length armour belt and a ship rig towering over her short funnel and flying bridges. She was a surprisingly successful ship but would have been improved if completed unrigged as originally designed. A similar low-freeboard turret ship was started in 1867 and was completed in 1870 as the *Captain*. She was heavily rigged for ocean service and passed trials successfully, although floating below designed waterline due to considerably increased construction weight. When only a few months old, on the night of 6th September 1870, the *Captain* was on passage through the Bay of Biscay with the Channel fleet, under reefed sail in a gale, when a severe squall capsized her with the loss of four hundred and seventy three officers and men; a disastrous end to an experimental ship, which dismayed the British public and checked turret ship development for several years.

Meanwhile the French were steadily building a fleet of armoured ships with generous freeboard and full sailing rigs. By 1869 Britain had twenty-nine armoured ships of which about eight were similar. France had twenty-six of eight similar types, several of which were being sent to foreign stations, leading to second class battleships being built by Britain to counter this threat to her colonies and trade routes. The 280ft *Audacious*, *Swiftsure* and *Triumph* were built with an amidship battery and came out during 1870-1 fully rigged, and the 9,270-ton first class rigged ironclad *Sultan* of 1871 had similar gun arrangements. After several years of reversion to muzzle-loading guns an attempt was made to reintroduce breech-loading in the British fleet but this failed from conservatism as did the attempts of naval constructors to abolish the sailing rig of new battleship construction for sea work.

However, during 1869 Edward Reed, a brilliant British naval constructor, directed design of the mastless turret ships *Devastation* and *Thunderer* – prototypes for the typical battleship at the end of the nineteenth century. The 285ft long *Devastation (Plate 3)* was well armed with four 35-ton guns in two round turrets, forward and aft of an amidship superstructure with bridge, funnels and mast. She had no secondary armament, was adequately armoured, and steamed at about 14 knots with twin screws which gave reliability and better manoeuvring than the earlier single screw ironclads. She was a type suited to action in European waters and the Mediterranean. While her armour was proof against almost all contemporary shells, her guns could pierce any other ship's armour, and 1,800 tons of bunker coal gave her wide radius of action.

There was limited opposition to the *Devastation*'s low freeboard design when she was started in 1869, but the tragic loss of the low freeboard turret ship *Captain* caused serious questioning of her design although she had sufficient stability. Reed resigned and was replaced by Nathaniel Barnaby, and the *Devastation*'s trials were held in an atmosphere of cynical pessimisim. However, they were wholly successful. She proved herself a truly revolutionary sea-going battleship and confirmed Britain's lead in battleship design. The same year the French commenced construction of the "Colbert" class, battery or barbette type ships, with armoured wooden hulls, fully rigged, and comparing poorly with the *Devastation* or even the earlier *Monarch*.

However, Britain and most other fleets continued to build some fully-rigged battleships with an amidship armoured battery and Barnaby supervised the design of the graceful 9,490-ton *Alexandra*, laid down in 1873. Her gun arrangements were copied from the Austrian ironclad *Custozza*, designed four years before; large recesses in the ship's side allowed the amidships battery direct ahead or astern fire *(Plate 5)*. The same year the brig-rigged battleship *Temeraire* was started, with an amidship battery and a 25-ton gun mounted forward and aft in armoured redoubts which raised the guns hydraulically to the firing position after loading in protection below.

Battle fleets contributed little to the Franco-German war of 1870-1, except that the powerful French fleet blockaded German ports and secured unhindered passage of large French armies from North Africa to France.

At that time France was the only naval power which could seriously challenge Britain, as the Russian fleet, which was then thought certain to be allied to France in war with Britain, had few ironclads. The Russian Navy was deployed in two principal fleets, one in the Baltic, the other in the North Sea, with a squadron in the Far East. Russian battleship construction suffered even more than the French from changes in design policy, and political ties with France influenced the design of Russian warships for many years.

The American fleet was then largely composed of shallow draught monitors and a few cruising ships, but that nation was in no mood for fighting anyone.

Austria and Italy did not seriously develop their fleets after the war of 1866 and the Turkish fleet was probably the strongest in the eastern Mediterranean at the time. Spain had several ironclads and the Navy of the North German confederation had the 9,600-ton *König Wilhelm* which was built in England in 1868 as one of world's most powerful warships.

Japan was only awakening to western influence and had no large modern ships.

During the 1870's and 80's the British Admiralty and to some extent the French naval ministry attempted to restrict the size of battleships, not only for economy but for manoeuvrability and shallow draught work in European waters. However, as experience with operation of ironclads individually and in fleets increased, better judgements could be made and more rational ships emerged from the experimental excesses of the 1870's, when foreign gun developments and improved armour made ships obsolete before they were launched. Warship design was full of contradictions: big guns and thick armour versus moderate displacement; wide arcs of fire incompatible with masts and sails.

The mounting of heavy guns in an armoured redoubt was introduced, and soon developed to the full "barbette" system, with a revolving turntable inside the barbette, with the guns mounted on it. Gun and crew were unprotected from above, but it was thought to enable clearer sighting and better aim in action. Barbette mounting of battleship guns survived in many navies into the 1890's, as the weight of a turret was saved and guns could be mounted correspondingly higher without raising the acceptable centre of gravity of armament weights.

After the disastrous land war with Germany, France recommenced battleship construction in 1872 with the *Redoutable*, a 9,200-tonner which had a 14-inch armour belt, above which the sides tumbled in to a short amidship battery with 9½-inch armour. At each quarter of this a 38½-ton gun was mounted to fire through ports angled to permit broadside or longitudinal fire and two smaller guns were mounted on the deck above. She was fully rigged and was the first armoured ship to have steel framing. Her hull plating was of iron, with armour of steel and she had extensive internal subdivision.

Contemporary French battleships had exaggerated shape in the sides above water, sweeping in with "S"-shaped tumble home, which enabled the heavy guns to fire longitudinally with better effect and was thought to improve resistance to shell hits, but it complicated construction, decreased stability in some conditions and greatly reduced deck area. These ships differed in size, speed and armament and for almost thirty years most were experimental designs, difficult to work together as a fleet.

The 8,650-ton *Richelieu* of 1873 was the first French "central battery" ship, joined in 1875 by the *Colbert, Friedland* and *Trident;* similar but with differing armament and arrangement. The larger battleships *Foudroyant* and *Devastation* were laid down in 1876 and that year a new concept of barbette battleship was started, to be named *Admiral Duperre*. This 11,100-tonner had a complete waterline armour belt 21½-inches thick but was unprotected above. Despite having twin-screw, triple expansion engines and 14 knots speed, she was fully rigged. Two of the four 13.5-inch guns were carried in barbettes, sponsored out at the sides forward, allowing clear ahead fire. The other two guns were mounted in barbettes on the centreline before and abaft the mizzen. She also carried fourteen 5.5-inch broadside guns for attack of an adversary's unarmoured areas, besides many 3-pounders for defence against the new torpedo boats. Although the big guns were well above the waterline, affording good aim, the full rig was cumbersome and she was still an inferior type to the British *Devastation*.

The *Thunderer (Plate 4)* the second ship of the "Devastation" type of unrigged British battleship, was not completed until 1877. A third, the *Dreadnought*, was commenced in 1872 and completed in 1879. She was the first British warship to have artificial ventilation, so necessary at sea in these low freeboard ships.

Italy had become a naval power shortly after unification but at first ordered warships from abroad and to foreign designs. At the battle of Lissa in 1866, none of the Italian ships was built in Italy. However, when the government introduced a programme of naval development in 1872, some distinguished Italian naval architects emerged, with ideas in the forefront of international warship construction.

Italy was then in the same naval position relative to France as France was to Britain, and to compensate for her industrial and financial limitations Italy built very powerful individual ships with extremely heavy guns to smash any known armour and have high speed and sufficient radius and seakeeping to meet all comers in the Mediterranean.

Her most noted early designer was Benedetto Brin, whose first major warships were the 12,000-ton battleships *Duilio* and *Dandolo,* in which some armour protection was combined with the largest guns then carried at sea: two *en echelon* amidships turrets each mounting two 17.7-inch Armstrong guns, resulting in the most powerful battleships afloat. Trials of the 100-ton guns for the *Duilio* breached all available armour, but the Creusot company produced 22-inch thick steel plate which stopped the shell, so this was chosen for the new ships' protection, making Italy the first to use steel armour, which soon replaced wrought iron.

The *Duilio* and *Dandolo* were commenced in 1873 and prompted the design of the broadly similar British battleship *Inflexible* of 11,900 tons, with thicker armour and four 81-ton guns in two turrets. She was launched in 1876 and her armoured citadel was small compared to the unprotected ends, which were well divided into watertight compartments.

The *Inflexible* was the first British battleship to have submerged torpedo tubes, one at each bow. She steamed at 14¾ knots – a very slight advance on the *Warrior* of twenty years earlier. As a practical fighting ship she would have been vulnerable in action but this did not stop four smaller ships of the same type being built: the 8,510-ton *Ajax* and *Agamemnon* in 1876 and the 9,150-ton *Colossus* and *Edinburgh* in 1879 *(Plates 6 and 7)*. With twin turrets *en echelon* amidships, above an armoured area over the engine and boiler spaces and high, unarmoured superstructures at each end, these ships exemplified the instability of warship design caused by the constant development of guns and armour.

While Britain was building armoured "Inflexible" type ships, Benedetto Brin was discarding armour altogether in the large, fast, mastless and very heavily gunned battleships *Italia* and *Lepanto (Plate 8)*, which were 400ft long and displaced 13,480 tons. These ships were ordered in 1876 and construction included items from many European countries. The concept foreshadowed the battlecruisers of the early twentieth century in having minimal armour, mounting four 17.7-inch guns on *en echelon* turntable barbettes amidships and attaining a then unprecedented speed of almost 18 knots. Some credit for their conception was due to the discerning minister of marine, Admiral di Saint Bon, and they were principally intended for defence of the long and vulnerable Italian coast, for which provision was made to embark large numbers of troops in a prophetic "combined operations" role.

However, the next two Italian battleships, the "Andrea Doria" class *(Plate 20)*, reverted to the protection and lower speed of the "Duilio" type, though Italian constructors continued to produce battleships which did not conform to the emerging pattern of "pre-Dreadnought" battleship design until 1899, when the appropriately named *Benedetto Brin* was commenced, arranged with the by then conventional four 12-inch guns, disposed in paired turrets forward and aft.

Despite Italian innovation and concentration of force in four powerful battleships, Britain and France remained the two major naval powers in the early 1880's. The British fleet could rely on the strength of the turret ships *Inflexible, Dreadnought, Thunderer* and *Devastation* and the belt and battery types *Monarch, Neptune, Alexandra, Triumph* and *Superb* as being the finest first class battleships in the world and representing half of the type existing. They were greatly superior to the contemporary French *Admiral Duperre*, and to the *Devastation, Foudroyant* and *Redoutable*.

Britain had not quite such an advantage with second class battleships, but their French equals were smaller and timber-hulled, while France's natural allies, Russia and America, had not one second class battleship. As growing Germany had concentrated on a powerful short sea or coastal fleet of well protected and armed second class battleships, Britain was secure in her maritime supremacy.

Many naval officers and constructors thought ramming a powerful method of attack, reinforced by its success at Lissa, and most battleships had bows designed and strengthened for this. Its use was subsequently indecisive in war but was forcefully demonstrated by several notable peacetime accidents. In 1875 the British ironclad *Iron Duke* rammed the *Vanguard* in fog and sank her. Three years later the German battleship *König Wilhelm* rammed the battleship *Grosser Kurfürst* in the English Channel, due to helm confusion while avoiding a small vessel, and sank her with heavy loss of life.

Prior to 1864 the Prussian Navy comprised various minor warships intended for coastal and Baltic operation. Thereafter, the founding of the Germany Navy encouraged growth of a seagoing fleet. At first a few armoured ships were built in England and France but after the Franco-Prussian war, which raised German ambitions, a squadron of armoured ships was ordered. The *Kaiser* and *Deutschland* were built in England to designs of E.J.Reed and were conservative armoured frigates of the time, fully rigged and having a maximum speed of 14½ knots. Meanwhile, German shipyards were completing their first three major warships – the *Grosser Kurfürst*, *Friedrich der Grosse* and *Preüssen*, turret battleships which were fully rigged in contemporary fashion. The four "Sachsen" class of 1877 had six 10¼-inch breech-loading guns mounted in an armoured battery amidships, the ends of the ship being unprotected. These early German battleships mounted smaller guns than their foreign contemporaries but had improved protective armour.

In 1877 the British Navy had its first and only action experience until 1914 against an armoured ship when the unarmoured frigate *Shah* and the unarmoured corvette *Amethyst* fought the Peruvian turret ironclad *Huascar*, whose crew had mutinied and committed piracy on British shipping off the west coast of South America.

The *Huascar* had been designed on the principles of Captain Coles and was built by Lairds at Birkenhead in 1864 with a single turret mounting two 12½-inch guns. The *Shah* had two 12-ton and eight 6½-ton guns and some smaller. The *Amethyst* had a relatively light armament. Both had to keep steaming and maintain long-range fire as they were no match for the ironclad. After two hours and forty minutes the *Shah* had fired 241 rounds and made 30 hits, with about the same number by the *Amethyst*. As the *Huascar* was steaming at 11 knots and was hulled by six hits this was creditable shooting for the time. The *Shah* also fired the first torpedo used in action, at 400 yards range, but the *Huascar* could steam faster than it ran and left it astern! She then retired into shallow water and afterwards surrendered to Peruvian authorities.

Two years later the *Huascar* participated in a war between Peru and Chile in which the navies were prominent. In May 1879 she was caught between two squadrons of Chilean ships off Iquique, including the belt and battery ironclads *Blanco Encalada* and *Almirante Cochrane* – 3,500-tonners mounting three 12-ton guns on each side of their armoured batteries. These ships fired 76 shells at close range, of which 27 wrecked and disabled the *Huascar* causing her surrender. She is preserved as a Chilean naval relic at Talcahuano.

In 1860 Commander Luppis, an Austrian naval officer, devised a self-propelled torpedo and during 1864 engaged the assistance of Robert Whitehead, English manager of an engineering works at Fiume, in solving the technical problems to perfect it. This 14ft long, fish-shaped weapon was to revolutionise sea warfare and has developed constantly since.

In 1878 Thornycroft built the first practical British torpedo boat – a small fast steam launch discharging a torpedo from a tube forward and initiating a new and comparatively inexpensive attack craft which, if lucky, might damage or sink a large warship. These were ordered to counter large numbers of torpedo boats which had been built for the Russian Navy during the previous four years.

Torpedoes also appealed to French naval thought as a method of attacking a fleet and offsetting Britain's considerable advantage in modern battleships. Large numbers of torpedo boats were built, to attack in flotillas, preferably at night and against an anchored battle fleet. Britain continued to develop and build the type and experiment with torpedoes launched from above water carriages and tubes in new warships.

By 1875 British battleships were prepared for possible torpedo attack and were equipped with anti-torpedo nets of steel to be suspended on booms around the ship at anchor or at slow speeds. Searchlights, Gatling guns and guard boat patrols for anchorages were also used as torpedo boat defence.

The war between Russia and Turkey during 1877-8 caused a squadron of British ironclads to be deployed in the eastern Mediterranean and, when Constantinople became threatened, these were ordered to the Dardanelles. But it was the rapid movement of troops from India to concentrate at Malta in the Mediterranean, their movements covered by three ironclads, which forced a settlement of peace and caused Russia, that vast land power, to seek a powerful fleet to enforce her policies, though she had little ocean trade.

During the 1880's the term "ironclad" was dying out and "battleships" crystallised as a type in major navies. In the British fleet the decade saw the end of sail in warships, an end to experimental designs, and the commencement of naval strength founded on balanced battle squadrons, capable of seakeeping in all weathers and relying on gun power to conquer.

Reliable breech-loading guns were developed, made of steel and with high muzzle velocities and improved breech-closing mechanism. The British Navy re-adopted breech-loading after having reverted to muzzle-loading for some years. France had led for some time with breech-closing mechanism and the Italian Navy followed. Turkish and American ships continued with muzzle-loading for a few years, until their fleets were modernised.

The menace of torpedo boat attack stimulated development of the quick-firing gun as protective secondary armament for battleships and to provide a hail of fire at close range to damage unarmoured areas and demoralize an opponent's crew.

To counter first rate French ships, the British Admiralty laid down a series of battleships, commencing with the *Collingwood (Plate 10)*, in which the main guns were mounted in barbettes, enabling them to be carried higher as the weight of turrets was saved. The armour was

14

disposed amidships and generally she resembled an improved "Devastation" type, with displacement of 9,500 tons. The *Collingwood* mounted four 12-inch guns. The following four "Admiral" class ships, *Anson, Camperdown, Howe* and *Rodney (Plates 11-13)*, had four 13.5-inch guns and the later and similar *Benbow* two 16.25-inch monsters *(Plate 14)*. The ships had too limited a displacement, the armour was not sufficiently extensive and they were not considered ocean-going battleships, being very wet at sea.

In contrast, French designers retained ample freeboard in their large battleships, which forced the big guns to be mounted singly in barbettes. They also produced second class armoured coast defence ships which were not rigged and had low freeboard.

Britain was involved with the problems of the big gun, and the *Victoria* and *Sanspareil (Plate 16)*, laid down in 1885, had two 16.25-inch guns in a single turret, but the same armour protection as the "Admirals". The secondary battery were 6-inch guns. These ships were developed from the coast defence ships *Hero* and *Conqueror (Plate 9)* and the big guns had a satisfactory rate of fire for the unlikely chance of dealing a smashing shell at an enemy. In 1886 William White became Director of Naval Construction, succeeding Nathaniel Barnaby.

A year later the "improved" battleships *Nile* and *Trafalgar* were started, but were almost of monitor type *(Plates 17-19)* with short unarmoured ends and four 13.5-inch guns in two turrets. The great weight of these ships' armour and the restricted dimensions for manoeuvrability reduced their freeboard and the height at which the main guns could be mounted, contributing to the resignation of Naval Constructor Barnaby. However, they were probably more effective than contemporary French battleships, against which they were designed. In 1880 France was building a class of four: *Magenta, Marceau, Neptune* and *Hoche,* with less protection than their predecessors but with the same exaggerated tumble home to improve side longitudinal fire. Four 13.4-inch guns were mounted singly in barbettes; one forward, one aft and one each side amidships.

During the years 1870-1900 France had thirty-one different ministers of marine, each usually having different ideas. This caused French naval policy to change continually from a fleet intended to be capable of meeting the British battle fleet, to a huge torpedo boat force, or a cruiser and torpedo boat force for raiding commerce, backed by smaller coast defence battleships and torpedo boats. Others wished the fleet to be principally directed against Italy in the Mediterranean and Germany in the North Sea, with Austria and the Adriatic as a remote possibility. This confusion was worsened by the French dockyards' inability to build as quickly as British shipbuilders, or for a comparable price.

By 1886 French naval opinion had swung temporarily against battleships in favour of large numbers of seagoing torpedo boats for potential attack on the British fleet but after poor results with torpedo craft during

annual French manoeuvres of 1887, held in bad weather, this trend was checked and gradually the French returned to faith in battleships as the major fleet force.

Victory

BRITISH FIRST RATE SHIP OF THE LINE 1778 *Plate 1*

Built	Royal Naval dockyard, Chatham
Laid down	July 1759
Launched	May 1765
Completed	1778
Dimensions	*Length,* figurehead to taffrail 226ft 6in
	Length of keel 152ft 3in
	Breadth 51ft 10in
	Depth of hold 21ft 6in
Displacement	2,162 tons
Armament	Thirty 32-pounder muzzle-loading. On lower gun deck
	Twenty-eight 24-pounders, muzzle-loading. On middle gun deck
	Thirty 12-pounders. On upper gun deck
	Twelve 12-pounders, muzzle-loading. On quarter deck
	Two 12-pounders, muzzle-loading. Two 68-pounder carronades, muzzle-loading. On forecastle
Complement	850
Designed	Thomas Slade, senior surveyor to the Royal Navy
Original cost	£57,748

Since 1805 the first rate ship of the line HMS *Victory* has symbolised Britain's naval strength and pride. Raised to fame as Admiral Nelson's flagship at the battle of Trafalgar, she remains preserved in dry dock at Portsmouth dockyard and still serves as the nominal flagship of the commander-in-chief Portsmouth.

The *Victory* was already an old ship when she fought at Trafalgar and had seen other actions.

In 1805 the British had finally succeeded in blockading the French Admiral Villeneuve in Cadiz. When Villeneuve came out to fight Nelson was commanding a fleet of twenty-seven ships; the French had a total force of thirty-three French and Spanish ships of the line.

At dawn on 21st October 1805 the two fleets were in sight, about twenty miles from Cape Trafalgar, thirty-miles south-west of Cadiz. Nelson signalled to attack, leading one line of the British fleet with *Victory.* Collingwood in the *Royal Sovereign* led the other. The light west wind allowed the British ships to bear down on the French and Spanish under full sail.

At 11.50 am the French fired on the *Victory,* and soon after the action

1 VICTORY, BRITISH FIRST RATE SHIP OF THE LINE, 1778

became general. Nelson ran up the signal, "Engage the enemy more closely", and as the *Victory* passed the *Bucentaure*, Admiral Villeneuve's flagship, she fired a close-range broadside into her which killed about four hundred men and disabled the ship. The *Victory* then went alongside the French *Redoutable*, both ships firing into each other. The British *Temeraire* came alongside the *Redoutable's* disengaged side while the *Victory* repeatedly fired broadsides into the French ship and at the same time her other side guns fired at the *Bucentaure* and the four-decked line of battleship *Santissima Trinidad*.

The French ship *Fougeux* came up and engaged the *Temeraire* on her other side and there were then four ships locked in close action. Twice the *Victory's* guns were ordered to cease firing on the *Redoutable*, whose big guns were silent, but the many soldiers and marines in the tops and rigging of the *Redoutable* continued to pour out musket and rifle fire and one shot struck Nelson, who was carried below mortally wounded.

About twenty minutes after Nelson fell the *Redoutable* surrendered and two hours later Hardy was able to tell the dying Nelson that the French and Spanish fleets were captured, sunk or fleeing. Many of the fleeing survivors were afterwards intercepted and successfully fought by an English squadron off Cape Ortegal on November 4th.

The *Victory* returned to Portsmouth with Nelson's body on board, to a nation mourning for a hero. His victory at Trafalgar confirmed Britain's superiority at sea, and though the war did not end until 1815 and the French fleet was rebuilt and regained its offensive potential, the British Navy was not again seriously challenged for the next hundred years. Competition was to lie in the field of advancements in warship construction, and Britain's reputation enabled her to maintain a century of international freedom from large-scale wars at sea and to embark on her enormous industrial and economic expansion and the enlargement of her empire.

The *Victory* remains the only surviving ship of the line and although an old vessel in 1805, she typifies the three-decked first rate which was improved only gradually until steam auxiliary engines and single screws were installed in existing and new ships of the line in the 1840's. These remained the principal force of the British fleet until the iron-hulled steam "frigates" *Black Prince* and *Warrior* were built in 1859 to counter the French ironclad ship *La Gloire*, which had been completed the year before. The era of the ironclads had commenced and would radically change all concepts of sea war.

The *Victory* remained afloat until 1922 when, through the efforts of the Society for Nautical Research, she was docked and restored to her condition at the time of Trafalgar and remains a serving warship and a considerable attraction to the thousands who visit her annually in Portsmouth dockyard.

This photograph was taken in 1890 and shows the *Victory* on moorings in Portsmouth harbour, surrounded by Victorian warships, troopships and yachts.

Minotaur

BRITISH 1865 *Plate 2*

Built	Milwall Shipbuilding Co., London
Laid down	1861
Launched	December 1863
Completed	1865
Dimensions	*Length between perpendiculars* 400ft
	Breadth 59ft 3in
	Draught 27ft full load
Displacement	10,690 tons
Machinery	Single screw
	2-cylinder trunk type engines by Penn
	58 revolutions per minute
	Ten rectangular, return fire-tube type boilers
	Speed 14¼ knots mean, on trials at full load
Bunkers	Coal. 750 tons
Endurance	1,500 miles at 7½ knots. 1,000 miles at 14¼ knots
Armament	*Original*
	Four 9-inch rifled muzzle-loading. On main deck broadside
	Twenty-two 7-inch rifled muzzle-loading. On main deck broadside
	Two 7-inch rifled muzzle-loading. One under forecastle. One under poop
	Eight 24-pounders. Saluting
	Re-armed 1875
	Fourteen 9-inch rifled muzzle-loading. On main deck broadside
	One 9-inch rifled muzzle-loading. Under poop
	Two 9-inch rifled muzzle-loading. Under forecastle
Armour	Wrought iron
	Belt 5½-inch amidships to 4½-inch at ends. Extending from upper deck to 5ft below waterline (Sufficient to resist contemporary shot)
Complement	705

The *Minotaur*, with her sister battleship *Agincourt* and the *Northumberland* of similar dimensions, were the longest major warships built with a single screw. They were also the only warships rigged with five masts and were identical except for machinery.

The *Minotaur's* iron hull had a ram bow, a semi-circular and almost vertical stern above a low counter, a straight sheer and little tumble home in the sides. Her underwater lines were fine for contemporary warships and she was an excellent sea boat and steady gun platform, but was unhandy under steam and almost unmanageable under sail, except

2   MINOTAUR, BRITISH 1865

with the wind abaft the beam.

There were three complete decks – upper, main and lower – an open topgallant forecastle and a poop and sternwalk. She was divided by bulkheads below the main deck.

The Penn trunk engines were a successful and compact type which obviated piston rods and were installed in the majority of British battleships of that time. Maximum revolutions were 58, driving a 24ft-diameter, four-bladed propeller. The boilers were arranged in two rows, with stokeholds between them, and uptakes led to two telescopic funnels. As completed there was a steam capstan for weighing anchor but no other mechanical aids; the rest was square-rig seamanship.

The *Minotaur* and *Agincourt* were the worst sailers in the fleet. The five masts were at first known as fore, second, main, fourth, and mizzen. Originally the first four carried yards but these were removed from the fourth mast during her first commission. Afterwards the masts were renamed fore, second, main, mizzen and jigger. Her main truck was 153ft above deck and the lower yards were 91ft long. Despite a large sail area her best sailing speed was 9½ knots with wind abeam and the propeller disconnected. Two of the five masts were removed after 1877.

Although classed as a third rate ship of the line for purposes of complement, the *Minotaur* was a more powerful warship than the contemporary first rates. Her crew berthed on the main deck, between the guns – a system disliked by seamen accustomed to the close atmosphere of the orlop deck berthing then common, as mess tables and gear had to be cleared away for quarters and drills, disturbing the watch below. As there were no transverse battery bulkheads, the ships were open from end to end and the seven hundred men berthing there made it a striking scene at mess times. However, many additional crew were found to be necessary for handling the rig and the number of guns and there were often eight hundred on board. The officers' accommodation remained on the ill-ventilated and badly lit lower deck and would have been better arranged in the half deck, aft.

The *Minotaur* was ordered as the *Elephant*, but her name was altered while building. Launched in December 1863, her completion was delayed two years by design changes. For the next eighteen months she carried out experimental trials and was altered in rig and armament. Many types of new, heavy gun mountings were tried on board for general service use.

She was commissioned into the fleet as flagship of the Channel squadron under command of Rear-Admiral Warden, and for the whole of her eighteen years in commission served as a fleet flagship; a unique career. As principal seagoing flagship in home waters she attracted considerable attention, and royalty and other important visitors were frequently on board.

Her sister *Agincourt* was built at Birkenhead by Laird and spent most of her active life as leader of the second division, on the starboard beam of the *Minotaur*. *Minotaur*'s original hydraulic steering gear proved unreliable and she was steered by hand until steam gear was fitted after two commissions. Despite her unhandiness she was only once involved in a manoeuvring incident, almost ramming the battleship *Bellerophon*.

Both the *Minotaur* and *Agincourt* were of impressive appearance and although their careers were uneventful, their existence affected the policies of foreign fleets. The *Minotaur* saw no action; she arrived one day late for the bombardment of Alexandria, so missing the only fleet action for half a century. However, some of her crew participated in the following naval brigade operations ashore, and the *Minotaur*'s crew led the march past of the United Services at the Queen's review at the end of the Egyptian campaign.

From 1867 to 1873 she was continuously in commission, successively flying the flags of Admirals Warden, Symons, Yelverton, Wellesley and Hornby. During 1873 she paid off for refit and rearming, and in 1875 recommissioned as a flagship for twelve more years of sea service under Admirals Seymour, Hay, Hood, the Duke of Edinburgh, De Horsey, Fellowes and Hewett.

During the 1875 refit the *Minotaur* was fitted with the first searchlight in the British fleet, and later had the first type of Whitehead torpedo and tubes added.

Her last appearance at an historic event was on June 23rd 1887 when, although obsolete, she headed the southern line of ships at Queen Victoria's Jubilee review at Spithead, where this photograph was taken. She had been twenty-two years afloat and at the end of the year was paid off and relegated to the non-effective list.

In 1893 the *Minotaur* was converted for subsidiary training duties, and served in this way for the next twenty-nine years. During 1922 she was sold to be broken up.

Devastation

BRITISH 1873 *Plate 3*

Built Royal Naval dockyard, Portsmouth
Laid down   November 1869
Launched   July 1871
Completed   April 1873
Dimensions   *Length* 285ft
      Breadth 62ft 3in
      Draught 27ft 6in mean
Displacement 9,330 tons
Machinery   Twin screw
      Two, direct acting, 2-cylinder trunk type engines by Penn
      Eight rectangular boilers
      IHP natural draught = 6,650 = 13.84 knots

3   DEVASTATION, BRITISH 1873

	Speed 12.5 knots
Bunkers	Coal. 1,800 tons
Endurance	4,700 miles at 10 knots
Machinery	Altered 1891-2
	Two inverted, triple expansion engines
	Cylindrical tubular boilers
	IHP natural draught = 5,500 = 13.2 knots
	IHP forced draught = 7,000 = 14.2 knots
Bunkers	Coal. 1,200 tons
Armament	*Original*
	Four 12-inch 35-ton rifled muzzle-loading guns. Two in each turret, forward and aft. Improved Armstrong type. Projectile. 706 pounds
	Re-armed 1891
	Four 10-inch breech-loading guns. Two in each turret
	Six 6-pounder quick-firers
	Fourteen smaller guns
Armour	Iron
	Belt 12-inch – 10-inch – 8½-inch
	Turrets 14-inch – 10-inch
	Magazines 5-inch
	Deck 2-inch – 3-inch
	Conning tower 9-inch – 6-inch
Complement	358

During the period of mid-nineteenth century changes in warship design the success of the "Monitor" principle of armoured, mastless turret ships of moderate draught, devised during the American civil war, was observed closely by all navies, but British naval opinion remained divided. Conservatives wished to retain broadside mounted guns and fully rigged steamships; others backed the turret system of gun mounting which could reduce the armament of a battleship to two or four heavy guns capable of almost all round fire.

The sea-going turret ship *Devastation* was designed in 1868 by E.J. Reed. He impressed the Admiralty with his clean designed, armoured battleship mounting only four large guns, but before the *Devastation* was launched rival factions "proved" she would turn out to be a costly failure. However, she and her near sister ships *Thunderer* and *Dreadnought* were still giving excellent service twenty years later.

The *Devastion*'s turrets worked on the Coles principle of rollers fitted at the circumference of the turret bases. Two 30-ton Armstrong guns of improved types were mounted in each turret. Following the capsize of the masted turret ship *Captain*, the *Devastation* was altered during construction to increase amidship freeboard to about 12ft. When in seagoing trim her upper deck was only 4ft 6in above the waterline, except forward where a "sunk forecastle" increased the height to 9ft. The turret ports

were 13ft above the water so the guns were carried higher than in contemporary broadside ships, where they were usually 11ft above water.

The *Devastation*'s rolled iron armour was about seven times more effective than that of the first British ironclad *Warrior* of 1860. Her engines were the largest then built for a twin-screw ship and she was well compartmented and had a steel ram. As designed, two signal masts were to be stepped, one forward and one aft of the turrets, but she was finally more sensibly completed with one "military" mast stepped on the superstructure, the first of its kind.

She was commissioned during January 1873 for special service and was attached to the Channel fleet for sea trials in company with the rigged battleships *Agincourt* and *Sultan*. Although the *Devastation* shipped seas more readily than the broadside ships with greater freeboard, she pitched less and rolled no more, besides being a more powerful fighting ship. The trials were considered to be successful and Reed was vindicated, though he had by this time left Admiralty employment.

From May 1874 until April 1875 the *Devastation* served with the Channel fleet and was rammed by the battleship *Resistance* off Portland in July 1874. The *Devastation*'s armour was displaced but unbroken, and after refitting she joined the Mediterranean fleet, where her poor ventilation was hard on the crew. During November 1878 she returned to refit at Portsmouth, when searchlights, Nordenfelt guns and Whitehead torpedoes were fitted. On completion she was in reserve until April 1885 when she commissioned for special service with Admiral Hornby's "evolutionary squadron". She became portguard ship at Queensferry from August 1885 until May 1890, but took part in the 1887 Jubilee naval review at Spithead and suffered collision with the battleship *Ajax* immediately before it.

The *Devastation* underwent a lengthy refit at Portsmouth during 1891-2, being re-armed with four 10-inch breech-loading guns, two in each turret.

From 1893 until January 1898 she was port guardship at Devonport and then remained there in reserve until April 1898 when she sailed for Bantry, Ireland, to become coastguard ship until June. She then returned to the reserve at Devonport. From November 1898 to April 1902 she was port guardship at Gibraltar, but spent much time actively at sea with the fleet.

The *Devastation* returned to reserve at Portsmouth during April 1902 and was declared non-effective in 1905. In May 1908 she was sold for £21,700 to be scrapped. The photograph was taken in about 1896.

*4	THUNDERER, BRITISH 1877*

Thunderer

BRITISH 1877 *Plate 4*

Built	Royal Naval dockyard, Pembroke
Laid down	June 1869
Launched	March 1872
Completed	May 1877
Dimensions	*Length* 285ft
	Breadth 62ft 3in
	Draught 27ft 6in mean
Displacement	9,330 tons
Machinery	Twin screw
	Two horizontal direct-acting engines by Humphrey and Tennant
	Eight rectangular boilers
	IHP natural draught = 6,270 = 13.4 knots
	Maximum speed 12.5 knots
Bunkers	Coal. 1,600 tons
Endurance	4,700 miles at 10 knots. 2,700 miles at 12½ knots
Machinery	Altered 1891
	Two inverted triple expansion engines by Maudslay
	Cylindrical boilers
	IHP natural draught = 5,500 = 13.2 knots
	IHP forced draught = 7,000 = 14.2 knots
Bunkers	Coal. 1,200 tons
Armament	*Original*
	Two 12.5-inch 38-ton rifled muzzle-loaders. In forward turret.
	Two 12-inch 35-ton rifled muzzle-loaders. In turret aft
	Re-armed 1891
	Four 10-inch breech-loaders. Two in each turret
	Six 6-pounder quick-firers
	Eight 3-pounder quick-firers
	Four machine-guns
	Two 14-inch diameter torpedo tubes. Submerged
Armour	Iron
	Belt 12-inch – 10-inch – 8½-inch
	Turrets 14-inch – 10-inch
	Magazines 5-inch
	Deck 2-inch – 3-inch
	Conning tower 9-inch – 6-inch
Complement	358
Hull	Wood sheathed and coppered

The *Thunderer* took almost nine years to complete. Opinion had swung

against these "mastless seagoing monitors" as they were derisively called, which accounted both for the *Thunderer*'s delay and for the building of a number of retrograde central battery and fully rigged battleships. The *Thunderer* differed from the slightly earlier but very similar *Devastation* in mounting two 38-ton, 12.5-inch guns in the forward turret and two 12-inch in the after one. The turrets were rotated by hydraulic machinery powered by steam engines.

She was an unlucky ship. An explosion occurred in one of her boiler-rooms during trials in July 1876 and delayed her completion still further. In May 1877 she was commissioned in the reserve fleet, subsequently serving in the "particular service" squadron of the Channel fleet during June-September 1878. She was then fitted with 16-inch diameter torpedoes of experimental type and sailed for the Mediterranean later in the year. On January 2nd 1879 she suffered a gun explosion which killed eleven men and wounded thirty. The 12.5-inch guns were loaded by rotating the turret so the muzzles, which were run in and fully depressed, aligned with two loading tubes raking up from the deck below into the turret. A hydraulically-operated rammer forced the shell and the cartridge up the tube and into the muzzle. Following a misfire the gun had been mistakenly loaded with a second shell and charge, leading to its bursting on firing.

In 1881 the *Thunderer* went into reserve at Malta, where 14-inch diameter torpedo tubes were fitted and the charthouse was enlarged. She continued to serve in the Mediterranean fleet during 1885 and 1886, returning to Chatham to pay off for refitting. In January 1888 she was placed in reserve at Portsmouth and during 1889-91 was thoroughly refitted. Like the similar ships *Devastation* and *Dreadnought (Plate 3)* she was in advance of her time when she was built and could still be considered a useful ship. Four 10-inch breech-loading guns were installed in her turrets and smaller guns were also fitted.

In March 1891 the *Thunderer* returned to the Mediterranean fleet, but constant trouble with her boiler tubes resulted in her being ordered back to England, where she paid off into reserve at Chatham during 1892.

In 1894 her superstructure was painted in black and white chequers, like the warships of Nelson's time. Considerable latitude was still allowed in painting ships' upperworks at this time, though hull colours had been standardized.

In May 1895 the *Thunderer* became port guardship at Pembroke, remaining there until December 1900 when she returned to fleet reserve at Chatham. A refit during 1903 was followed by her being declared non-effective in 1907 and she transferred to Portsmouth to be sold. In July 1909 she was purchased for £19,700 to be broken up.

This photograph was taken about 1899. The *Thunderer* could be distinguished from her sister ship *Devastation* by her shorter funnels.

Alexandra

BRITISH 1877 *Plate 5*

Built	Chatham dockyard
Laid down	March 1873
Launched	April 1875
Completed	January 1877
Dimensions	*Length* 325ft
	Breadth 63ft 4in
	Draught 26ft 6in maximum
Displacement	9,490 tons
Machinery	Twin screw
	Two 3-cylinder vertical compound engines by Humphrys, Tennant and Co
	Twelve cylindrical boilers
	Trial speed 15 knots
Bunkers	Coal. 670 tons
Endurance	3,800 miles at 8 knots
Armament	*Original*
	Two 11-inch 25-ton rifled muzzle-loading. 540-pound shell. On carriages and skids
	Ten 10-inch 18-ton rifled muzzle-loading. 400-pound shell
	Six 13 cwt breech-loading
	Four launching carriages for torpedoes
	Re-armed 1891
	Four 9.2-inch breech-loading
	Eight 10-inch rifled muzzle-loading
	Six 4.7-inch quick-firers
	Re-armed 1897
	Four 9.2-inch
	Eight 10-inch rifled muzzle-loading
	Six 4.7-inch quick-firers
Armour	*Belt* 12-inch amidships. 6-inch at ends. 10ft 6in wide
	Battery sides. 8-inch upper tier
	Upper transverse bulkheads 6-inch
	Lower transverse bulkheads 8-inch forward. 6-inch aft
	Battery division 6-inch
	Engine-room aft bulkhead 5½-inch
Complement	665. Later 685

Like many major warships in that period of rapid change in ships and armament the *Alexandra* was designed as an individual ship. She was the largest, fastest and longest serving of the eighteen central-battery ships which formed the backbone of the British Navy during its transition from the full broadside armoured vessels with many light guns, to the turret battleships.

She had moderately fine lines with a full midship section and almost vertical sides, steered well and was a steady sea boat. Deck space was restricted due to the recesses in its breadth to allow gun traverse from the upper battery. The battery divided the berthing and storage areas in two. Most of the crew berthed forward of it and some, with the marines, in the battery itself, between the guns. The stokers' messes were on the forward lower deck. The main deck abaft the battery was officers' accommodation which was superior to that of most earlier ships. In contrast, the crews' quarters were inferior.

Her main armament was mounted in an armoured citadel amidships, on two decks; an arrangement known as the "central battery" principle. The *Alexandra*'s battery was unusual in having two decks, embrasured to afford ahead fire.

The central battery system reduced the extent of side armour required but restricted and congested the methods of ammunition supply from the magazines, which could not be placed beneath the battery due to the boiler-rooms being sited there, so ammunition had to be manhandled along passageways to the battery hoists, along with the powder charges.

The battery had a slice cut off each corner for a gun port. The two 11-inch guns were mounted forward and the two 10-inch aft. The remaining 10-inch guns were the main deck or lower tier armament. The battery had arcs of fire from four guns ahead, six on each beam and two astern, but only half the total could be concentrated on one target.

During a refit the four muzzle-loading guns in the upper battery were replaced by 9.2-inch breech-loaders on carriages. These had double the range and rate of fire. Secondary batteries, later developed in battleships, were then unknown and the *Alexandra* typically mounted a few small guns as defence against attack by spar torpedo boats or boarding.

The *Alexandra* was the world's fastest battleship when new, exceeding 15 knots on trials, unapproached by any comparable ship for ten years. She and the *Dreadnought* were the first two battleships to have vertical compound engines and cylindrical boilers, doubling steam pressures to 60 pounds per square inch. A steam capstan and steering engine were fitted.

Her barque rig was insurance against seagoing machinery breakdown. It had great breadth to height and set about 27,000 square feet, but like many twin screw ships she was a poor sailer, never achieving more than 6 knots.

The *Alexandra* was named by Princess Alexandra, wife of the Prince of Wales, later King Edward VII. Commissioned for sea in February 1877 she sailed under Vice-Admiral Hornby as flagship of the Mediterranean fleet, and did not return to England for twelve years. Her arrival in the Mediterranean coincided with a threat by Russia to occupy Turkey and seize the Dardanelles, so for two years the British fleet was based on the roadstead of Besika Bay, in constant readiness to proceed to the Dardanelles if the Russians attacked. When this finally occurred the *Alex-*

5 ALEXANDRA, BRITISH 1877

6 COLOSSUS, BRITISH 1886

andra led six British battleships through the straits in a severe snowstorm, which caused her to ground, but she got off with assistance from the battleship *Sultan*. When this force arrived off Constantinople, the Russians were induced to make a political settlement, and while negotiations proceeded the British fleet was stationed in the Sea of Marmora, all being relieved at intervals except the *Alexandra*. They finally withdrew in 1879.

The *Alexandra* cruised the Levant and paid off at Malta during 1880, to recommission with a new crew sent out from Britain. Hornby was succeeded by Sir Beauchamp Seymour. At the end of this commission, in 1884, there was an army rebellion in Egypt and the British Mediterranean fleet anchored off Alexandria to receive British and European refugees. When a demand for the withdrawal of Eygptian troops from Alexandria was ignored, on July 11th 1882, the fleet bombarded the forts, Seymour transferring to the lighter draught battleship *Invincible* for the attack. The *Alexandra* fired the first shot and fierce firing went on for nine hours until the forts were silenced and the city was evacuated by the Egyptians. The *Alexandra* was hit thirty-four times and suffered damage to boats and gear, losing one man killed and three wounded, but her armour was unpierced. A party of her officers and men subsequently embarked in Nile steamers to participate in the attempted relief of Khartoum.

The *Alexandra* paid off at Malta and again recommissioned there with a fresh crew sent out in March 1886. The Duke of Edinburgh became commander-in-chief Mediterranean, and Prince George, later King George V, was one of her lieutenants. She was then painted white to minimise heat discomfort. During 1887 the *Alexandra* led an international squadron blockading Greek ports to prevent a war between Greece and Turkey. In May 1889 she sailed for England to pay off and was refitted at Chatham until February 1891, altered in armament and rig. She then commenced a period of continuous service in home waters as flagship of Rear-Admiral Fitzroy, commanding the first reserve fleet based at Portland, but only putting to sea for the summer cruise or for fleet manoeuvres or routine gunnery practice. She continued in this service under successive admirals and participated in the Diamond Jubilee naval review of 1897, when this photograph was taken, appearing as the sole survivor of her type.

During 1901 the *Alexandra* paid off at Chatham to be disarmed and placed in low catagory reserve for use as a mechanical training ship. She was broken up in 1908.

Colossus

BRITISH 1886 *Plate 6*

Built	Royal Naval dockyard, Portsmouth
Laid down	June 1879
Launched	May 1882
Completed	October 1886
Dimensions	*Length* 325ft
	Breadth 68ft
	Draught 25ft 9in mean
Displacement	9,150 tons
Machinery	Twin screw
	Two 3-cylinder vertical, inverted compound engines by Maudslay
	Ten elliptical boilers
	IHP natural draught = 5,500 = 14.2 knots
	IHP trials = 7,488 = 16.5 knots (light condition)
Bunkers	Coal. 850 tons normal. 950 tons maximum
Endurance	6,200 miles at 10 knots
Armament	*Original*
	Four 12-inch 25 calibre 45-ton breech-loading guns. Two in each turret
	Five 6-inch breech-loading quick-firers
	Added later
	Four 6-pounder quick-firers
	Ten 3-pounder quick-firers
	Two 14-inch diameter torpedo tubes above water
Armour	Compound
	Citadel 18-inch – 14-inch. 108ft long by 15ft 6in broad
	Bulkheads 16-inch – 13-inch
	Turrets 16-inch – 14-inch
	Deck 3-inch – 2½-inch
	Conning tower 14-inch
Complement	396

The *Colossus* and her sister ship *Edinburgh (Plate 7)* were the first British battleships to mount breech-loading main guns, the first to have compound armour in place of iron, and the first to be generally constructed of steel. The four 12-inch guns were carried in two turrets placed *en echelon* on an armoured "citadel" amidships. Forward and aft of this a forecastle and poop extended to stem and stern, with flying bridges above the turrets to the funnel casing, giving these ships a distinctive and peculiar appearance.

The *Colossus* took over seven years to build and cost £661,716. She commissioned at Portsmouth in 1886 for special service, joining the Channel fleet in August for further trials. During October she was detached for special duties and after being formally accepted, sailed for the Mediterranean in April 1887, remaining there for six years.

The *Colossus* returned to become coastguard ship at Holyhead in November 1893 until she was paid off into the fleet reserve at Portsmouth in 1901. The photograph of her in Victorian livery was probably taken

7   *EDINBURGH, BRITISH 1887*

when she attended the naval review at Spithead in 1897.

She was transferred to dockyard reserve in 1902 but in July 1904 refitted to become tender to HMS *Excellent,* the naval gunnery school at Portsmouth. In August 1904 she acted as guardship in Cowes Roads. The *Colossus* was offered for sale in September 1906 and was sold for £18,500 in October 1908 to be scrapped.

Edinburgh

BRITISH 1887 *Plate 7*

Built	Royal Naval dockyard, Pembroke
Laid down	March 1879
Launched	March 1882
Completed	July 1887
Dimensions	*Length* 325ft
	Breadth 68ft
	Draught 25ft 9in mean
Displacement	9,150 tons
Machinery	Twin screw
	Two 3-cylinder vertical inverted compound engines by Humphrys and Tennant
	Ten elliptical boilers
	IHP natural draught = 5,500 = 14.2 knots
	IHP trials = 6,808 = 16 knots (light condition)
Bunkers	Coal. 850 tons normal. 950 tons maximum
Endurance	6,200 miles at 10 knots
Armament	*Original*
	Four 12-inch 25-calibre 45-ton breech-loading guns. Two in each turret
	Five 6-inch breech-loading quick-firers
	Added later
	Four 6-pounder quick-firers
	Ten 3-pounder quick-firers
	Two 14-inch diameter torpedo tubes above water
Armour	Compound
	Citadel 18-inch – 14-inch. 108ft long by 15ft 6in broad
	Bulkheads 16-inch – 13-inch
	Turrets 16-inch – 14-inch
	Deck 3-inch – 2½-inch
	Conning tower 14-inch
Complement	396

The *Edinburgh* ran trials during September 1883, proving, like her sister *Colossus (Plate 6),* to have poor manoeuvring characteristics and a large turning circle. Both ships were unsteady gun platforms and with the 12-inch guns trained abeam in a seaway the muzzles were frequently rolled into the waves. Delivery of her guns was delayed and the *Edinburgh* first commissioned at Portsmouth for the Jubilee naval review of 1887 and sailed for the Mediterranean in September, remaining there until January 1894. In February 1894 she became coastguard ship at Hull but was soon transferred to Queensferry.

During September 1897 the *Edinburgh* went into fleet reserve at Chatham and was partially reconstructed. In May 1899 she became temporary flagship at the Nore and in October commenced service as gunnery tender to HMS *Wildfire* at Sheerness. In 1905 she was transferred to special reserve at Chatham. This photograph was probably taken about 1902.

In 1908 the *Edinburgh* was used as a fleet gunnery target in the Channel, being fitted with sample armour plating and subjected to more devastating gunfire than she would have had to endure as an active warship. She proved remarkably durable and was towed back to Portsmouth with her ends little damaged and on an even keel.

Lepanto

ITALIAN 1887 *Plate 8*

Built	Orlando, Livorno
Laid down	October 1876
Launched	March 1883
Completed	August 1887
Dimensions	*Length waterline* 400ft 3in
	Breadth 75ft 6in
	Draught 31ft 2in mean. 33ft maximum
Displacement	15,900 tons
Machinery	Twin screw
	Four 3-cylinder vertical compound engines. Two on each shaft
	Sixteen locomotive type boilers. Eight oval
	IHP forced draught = 15,797 = 18.4 knots (on trials)
Bunkers	Coal. 1,650 tons normal. About 3,000 tons maximum
Endurance	5,000 miles at 10 knots
Armament	*Original*
	Four 17-inch 102-ton Armstrong guns. 27 calibre. In pairs in *en echelon* barbettes
	Eighteen 6-inch. 26 calibre
	Four 14-inch torpedo tubes above water
	Later amendments
	Four 17-inch

8 LEPANTO, ITALIAN 1887

Eight 6-inch (modified to quick-firers)
Four 4.7-inch quick-firers
Twelve 6-pounder quick-firers
Twenty-eight 1-pounders
Two machine-guns

Armour   Compound. No side armour on hull
Redoubt for main guns 18-inch
Hoist amidships 18-inch
Funnel bases 16-inch
Protective deck 3-inch

Complement   744

Following two already unusual battleships, the *Duilio* and *Dandolo*, the Italian Navy ordered the *Italia* and *Lepanto*, two ships of revolutionary design which were to dominate thought on large warships for several years.

The requirements were for a steel-hulled battleship, faster and more seaworthy than the "Duilio" type, with an armament superior to any then afloat. These ships had also to be capable of carrying a large number of troops in an unusual anti-invasion role. They were prophetic craft, foreshadowing the battlecruiser and the present commando ships.

The *Italia* and *Lepanto* were designed under the direction of Benedetto Brin, one of several brilliant naval architects produced by Italy. The design accepted that no armour could withstand very large guns and the customary belt and citadel armour was not fitted, so that only the heavy gun positions, ammunition hoists, funnel bases and lower protective deck were armoured. The 3-inch thick deck was carried 6ft below the waterline, with bunker coal stowed above it as further protection. A large armoured barbette was arranged amidships, diagonally across the deck, with two 17-inch guns mounted on turntables at each end, 33 feet above the waterline. These very large weapons could fire only one shell every five minutes and the adjacent 6-inch secondary guns could not be worked while they were in use.

The *Lepanto* cost about £1,200,000 in contemporary value. Her designed displacement of 13,850 tons was later increased to 15,000 tons and bunker capacity was modified to 1,700 tons. The secondary armament was also quickly reduced to eight six-inch guns. Subsequently there were other alterations. Unfortunately the emergence of the quick-firing gun and the development of high explosive shells coincided with the completion of these ships and quickly rendered them almost ineffective as battleships. They were afterwards regarded as huge protected cruisers.

With her four funnels and generous freeboard the *Lepanto* was a striking ship. She saw no action during her life. This photograph, taken in 1902, shows the extensive awnings used in the Mediterranean.

The arrangement of funnels in pairs to suit the boiler-rooms placed at each end of the central ammunition hoist and barbettes, the mast

position and the flying bridges resulted in a symmetrical appearance. The large number of side ports for light and air was unusual.

As late as 1906 the *Lepanto* and *Italia* were considered worth renovating but were almost ineffective. In 1913 the *Lepanto* was a gunnery schoolship and in July 1914 she was sold to be broken up.

The *Italia* differed in several ways from the *Lepanto* and had six funnels when built. She was laid up in June 1914 and was removed from the navy list. However, in April 1914 she was towed to Brindisi to serve as a floating battery for harbour defence. In December 1917 she was taken to La Spezia for conversion to a merchant ship for grain carrying, and was finally discarded in November 1921.

Hero

BRITISH 1888 *Plate 9*

Built	Royal Naval dockyard, Chatham
Laid down	April 1884
Undocked	November 1885
Completed	May 1888
Dimensions	*Length between perpendiculars* 270ft
	Breadth 58ft
	Draught 25ft 9½in
Displacement	6,440 tons
Machinery	Twin screw
	Two 3-cylinder inverted compound engines by Rennie
	Eight cylindrical boilers
	IHP 4,500
	Speed 14 knots
Bunkers	Coal. 500 tons normal. 620 tons maximum
Armament	Two 12-inch 45-ton breech-loading rifled 25 calibre. In turret forward
	Four 6-inch 89-cwt breech-loading rifled. Behind gun shields on sponsons on boat-deck
	Seven 6-pounder quick-firers
	Thirteen smaller guns
	Six 14-inch torpedo tubes above water
Armour	*Belt* 12-inch – 8-inch
	Citadel 12-inch – 10½-inch
	Turret 14-inch – 12-inch
	Conning tower 12-inch – 6-inch
	Decks 2½-inch – 1¼-inch
	Bulkheads 11½-inch – 11-inch – 10½-inch
Complement	330

9   HERO, BRITISH 1888

33   *10*   COLLINGWOOD, BRITISH 1887

The *Hero* and her sister ship *Conqueror*, completed in 1886, were designed as improvements on the ram ship *Rupert*, but were more heavily armed and not principally intended as rams. The two ships differed only in that the secondary armament of the *Hero* was mounted at boat-deck height, while two of the *Conqueror*'s 6-inch guns were carried on the main deck, inside the superstructure, which in both ships occupied the whole after part above that deck – a feature reproduced in several classes of subsequent British battleships.

The *Hero* and *Conqueror* were regarded as coast defence battleships, and the low freeboard, coupled with the weight and windage of the superstructure, limited their seaworthiness. At sea in bad weather the *Conqueror* once lost a cutter carried at boat-deck level, which was washed out of the chocks by her heavy rolling. Most of their careers were spent as harbour service gunnery tenders; the *Hero* at Portsmouth and the *Conqueror* at Devonport. After about ten years' service they were considered of little value, though the *Hero* had cost £388,746 to build.

During November 1907 the *Hero* was made a target ship and was sunk during gunnery practice off the Kentish Knock in February 1908.

The *Conqueror* was paid off during July 1902, was sent to Rothesay in 1905, and was sold during 1907 for £16,800 to be broken up.

The photograph shows the *Hero* commissioned for naval manoeuvres for a month during 1891. These ships were seldom away from dockyard waters, the *Hero* participating in manoeuvres only during 1888, '89, '90 and '91.

Collingwood

BRITISH 1887 *Plate 10*

Built	Royal Naval dockyard, Pembroke
Laid down	July 1880
Launched	November 1882
Completed	July 1887
Dimensions	*Length* 325ft
	Breadth 68ft
	Draught 26ft 10in mean
Displacement	9,500 tons
Machinery	Twin screw
	Two 3-cylinder inverted compound engines by Humphrys, Tennant and Co
	Twelve oval type boilers
	IHP natural draught = 7,000 = 15 knots
	IHP force draught = 9,500 = 16.5 knots
Bunkers	Coal. 900 tons normal. 1,200 tons maximum
Endurance	6,000 miles and 8,500 miles at 10 knots
Armament	Four 12-inch 45-ton breech-loading. Two forward and two aft
	Six 6-inch quick-firers
	Twelve 6-pounder quick-firers
	Eight 3-pounder quick-firers
	Six machine-guns
Armour	*Belt* 18-inch to 8-inch. 150ft long by 7ft 6in wide
	Bulkheads at ends of belt. 16-inch to 6-inch
	Barbettes 14-inch to 12-inch
	Hoists to barbettes 12-inch
	Deck 2½-inch
	Conning tower 14-inch
Complement	460

The *Collingwood* was an individually designed battleship, forerunner of the "Admiral" class which comprised the *Howe, Rodney, Camperdown* and *Anson,* and followed by the similar individual ship *Benbow*.

Essentially they were of one type, developed from the *Devastation*, but with heavier guns. They differed only in armament and detail, and were often regarded as a reply to the Italian *Italia* and *Lepanto*. All were constructed of steel and were armoured for slightly less than half their length, with the forward and after parts being protected by an armoured deck. The large guns were mounted in armoured barbettes, without protective hoods, one forward and one aft of a superstructure mounting the secondary guns which varied from six to ten 6-inch quick-firers, besides smaller weapons.

This type of low freeboard battleship was criticised for having a comparatively short and narrow armour belt, leaving more than half the length at the ends unprotected. With the end compartments holed in action, a slight heel with such low freeboard would completely submerge the side armour. There was also the possibility of capsize in those conditions.

Despite their faults, these ships did provide the British fleet with a squadron of battleships of one type, with similar tactical characteristics.

The *Collingwood* arrived at Portsmouth in July 1887 to participate in Queen Victoria's Jubilee review but paid off into reserve during August. She recommissioned for manoeuvres during July-September 1888 but returned to reserve until the 1889 manoeuvres, after which she was prepared for the Mediterranean, arriving there in November 1889 and returning to England during March 1897, having been refitted at Malta in 1896. She became coastguard ship at Bantry, Ireland, from March 1897 until June 1903 and was then placed in "B" reserve at Devonport. In July 1905 the *Collingwood* was transferred to the East Kyle, on the Clyde, remaining there until sold in March 1909 for £19,000 to be broken up.

This photograph was taken in 1902 and clearly shows the angular barbettes for her main armament.

11   HOWE, BRITISH 1889

Howe

BRITISH 1889 *Plate 11*

Built	Royal Naval dockyard, Pembroke
Laid down	June 1882
Launched	April 1885
Completed	July 1889
Dimensions	*Length* 325ft
	Breadth 68ft
	Draught 27ft 3in mean
Displacement	10,300 tons
Machinery	Twin screw
	Two 3-cylinder, inverted compound engines by Humphrys, Tennant and Co
	Twelve oval type boilers
	IHP natural draught = 7,500 = 15.5 knots
	IHP forced draught = 11,500 = 16.7 knots
Bunkers	Coal. 900 tons normal. 1,200 tons maximum
Endurance	5,000 and 7,200 miles at 10 knots
Armament	Four 13.5 67-ton breech-loading guns. Two forward and two aft
	Six 6-inch quick-firers
	Twelve 6-pounder quick-firers
	Ten 3-pounder quick-firers
	Seven machine-guns
Armour	*Belt* 18-inch – 8-inch. 150ft long by 7ft 6in wide
	Bulkheads at ends of belt 16-inch – 6-inch
	Barbettes 11½-inch – 10-inch
	Hoists to barbettes 12-inch
	Deck 3-inch – 2½-inch
	Conning tower 14-inch
Complement	510

Very similar to the earlier *Collingwood*, the *Howe*, with her sister ship *Rodney*, the *Camperdown* and *Anson*, was one of the "Admiral" class battleships. These ships were very completely divided, having ninety-eight watertight doors in the hull.

The *Howe* was delivered to Portsmouth during November 1885 to have her guns fitted, being first commissioned in July 1889 for fleet manoeuvres. In May 1890 she replaced the battleship *Iron Duke* in the Channel fleet, and during the fleet's Mediterranean cruise in November 1892, she stranded on a rock off Ferrol, Spain – a great blow to British pride. Salvage was difficult and was eventually successfully undertaken by a Swedish company, who refloated her in March 1893. Temporary repairs were made at Ferrol during April, after which she returned to

Chatham for complete refitting, which cost £45,000. During October 1893 the *Howe* relieved the *Edinburgh* in the Mediterranean fleet. She returned to England in December 1896 and was ordered to Queenstown, Ireland, as portguard ship, serving there except when absent on manoeuvres. In October 1901 she was transferred to reserve at Devonport. She recommissioned during the July-September manoeuvres of 1904 for her last seagoing service and returned to reserve until sold in October 1910 for £25,100 to be scrapped.

The photograph, taken in 1897, shows one of her steam torpedo-carrying launches alongside. Usually two of these were carried on board British battleships of the time, and were fitted with dropping gear for 14-inch diameter torpedoes. They served as picket boats when not on exercises.

Anson

BRITISH 1889 *Plate 12*

Built	Royal Naval dockyard, Pembroke
Laid down	April 1883
Launched	February 1886
Completed	May 1889
Dimensions	*Length* 330ft
	Breadth 68ft 6in
	Draught 26ft 9in mean. 28ft 5in maximum
Displacement	10,600 tons
Machinery	Twin screw
	Two 3-cylinder inverted compound engines by Humphrys, Tennant and Co
	Twelve cylindrical boilers
	IHP natural draught = 7,500 = 15.7 knots
	IHP forced draught = 11,500 = 17.4 knots
Bunkers	Coal. 900 tons normal. 1,200 tons maximum
Endurance	5,000 miles and 7,100 miles at 10 knots
Armament	Four 13.5-inch 67-ton breech-loading guns.
	Two forward to aft, in barbettes
	Six 6-inch breech-loading quick-firers. 26 calibre
	Twelve 6-pounder quick-firers
	Ten 3-pounders
	Seven machine-guns
	Five torpedo tubes above water
Armour	*Belt* 18-inch amidships – 8-inch at ends. 150ft long by 7ft 6in wide
	Bulkheads at ends of belt 16-inch – 6-inch
	Barbettes 14-inch – 12-inch
	Hoists to barbettes 12-inch

12   *ANSON, BRITISH 1889*

Deck 3-inch – 2½-inch
Conning tower 12-inch
Complement 525 – 536

The *Anson* and her sister ship *Camperdown* were two more of the "Admiral" class battleships.

The *Anson* was delivered to Portsmouth dockyard from Pembroke during March 1887, complete except for the main armament. She was not ready for sea until May 1889, when she commissioned as rear-admiral's flagship, Channel fleet. In September 1893 she joined the Mediterranean fleet and was refitted at Malta during 1896. She returned to England in July 1900 to pay off at Devonport into "C" reserve, but in February 1901 the *Anson* was transferred to the "A" reserve. Her torpedo tubes were removed about this time and maximum speed had fallen to about 13.5 knots. As a third class battleship she was almost obsolete but during March 1901 was commissioned to join the newly formed Home fleet and served until May 1904, when she was relegated to "B" reserve at Chatham, remaining there until sold in July 1909 for £21,200 to be scrapped.

Taken about 1902, in the last years of the smart Victorian colouring, this photograph shows the vulnerability of barbette-mounted guns.

Camperdown

BRITISH 1889 *Plate 13*

Built	Royal Naval dockyard, Portsmouth
Laid down	December 1882
Launched	November 1885
Completed	July 1889
Dimensions	*Length* 330ft
	Breadth 68ft 6in
	Draught 26ft 9in normal. 28ft 5in deep-loaded
Displacement	10,600 tons
Machinery	Twin screw
	Two 3-cylinder inverted compound engines by Maudslay, Son and Field
	Twelve cylindrical boilers
	IHP natural draught = 7,500 = 15.5 knots
	IHP forced draught = 11,500 = 17.2 knots
Bunkers	Coal. 900 tons normal. 1,200 tons maximum
Endurance	5,000 miles and 7,100 miles at 10 knots
Armament	Four 13.5-inch 67-ton breech-loading guns.
	Two forward and two aft, in barbettes

Six 6-inch breech-loading quick-firers. 26 calibre
Twelve 6-pounder quick-firers
Ten 3-pounder quick-firers
Seven machine-guns
Five torpedo tubes above water

Armour	Compound
	Belt 18-inch – 8-inch
	Bulkheads 16-inch – 7-inch
	Barbettes 14-inch – 12-inch
	Screens to battery 6-inch
	Upper deck amidships 3-inch
	Lower deck 2½-inch
	Conning tower 12-inch – 2-inch
Complement	515

Sister ship of the *Anson (Plate 12)*, the *Camperdown* was another of the six "Admiral" class battleships. She cost £677,724 to build and first commissioned at Portsmouth in July 1889 for the Home fleet manoeuvres, but during September went into reserve. In December 1889 she sailed to become flagship of the Mediterranean fleet and in May 1890 transferred to the Channel fleet as flagship, replacing the ironclad *Northumberland*. In May 1892 the *Camperdown* went into fleet reserve "A" but was commissioned for manoeuvres in July and subsequently returned to the Mediterranean fleet.

On 22nd June 1893 the Mediterranean fleet was steaming between Beirut and Tripoli, off the Syrian coast, in fine weather, manoeuvring before anchoring off Tripoli. Admiral Sir George Tryon, leading the starboard division in the flagship *Victoria*, ordered his two columns of ships to turn 16 points (a half circle) inwards towards each other, when steaming only 6 cables apart. He had previously decided on carrying the manoeuvre out at 8 cables, a safe distance, as the turning circle of these ships was about 800 yards. 10 cables (2,000 yards) would have been prudent to bring the ships to the usual distance apart for anchoring.

Tryon frequently ordered complicated manoeuvres which were not explained beforehand, though fully discussed afterwards. All executive officers in the fleet knew that the 6 cables order made collision almost certain and Rear-Admiral Hastings Markham, leading the port column in the *Camperdown*, ordered à semaphored query to be made to the flagship, keeping his answering signal at the dip. Before this was sent, the *Victoria* signalled to know why he was hesitating. Markham had the signal acknowledged, concluding he had misunderstood the purpose of the order. He had confidence in Tryon though, like many others in the fleet, he was extremely unhappy about this manoeuvre.

The *Victoria* and the *Camperdown*, the leading ships, turned inwards at 3.31 pm and it quickly became obvious that disaster was imminent. As they closed, the port engine of the *Victoria* was put astern and when two-thirds of the turn was completed and collision was seen to be

13   CAMPERDOWN, BRITISH 1889

inevitable, both engines were at full astern. The *Victoria* had a slightly smaller turning circle than the *Camperdown*, which struck her starboard side, forward, at an acute angle, both ships moving at about 6 knots. The *Camperdown*'s ram proved its effectiveness and tore a hole in the *Victoria*'s hull, swinging round to enlarge it and rupture two vital watertight bulkheads abaft it. The order to close watertight doors and hatches was not given until one minute before impact, and usually three minutes were needed to achieve this, so many compartments were flooded.

The *Victoria* listed to starboard and with her bow well under water was steamed slowly towards shallow water, hoping to beach, but her deck was immersed to the superstructure, where doors and other openings were not closed. A lurch brought an inrush of water into the battery and through open hatches into the hull which heeled slowly until the port propeller emerged and she capsized and sank by the bow, drowning Tryon and three hundred and twenty-one officers and men in the greatest peacetime disaster the Royal Navy had suffered for generations.

The cause of the confusion of orders has never been satisfactorily explained but it is thought to have been an error of judgement by Admiral Tryon. The fleet was accustomed to making quarter turns, whereas half turns were seldom executed and required more space between ships, so it is probable that Tryon ordered the manoeuvre in good faith but erred in the distance calculation for the half turn. Although many officers realised the error in the order, discipline and faith in the Admiral were such that it was obeyed.

The *Camperdown* was refitted from July to September 1893 and underwent a major refit during 1896-7, when a signal mast was stepped and the charthouse was altered. This photograph was taken in 1897 and shows the breeches of the forward guns. She paid off at Portsmouth in September 1899 and went into "B" reserve. The following May she transferred to the "C" reserve but commissioned in July 1900 as coastguard ship at Lough Swilly, Ireland. In May 1903 she reverted to "B" reserve at Chatham and was prepared to be a submarine depot ship to be stationed at Harwich, where she served from October 1908 until sold in July 1911 for £28,000 to be broken up.

Benbow

BRITISH 1888 *Plate 14*

Built	Thames Ironworks, Blackwall, London
Laid down	November 1882
Launched	June 1885
Completed	June 1888
Dimension	*Length* 330ft
	Breadth 68ft 6in

	Draught 27ft 5in. 28ft 5in deep-loaded
Displacement	10,600 tons
Machinery	Twin screw
	Two 3-cylinder inverted compound engines by Maudslay, Son and Field
	Twelve cylindrical boilers
	IHP natural draught = 7,500 = 15.7 knots
	IHP forced draught = 10,860 = 17.5 knots
Bunkers	Coal. 900 tons normal. 1,200 tons minimum
Endurance	5,000 and 7,100 miles at 10 knots
Armament	Two 16.25-inch 110-ton breech-loading Armstrong guns. One forward one aft in barbettes
	Ten 6-inch quick-firers
	Twelve 6-pounder quick-firers
	Ten 3-pounder quick-firers
	Seven machine-guns
	Five torpedo tubes. One bow. Four broadside
Armour	Compound
	Belt 18-inch – 8-inch. 150ft by 7ft 6in
	Bulkheads 16-inch – 6-inch
	Barbettes 14-inch – 12-inch
	Screens to battery 6-inch
	Upper deck amidships 3-inch
	Upper deck at ends 2½-inch
	Conning tower 12-inch – 2-inch
Complement	525

The *Benbow* was ordered with the later "Admiral" class battleships, but due to pressure of work in the Royal dockyards, was placed with the Thames Ironworks at Blackwall, delivery being stipulated within three years. As Woolwich Arsenal could not construct the necessary number of 13.5-inch guns in time for her completion, the alternative was to use either 12-inch, as in the *Collingwood*, or the Elswick 105-ton, 17-inch, breech-loading monsters which the firm had been supplying for the new Italian battleships of the "Andrea Doria" class.

Weight and structural considerations allowed only one 16.25-inch gun to be mounted in each of the *Benbow's* two barbettes. However, ten 6-inch guns could be carried in the battery instead of the six 6-inch of the other ships. The *Benbow* was always regarded with awe because of her huge guns, but they were slow in action, only managing one round every five minutes, and had a much shorter life than the 13.5-inch pieces.

The *Benbow* cost £764,022 to build and was delivered to Chatham during August 1886. She did not commission until June 1888, for the Mediterranean fleet, serving there until October 1891, when she paid off into reserve at Chatham, having proved a good steamer and a reasonably good sea boat. In June 1892 she commissioned for manoeuvres, and again from July to September 1893, reverting to fleet reserve "B" until

41   *14* *BENBOW, BRITISH 1888*

42 BATTLESHIPS AT THE CORONATION NAVAL REVIEW, 1902

March 1894, when she was sent to Greenock as coastguard ship, stationed there until April 1904 but participating in fleet manoeuvres. During those of 1903 the exercising fleet encountered a gale which shook the fleet out of station, but the old *Benbow* kept up with the flagship *Revenge*, leaving more "seaworthy" ships well astern, and the battleship *Royal Sovereign* hull-down.

The *Benbow* returned to "B" reserve at Devonport until sold in July 1909 for £21,200 to be scrapped. This photograph shows her at the Coronation naval review at Spithead, 1902, and expresses the size of her main guns which dwarfed the light quick-firers mounted on the superstructure and barbette top.

Battleships at the Coronation Naval Review, Spithead, 1902.

Plate 15

Many naval reviews have been held at Spithead, that arm of water between the eastern part of the Isle of Wight and the mainland of southern England, close to Portsmouth harbour with its centuries old naval dockyard. Reviews were held to commemorate important events, occasionally to impress important foreign visitors and particularly to mark coronations, when the new sovereign sails through the fleet to the cheers of its officers and men and the thunder of salutes. The last major review of British and foreign warships was held at Spithead in 1953, to mark the coronation of Queen Elizabeth II.

Many naval reviews were held during the long reign of Queen Victoria, notably the Jubilee reviews of 1887 and 1897. These two great gatherings of British and foreign warships brought striking contrasts: sails and rigging were conspicuous in 1887 but had almost disappeared ten years later.

Queen Victoria died in 1901, and when her son, King Edward VII, was crowned in 1902 another review assembled at Spithead, with many foreign warships attending. Britain not only put on show her newest and finest battleships and cruisers, besides scores of smaller craft, but also swelled the long review lines with older battleships, normally relegated to portguard and coastguard duties around her coasts. Almost obsolete battleships and other major vessels were even sometimes temporarily commissioned from the dockyards to fill the lines and avoid having to withdraw modern ships from the Mediterranean fleet.

The ageing battleship *Benbow* occupies the foreground of this typical review scene in 1902, with the *Sanspareil* and other similar battleships astern. These low freeboard ships of the 1880's contrast with the healthy freeboard and 15,000-ton bulk of the newly completed battleship *London*, extreme right, flagship of the review and just commissioned at Portsmouth dockyard. The crossed yards on the tall masts were still necessary for the extensive flag and seaphore signalling needed before wireless brought a new dimension to war at sea. The sailing tradition died hard in a navy which had seen no fleet against fleet action for almost a century and patrolled the oceans secure in its overwhelming superiority of numbers, and the *London* carried topmasts, with their associated weight, windage and rigging.

A signal has broken out from the *London*'s yard arm, bringing officers of the watch on the alert and signalmen ready with the acknowledgement. A steam yacht slices through the lines of warships and a cargo-carrying spritsail barge beats up from the eastward. Boats lie to the booms, paintwork glistens, canvas dodgers stretch taut and ships lie at anchor in mathematical precision of review order.

Sanspareil

BRITISH 1889 *Plate 16*

Built	Thames Ironworks, Blackwall, London
Laid down	April 1885
Launched	May 1887
Completed	1889
Dimensions	*Length between perpendiculars* 340ft
	Breadth 70ft
	Draught 27ft 9in mean
Displacement	10,470 tons
Machinery	Twin screw
	Two triple expansion engines by Humphrys, Tennant and Co
	Eight boilers
	IHP natural draught = 7,500 = 15.6 knots
	IHP forced draught = 14,000 = 17.5 knots
	Trials achieved 17.75 knots
Bunkers	Coal. 900 tons normal. 1,200 tons maximum
Endurance	at 10 knots from above = 5,000 miles and 7,000 miles
Armament	Two 16.25-inch 110-ton guns. Pair mounted in turret forward
	One 9.2-inch 29-ton gun. Aft
	Twelve 6-inch quick-firers. In battery amidships
	Twelve 6-pounders
	Twelve 3-pounders
	Eight machine-guns
	Three 14-inch torpedo tubes. Two submerged. Carried twenty-four torpedoes
Armour	Compound
	Belt 18-inch – 16-inch. 152ft long by 8ft 4in wide.

44   *16 SANSPAREIL, BRITISH 1889*

Redoubt 18-inch
Bulkheads 16-inch
Turret 18-inch
Shield to 9.2-inch gun 6-inch
Battery bulkheads 3-inch
Deck 3-inch
Conning tower 14-inch
Complement   630

By the 1880's British battleship design had moved towards the mounting of the largest guns, protected by the heaviest armour it was possbile to produce. This policy reduced the number of large guns to two, which in turn influenced the design of the *Sanspareil* and her sister ship the *Victoria*.

They were the last of a series of battleships of this general type built for the fleet, were the first to have triple-expansion engines instead of the compounds of their predecessors, and had the heaviest armour protection since the *Dreadnought*. The design was intended as an improvement on the *Conqueror* and *Hero (Plate 9)* and the ships were built with use in the Mediterranean in mind; possibly in having to force the 'Dardanelles, then a contingency of British naval policy. Construction took nearly four years due to Elswick having trouble making the 16.25-inch guns. These had a life of only 75 rounds at a very slow rate of fire, proved costly to repair and reline, and were described as "a highly respectable blunder". The ships had in all eight sizes of gun on board, which caused magazine difficulties.

At 6,000 tons launching weight the *Sanspareil* was the heaviest ship launched since the *Great Eastern*. She was completed with distinctive tall funnels abreast, and the *Victoria*'s being similarly raised after completion.

The *Sanspareil* was commissioned at Chatham in July 1891 but was immediately placed in reserve due to scarcity of men. She recommissioned in February 1892 for service with the Mediterranean fleet until April 1895, afterwards becoming port guardship at Sheerness. She became an independent command as guardship in May 1898 and remained in that service until December 1903. During January 1904 she went into reserve, and was sold for scrapping in April 1907 for £26,000. The loss of her sister *Victoria* was one of the most tragic and inexplicable events in British naval history (see under *"Camperdown", Plate 13)*. After the *Victoria*'s capsize the sub-division of the *Sanspareil* was improved. She was the best sea boat of the low freeboard battleships of the time.

This photograph, taken in 1898, shows considerable detail and illustrates the confused contemporary thought on gun mounting. The two 16.25-inch guns in the turret forward are not balanced by the single 9.2-inch aft. The battery consisted of six 6-inch quick-firers on each side, protruding through side ports which gave an almost "wooden wall" appearance to a steel and steam warship. The number of boats carried by a battleship can also be seen, from 52ft steam pinnaces to the slender gig of beautiful hull form slung on the starboard quarter. A small steam launch with dodgers rigged is returning to the parent ship.

Trafalgar

BRITISH 1890 *Plates 17 and 18*

Built	Royal Naval dockyard, Portsmouth
Laid down	January 1886
Launched	September 1887
Completed	March 1890
Dimensions	*Length* 345ft
	Breadth 73ft
	Draught 27ft 6in mean. 29ft maximum
Displacement	12,590 tons. At 28ft draught
Machinery	Twin screw
	Two vertical triple expansion engines by Humphrys and Tennant
	Six cylindrical boilers
	IHP natural draught = 7,500 = 15.1 knots
	IHP forced draught = 12,000 = 16.75 knots (17.2 knots trials)
Bunkers	Coal. 900 tons normal. 1,200 tons maximum
Endurance	1,050 miles at 16.25 knots. 6,500 miles at 10 knots
Armament	*Original*
	Four 13.5-inch 67-ton breech-loading guns. Two forward and two aft in turrets.
	Six 4.7-inch quick-firers
	Eight 6-pounder quick-firers
	Twelve 3-pounder quick-firers
	Torpedo tubes added 1890. 14-inch diameter. One bow. One, stern. Two sides
	Alterations 1896
	Six 6-inch quick-firing guns replaced 4.7-inch secondary armament
Armour	Compound
	Belt 20-inch amidships to 14-inch at ends. 8-inch – 6-inch at lower edge. 230ft long by 8ft 6in wide
	Bulkheads 16-inch forward and 14-inch aft
	Citadel 18-inch – 16-inch
	Turrets 18-inch
	Battery bulkheads 5-inch
	Battery sides 4-inch
	Deck 3-inch
	Conning tower 3-inch
Complement	520

45

46   *17   TRAFALGAR, BRITISH 1890*

47   *18   TRAFALGAR, BRITISH 1890*

In many respects the design of the *Trafalgar* and her sister ship *Nile* reverted to the best features of the "Devastation" type battleships of the 1870's, which were highly regarded by those serving in them.

The *Trafalgar* and *Nile* had improved protection compared to their immediate predecessors and a consequently greater displacement, almost one third of which was due to weight of armour.

When these ships were projected in 1885, fear of the dominance of naval warfare by the torpedo and torpedo boat led to predictions that they would be the last battleships to be built, but by the time they were ready for sea the torpedo had been brought into perspective and battleships were to survive for a further sixty years.

The 13.5-inch guns mounted in two turrets, forward and aft, foreshadowed the long line of subsequent British "pre-Dreadnought" battleships. Four single rounds could be fired in eight minutes.

The *Trafalgar* was completed with short funnels like the *Victoria*, but these were heightened 17ft in 1891, to obtain better draught.

The *Trafalgar* cost £859,070 ready for sea but was completed before her guns were ready and did not commission until April 1890, as second flagship of the Mediterranean fleet. She served there for seven years and received a new secondary armament of 6-inch guns during a refit in 1896. She returned to England and paid off at Portsmouth in October 1897, remaining there as portguard ship until August 1902, when she was relegated to fleet reserve "A", and during September 1903 to dockyard reserve.

In April 1905 the *Trafalgar* was transferred to the reserve fleet at Devonport and in March 1907 moved to Sheerness to become turret drill-ship until April 1909 when she joined the 4th division, Home fleet at the Nore. In March 1911 she was sold for £29,000 to be scrapped.

Plate 17 gives a general view of the *Trafalgar* in 1898 and *Plate 18* shows considerable detail and emphasises her low freeboard and the size of the turrets. The widely spaced funnels and spacious bridge indicate her beam.

The anchoring arrangements of contemporary British battleships were elaborate, the hawse pipes being comparatively short and the anchors stowed on recessed billboards with heavy catting davits. The chain cables led aft from the hawse and were an embarrassment at sea in bad weather. Although bowsprits and figureheads had long disappeared from warships, the custom of carrying a bow decoration persisted to the end of the nineteenth century in the British Navy, and the *Trafalgar*'s crown is clearly visible on the face of the stem.

Nile

BRITISH 1891 *Plate 19*

Built	Royal Naval dockyard, Pembroke
Laid down	April 1886
Launched	March 1888
Completed	July 1891
Dimensions	*Length* 345ft
	Breadth 73ft
	Draught 27ft 6in mean. 29ft maximum
Displacement	12,590 tons. At 28ft draught
Machinery	Twin screw
	Two vertical triple expansion engines by Maudslay, Son and Field
	Six cylindrical boilers
	IHP natural draught = 10,112 = about 16 knots trials
	IHP forced draught = 12,102 = 16.8 knots trials
Bunkers	Coal. 900 tons normal. 1,200 tons maximum
Endurance	1,050 miles at 16.25 knots. 6,500 miles at 10 knots
Armament	*Original*
	Four 13.5-inch 67-ton breech-loading guns. Two forward and two aft in turrets
	Six 4.7-inch quick-firers
	Eight 6-pounder quick-firers
	Twelve 3-pounder quick-firers
	Torpedo tubes added 1890. 14-inch diameter. One bow. One stern. Two sides
	Alterations 1897
	Six 6-inch quick-firers replaced 4.7-inch secondary armament
Armour	Compound
	Belt 20-inch amidships to 14-inch at ends. 8-inch – 6-inch at lower edge. 230ft long by 8ft 6in wide
	Bulkheads 16-inch forward and 14-inch aft
	Citadel 18-inch – 16-inch
	Turrets 18-inch
	Battery bulkheads 5-inch
	Battery sides 4-inch
	Deck 3-inch
	Conning tower 3-inch
Complement	520

The *Nile* was a sister of the *Trafalgar* (Plates 17 and 18) and cost £885,718 to build. She was completed in July 1890 but her guns and mountings were delayed, so she ran trials with compensating ballast. Submerged

19   NILE, BRITISH 1891

20   ANDREA DORIA, ITALIAN 1891

torpedo tubes were fitted to both ships at this time. The *Nile* commissioned in June 1891 for the naval manoeuvres and then proceeded to the Mediterranean to relieve the battleship *Benbow*, remaining there until January 1898.

During 1897 the secondary armament was replaced by 6-inch quick-firers.

The low freeboard of the *Nile* and *Trafalgar* was better suited to the Mediterranean seas and both were regarded as good fighting ships because of their heavy armour and gun power.

On return to England the *Nile* became portguard ship at Devonport. In February 1903 she was relegated to dockyard reserve but commissioned in the reserve the following month. On formation of the Home fleet she received a nucleus crew and became part of the 4th division at Devonport.

In June 1911 the *Nile* was transferred to the "E" division and was offered for sale. During July 1912 she was sold for £34,900 to be scrapped.

The *Nile* was distinguished from her sister by her funnels which were carried up in the form of cowls above the casings.

The bow form of both battleships caused considerable disturbance when steaming at speed and in a small sea spray drove in sheets over the foredeck and the turret.

Andrea Doria

ITALIAN 1891 *Plate 20*

Built	Royal Arsenal, Spezia
Laid down	January 1882
Launched	November 1885
Completed	May 1891
Dimensions	*Length waterline* 328ft 2in
	Breadth 65ft 4in
	Draught 27ft 2in mean. 30ft maximum
Displacement	11,204 tons
Machinery	Twin screw
	Two 3-cylinder vertical compound engines by Maudslay, Son and Field
	Eight cylindrical boilers
	IHP natural draught = 7,500 = 15 – 15.5 knots. Trials
	IHP forced draught = 10,200 16.5 – 17 knots. Trials
Bunkers	Coal. 850 tons normal (Oil fuel added by 1903)
Endurance	4,500 miles at 10 knots
Armament	Four 17-inch 105-ton guns. 27 calibre. Projectile about 2,240 pounds. Two in each barbette

	Two 6-inch breech-loading guns. 32 calibre
	Four 4.7-inch quick-firers. 32 calibre
	Ten 6-pounder quick-firers
	Seventeen 1-pounder quick-firers
	Three 14-inch diameter torpedo tubes. Two submerged. One above water
Armour	*Belt* Partial compound 17.7-inch
	Redoubt and barbettes 17.7-inch
	Bulkheads 14-inch
	Deck 2.9-inch
	Barbette hoods 1-inch
	Conning tower 17.7-inch
Complement	506

The *Andrea Doria* cost about £780,000 and was one of the "Ruggiero di Lauria" class battleships designed under the direction of Engineer Inspector General Giuseppe Micheli, the others being the *Ruggiero di Lauria* and the *Francesco Morosini*, which were completed in 1888 and 1889 respectively.

They carried two pairs of short 17-inch, 105-ton guns in hooded barbettes placed *en echelon* amidships. The general design may be compared with the British *Colossus* and *Edinburgh (Plates 6 and 7)* and with the earlier Italian *Duilio* and *Dandolo,* or the *Italia* and *Lepanto (Plate 8)*.

The *Andrea Doria* had the then fashionable low freeboard and symmetrical arrangement which resulted in some unusual ships. The large crane forward and derrick aft were prominent features and the tubular mast seemed heavy with crossed yards for signalling. The light signalling bridges are visible amidships in this photograph taken in 1902. These crossed the ship at the level of the catwalks between the forward and after superstructures.

The *Andrea Doria* was not in action throughout her existance but was regarded as a fleet unit until about 1904, thereafter being relegated. Her two sister ships were discarded in 1909 but the *Andrea Doria* remained on the list until May 1911 when she became a depot ship at Taranto. In February 1915 she was converted to a floating battery and was renamed *GR 104*, as a new battleship was to be named "Andrea Doria". She was towed to Brindisi for defence of its harbour and served there until the end of 1918. Afterwards she was converted to an oil hulk and retained the name *GR 104* until 1929, when she was broken up.

BATTLESHIPS II

British naval manoeuvres of 1888 resulted in a report that the fleet was inadequate to fight a major war against two great powers. This coincided with rumour of war with France, which was massing a battle fleet in the Mediterranean, and Russia was building battleships for the Black Sea fleet. Cordiality between these allies created anxiety in England and resulted in the Naval Defence Act of 1889, intended to boldly strengthen the Navy. It was the most important administrative event in the British Navy during the period covered by this book and provided for seventy new warships being ordered at the then incredible cost of £21,500,000 with treasury support. The intention was to remove seventy-two obsolete ships from the fleet, though eventually only thirty were struck off.

Britain had by far the world's largest and most powerful fleet but contemporary British naval administration was inefficient and uneconomical. There was no organisation for naval war policy or personnel, and logistic support was inadequate. There was little agreement on the need for developing and sustaining a naval programme and the attitude of many high-ranking officers was typified by Admiral Hood who stated he "would have preferred by the end of 1890 to have had six more fast cruisers, but did not consider it a point of vital importance!"

Britain then possessed fifteen effective battleships, with six building. France had nine and five building and Russia three effective and three building. All three nations had many more old ships. To protect trade routes and assure future supremacy Britain needed large numbers of modern cruisers, and a class of new battleships.

Eight first class and two second class battleships were commenced under the act and the eight "Royal Sovereign" class were the finest of the time, with four 13.5-inch guns mounted in two barbettes, forward and aft of the amidship superstructure and ten 6-inch quick-firers as secondary armament *(Plate 24)*. These were good sea boats of 14,360 tons, 380ft long, and steamed at 15 knots but were capable of 17 in short spurts. Belt armour was good but the crews of the main and secondary armament were unprotected, which was a serious weakness, particularly as armour represented 30 per cent of the displacement.

By then the French Navy had adopted cylindrical turrets for the main and secondary armament in the 11,400-ton battleship *Brennus*, designed before the "Royal Sovereign" type. Two large guns were mounted forward and one aft, with secondary guns on two levels and a waterline armour belt. She had the usual tumble home and heavy looking superstructure.

Russian and Italian battleships then building had similar big gun disposition. The three Italian ships were of 13,500 tons and unusual funnel arrangement. They were commenced without side armour but by the time the first was launched, the *Re Umberto (Plate 27)*, quickfiring gun development made armour essential and she had 3.9-inch side armour fitted, but had the barbette and deck armour reduced in compensation.

The "Royal Sovereign" class were all completed within five years and proved superior to any contemporary battleships in power of attack, protection, seakeeping and speed. They were also majestic in appearance, though most battleships then building were basically similar in arrangement.

A feature of the mid 1890's was the readoption of the old sailing navy "line ahead" formation of a battle fleet in action, used in manoeuvres by the British fleet and the German, with others following. Exercises were increasingly recognised as being vital to efficiency but excessive attention was still given in all fleets to paint schemes, cleanliness, and drills of little fighting value. By then square-rig seamanship was not possible in the active fleet and skill in seamanship meant steaming ships in formation and performing intricate manoeuvres. This contributed to the loss of the British battleship *Victoria* in 1893, when the Mediterranean fleet was ordered to execute an apparently impossible inward turning manoeuvre, resulting in collision between the battleship *Camperdown (Plate 13)* and the flagship *Victoria*, which rammed and sunk with great loss of life and prestige.

Russia and France drew closer during the early 1890's and expanded their fleets. This was prompted by growing relations between Germany, Austria and Italy, with France soon to be conscious of German colonial and industrial expansion and of Italy's naval construction, particularly of battleships. In the Black Sea Russia was building more battleships, presumably to join the French Mediterranean fleet in war. Both were building commerce-raiding cruisers, potentially aimed against the 12½ million tons of British shipping using ocean trade routes. France and Russia combined then owned only 1½ million tons of merchant ships.

However, the French and Russians could not and did not build battleships to equal the numbers and quality of the British, and the situation in 1893 was that Britain had sixteen modern battleships against France's ten and Russia's four. Battleships under construction were in the ratio of six, five and five. These statistics led to a further British programme for seven first class battleships, six cruisers and thirty-six destroyers.

The "Majestic" class ships were of 14,900 tons and were enlargements of the "Royal Sovereign" type but with four 12-inch guns protected by armoured shields above the barbettes and having a rapid rate of fire every 45 seconds. There were twelve 6-inch quick-firing guns in armoured casemates on two decks as secondary armament and other light guns as defence against torpedo boat attack. Speed was 17 knots and bunkers were sufficient to steam 7,600 miles at 10 knots. The Harvey armour belt was of improved steel, only 9 inches thick, which enabled it to cover two thirds of the length and be of greater than usual width. In addition a 3-inch thick sloping deck protected the magazines, boilers and engine-rooms amidships. The "Majestics" were the finest battleships of the time and were the forerunners of many subsequent classes of British battleships (Plates 32-33).

Nevertheless there were critics, worried by the increasing size and cost of such ships, which a few lucky hits or a mine or torpedo might destroy. Some factions in Britain and France favoured smaller capital ships to disperse this risk. Others, rightly, foresaw a competitive "race" between naval nations attempting to outbuild each other with larger and more powerful battleships, resulting in a drain of resources as smaller and older ships quickly became obsolete. These counter arguments were dismissed by most British naval authorities who emphasised that French battleships, for instance, could be smaller as they were intended to operate only in European or Mediterranean conditions, never far from coaling facilities, so did not need the bunker capacity of British ships. The Admiralty had achieved its intention of having a powerful battle fleet of sixteen ships of the combined "Royal Sovereign" and "Majestic" classes: a homogenous force with all the advantages of efficiency, calculated handling and seakeeping. It was the best battle fleet in the world.

In contrast, French battleships continued to be unusual and individual. The 12,000-ton Charles Martel, Masséna and Bouvet type of 1893-6 reverted to an arrangement of single big gun turrets, with a pair of secondary gun turrets close to them and other secondary guns amidships – a retrograde system as the main armament broadside was reduced to three big guns in favour of obtaining three-gun fire ahead or astern, a doubtful advantage. The usual heavily rounded sides, large military masts, boat decks and funnels made them appear unstable.

In 1894-6 came the three new "Charlemagne" type battleships with twin end turrets and a long, lightly protected battery between them. Tumble home was retained, with sides unprotected below the battery but with the armour belt carried barely above water. During 1898-9 the 12,000-ton Iéna and 12,700-ton Suffren were launched, with improved protection, but remained curious individual ships. France seemed to be falling behind in battleship design until the "République" class ships were commenced in 1901, when displacement rose to 14,800 tons, excessive tumble home was abolished and the distribution of armament and armour resembled contemporary British battleships, though the armour was more concentrated and many considered the "Républiques" as the best protected ships afloat.

The proving of contemporary battle methods and ships occurred unexpectedly in the Far East during a war between China and Japan in 1894. China had a modest fleet of mixed ships headed by two 7,430-ton battleships of German build and two smaller armoured ships. The small but efficient Japanese fleet was handicapped by having only three old armoured ships but had several modern protected cruisers with quick-firing guns. A dispute arose over troop concentrations in Korea and war resulted. Chinese warships clashed with Japanese off the river Yalu in September 1894 and a naval battle developed. The four Chinese armoured ships were supported by six cruisers of various types. The Japanese attacked with the fast protected cruisers which put rapid fire into the Chinese ships, backed by the larger guns of the armoured craft. They ended the action circling the two largest Chinese battleships which were almost disabled. However, the Chen Yuen put one 12-inch shell into the cruiser Matsushima, which caused tremendous destruction and put her out of action. Four Chinese ships were sunk by gunfire and one was lost in collison, but their battleships again proved the value of armour, as despite about two hundred hits by quick-firing guns it remained intact and casualties in both ships were low. The action also proved the "line ahead" formation best for contemporary fleet battles, which in this case was indecisive as both fleets retired, but the Japanese had gained control of the surrounding sea, enabling their offensive to continue.

Flushed with success, Japan had ambitions to become a naval power and during 1894 ordered the 12,300-ton battleship Fuji in Britain (Plate 38). She was virtually a reduced "Royal Sovereign". Two years later two more battleships of 15,000 tons were ordered in Britain, which became the naval mentor of the Japanese, who were regarded by the British government as a potential ally to offset Russian influence in the Far East.

Russia watched the emergence of a militant Japan with apprehension and, concerned for her Far East territory, commenced construction of eight battleships which had French influence in the design, with long or complete waterline belts, curvature of side, high freeboard, large areas of unprotected side and big superstructures. Their stability was suspect, probably due to the weight of the main and secondary armament being mounted in turrets.

The emergence of two major battleship-owning powers outside Europe shocked Britain, as they could not be blockaded in war or be fought by the British fleets in home or Mediterranean waters. However, the China station was immediately reinforced with second class battleships of the "Centurion" class *(Plate 29)*. The ships were of light draught, enabling them to use the Suez canal and steam quickly to the Far East.

Britain's world-wide naval superiority was now threatened and alliances were contemplated with America and Japan to cover the Pacific. The American fleet had lapsed into coast defence lethargy for twenty-five years following the civil war, placing faith in clumsy coast defence monitors and a few cruisers. America still regarded the Atlantic and Pacific oceans as sure bulwarks against foreign interference in the steady growth of industrial eastern America and the settling of the west. The real barrier, however, was the British Navy, though no true American would have admitted it. American fleet expansion commenced in 1890 and reflected the mood of the nation to assert itself, backed by the continent's great resources and expanding trade.

Three "Indiana" class battleships were laid down – 10,200-tonners similar to the later "Royal Sovereign" type but with paired turrets for the main and secondary armament, resulting in low freeboard. These ships were heavily armed with four 13-inch guns backed by eight, paired 8-inch and four 6-inch – all breech loading. But they were indifferent seaboats and top speed was 16 knots.

The *Iowa* followed in 1896, then the two "Kearsarge" class and three "Alabama" class battleships of 1898 *(Plate 44)*. The "Kearsarge" type were distinguished in having the 8-inch secondary gun turrets mounted above the main armament turrets and moving with them, which would have been a serious weakness in action. The "Alabama" type were much better ships with four 13-inch and fourteen 6-inch quick-firers as secondary armament.

Before these ships were completed the Spanish-American war began in April 1898, in which the two fleets played a considerable part. Insurgent action in Cuba, then a Spanish colony, contributed to the war which flared after the sinking of the American armoured ship *Maine* by an explosion in Havana harbour during February 1898, with great loss of life. A force of Spanish cruisers and destroyers cruised in the West Indies and entered Santiago de Cuba, where they were blockaded by an American squadron. In July this Spanish force attempted to break out, with orders to fight its way clear or certainly perish in a daylight battle between four armoured cruisers versus battleships and armoured cruisers in superior numbers. The American ships fired about 8,000 rounds but made only one hundred and twenty-one recognisable hits on the Spaniards, which nevertheless beached in flames after a gallant but hopeless fight. Most damage was inflicted with the 8-inch guns, causing subsequent American battleships to continue mounting them as secondary armament.

American naval victories at Santiago and against a weak Spanish squadron in Manila Bay further demonstrated the rapid development of sea power when backed by the resources of an industrial nation.

Spain then had only one battleship, the 9,950-ton *Pelayo*, and she was not involved in any action.

After cessation of hostilities America purchased the Philippine Islands in the Pacific and acquired Puerto Rico and Guam, besides establishing a naval base in Cuba. With new world power status America ordered new battleships and spent large sums on expanding the fleet, which by 1907 was second in numbers to the British.

During 1898 British and French relations reached flashpoint when colony-seekers from both countries met and clashed at Fashonda in the Sudan. The incident threatened war and the French fleet at Toulon mobilised and British warships and fleets were alerted. But the mobilisation was defensive; the French fleet were unprepared for a major war and when Russia would not become involved, the French withdrew from the Sudan. Britain had safeguarded her Suez Canal-Red Sea route to the East by flexing her sea power.

With his "Majestic" type battleships setting the trend, British naval constructor White directed the design of many subsequent classes of battleships developed from them: the six "Canopus" class *(Plate 41)*, three "Formidable" class *(Plates 42 and 43)*, five "London" class *(Plates 47 to 50)*, six "Duncans" *(Plate 51)* and eight "King Edward VII" class *(Plates 52 to 54)*.

These maintained Britain's lead over any other nation, or the traditionally feared combination of France and Russia. As by then France obviously could not hope to compete with the British battle fleet, she increasingly experimented with submarines, and in 1901 the *Gustav Zede* was the first successfully to "torpedo" a battleship moving during exercises. This, the French were convinced, was the weapon which could destroy or immobilise Britain's battle fleet. Britain remained faithful to the battleship as the ultimate naval vessel, but began to build submarines to gain experience with what was for many years regarded as an underhand weapon. However, before an extensive French submarine policy could develop, Britain and France came to a political understanding against Germany, which was emerging as a potential common enemy.

German trade and industry had expanded rapidly from 1880-1900, overtaking Britain in production of iron and steel. Germany was energetically pursuing a growing colonial and trade policy which began to impinge on British interests and affect British business. A bitter rivalry began to replace the friendly feelings which had existed between the two countries until the 1880's and soon grew to enmity.

Eight small armoured ships were built for German coast defence between 1889-95, the first armoured ships built for the fleet since 1880.

Four 10,000-ton battleships of the "Wörth" type were laid down in 1890 *(Plates 22 and 23)* and were more advanced in design than any contemporary ships, with six 11-inch guns in paired turrets on the centreline, backed by ten 4.1-inch quick-firers. The speed of 16 knots was low but they were well armoured and stable.

The five 11,000-ton "Kaiser" class which followed reverted to a small armament of four 9.4-inch and twelve 5.9-inch, with the after turret mounted on a low freeboard deck *(Plate 40)* but these ships steamed at 18 knots.

Naval expansion was avidly encouraged by the Emperor Wilhelm II and when Admiral Tirpitz was appointed minister of marine in 1897 the German fleet surged ahead. A year later a naval law required construction of a seagoing battle fleet to raise the German Navy from a coast defence force to one intended to rival Britain in her home waters and show Germany's new status as an industrial and mercantile power.

The war between Britain and the Boers in South Africa at the end of the century, which brought seizure of German shipping suspected of aiding the Boers, expanded German desire for sea power and during 1900 a supplementary naval bill increased the battleship programme to thirty-eight, and cruiser building to thirty-two, with four battleships and seven cruisers in reserve.

While French, Italian, Austrian and Russian fleets and naval administrations could be regarded with equanimity by Britain, this determined new German surge to naval might could not; it was well organised and backed by great industrial resources. But the Germans still had limits to their naval expenditure and battleship dimensions were restricted by the depth of the Kiel canal which linked her naval bases in the Baltic and North Sea.

The five "Wittelsbach" type battleships built under the 1898 programme had only four 9.4-inch guns, though these had a rapid rate of fire and were backed by eighteen 5.9-inch quick-firers. Five further battleships built under the 1900 programme had four 11-inch guns which, though still smaller than those of other fleets, were accurate and efficient in rate of fire. All German battleships were well subdivided to restrict damage and, hopefully, to enable them to return to port for repair.

All this was a new and potentially dangerous threat to Britain whose naval policy for many years had been directed at maintaining naval supremacy over France, the assumed immediate adversary, and against Russia which was then reckoned a secondary foe of unknown naval capability. Now all this was changing and the principal force of the British fleet would have to be concentrated in home waters instead of spreading its force throughout the world, and particularly in the Mediterranean. Meanwhile gunnery science was not advancing as fast as the development of hulls, gun construction and armour. Naval guns were still laid on the target independently, with elementary sights, and in a seaway it was good shooting to hit a target at 1,500 yards. Naval thought was that actions should be fought at the closest possible range and gun drills and gun cleanliness were more important than spotting the fall of shot and developing accuracy at sea. Paintwork was spoiled by

flash and gunsmoke, which annoyed officers to whom smart appearance of the ship and quick execution of drills and manoeuvres were the signs of efficiency.

After the long period of general peace most fleets were complacent about their gunnery, but range-finders were installed in British battleships in 1892 and in other fleets soon after, and some enthusiastic officers were attempting to raise the fleet's interest in gunnery, handicapped by firing orders still transmitted by bugle and exercises satisfied by a high proportion of near misses to the target. French naval gunnery was claimed to be superior to the British, and the American was worse.

The leader in developing efficient firing methods was Captain Percy Scott of the British Navy. His first command, the protected cruiser *Scylla (Plate 74)*, was used to develop his methods which scored 80 per cent hits at the annual 1898 prize firing, leaving the fleet feeling that the *Scylla* had cheated somewhere, as the average score was 30 per cent in ideal target conditions. Scott's zeal spread to others and a wave of gunnery enthusiasm and new methods spread rapidly through the British fleet. By 1903 its gunlayers were following targets in a seaway with telescopic sights.

American naval gunnery was poor before 1903 but after Scott had discussed his methods with a Lieutenant Sims, later a famous admiral and gunnery specialist, his theories spread throughout the American Navy which became proficient very quickly. This cooperation was typical of the growing friendly relations between the two navies, which has always existed since.

During 1902 Japan became allied to Britain in an attempt to limit Russian expansion in Korea and Manchuria. Russia then had seven battleships based on Port Arthur, in Korea. During February 1904 the Japanese attacked this naval anchorage with torpedo craft as a declaration of war, a situation not unlike that of Pearl Harbour almost forty years later. No offensive or defensive measures had been taken by the Russian ships, and as two battleships were damaged this brought near parity with the Japanese battleship force. This war developed into the largest involving major fleets since the evolution of the steam battleship and the naval battles were followed keenly by all fleets, particularly by the British observers on board many Japanese ships, which were largely British-built or designed and were manned by officers and men influenced by British training and traditions, while Russia's best battleships were heavily influenced by the French.

There were various early naval clashes, and meanwhile, Japanese troops had landed in Korea and were pushing towards Port Arthur, where Vice-Admiral Makaroff had taken command to instil spirit into the Russian squadron with seagoing exercises and sorties which rapidly raised efficiency. Unfortunately his flagship, the battleship *Petropavlosk*, struck a mine during a sortie and the admiral and all but thirty men were drowned. His ability had been the Russian fleet's hope, and Admiral Vitgeft who succeeded him was a cautious commander. As Japanese troops advanced on Port Arthur he decided to break out and attempt to steam the squadron to Vladistock before it was trapped by a combined military and naval blockade.

The Japanese main fleet, under its commander-in-chief Admiral Togo, met the six Russian battleships, four cruisers and destroyers, with four battleships and four armoured cruisers. Togo was fighting with the whole battleship strength of Japan; the Russians had more battleships in the Baltic and Black Sea. So Togo kept the range long at 7,000 yards, well beyond the range of the smaller guns in his fleet. The Russian ships made good shooting at this long range, repeatedly straddling the Japanese, and as the long daylight action went on the Japanese flagship *Mikasa* was being seriously damaged. The Russian squadron was punishing the Japanese as it escaped until a chance shell struck Vitgeft's flagship *Tsarevitch* in the conning tower, killing the admiral and damaging the ship, which turned towards the Japanese line, throwing other Russian ships into disorder. The admiral next in command ordered them to follow him back to Port Arthur and the Japanese closed in to quick-firer range but lost the pursuit in darkness, under cover of which the Russian ships split up. A few months later Japanese field guns were shelling the trapped Russian ships which took no further part in the war.

That night the *Tsarevitch* steamed south to the neutral German colonial port of Kiaochau and internment. Although struck by about fifteen 12-inch shells and lighter ones, her armour belt and turrets were intact. The cruisers *Askold*, *Novik* and *Diana*, with four destroyers, also reached neutral ports.

Had it not been for the chance hit on the *Tsarevitch* the Japanese would probably not have contained the Russian squadron and the course of the whole war would have altered – but history is punctuated with "ifs".

This clash made Russia determined to crush the Japanese fleet and ships were assembled from the Baltic fleet for an epic voyage round Europe and Africa, across the Indian Ocean and round Asia to attempt an avenging defeat on the Japanese. Lacking homogeneity, this large force of battleships, cruisers, destroyers, supply ships and colliers was headed by four new "Borodino" class battleships of 13,500 tons, which were similar to the *Tsarevitch* with four 12-inch and seven 6-inch guns in paired turrets and a complete waterline armour belt 10-inches thick. Tumble home and a large superstructure, added to overloading with coal and stores for the long voyage, made them bad sea boats for this passage.

This "2nd Pacific squadron" sailed from Kronsdat in September 1904 commanded by Admiral Rozhestvensky. During passage of the North Sea in October they sighted the working flares of English trawlers on the Dogger Bank, and due to the close relations of the British and Japanese fleets, these were thought to be signals between Japanese destroyers, perhaps British-built, which were waiting in the North Sea. Nothing else could explain why the flagship *Suvoroff* opened fire towards the flares, followed by the rest of the fleet. Four Hull trawlers were set on fire and

another was sinking, there were dead and injured trawlermen and England was in a ferment. The Channel squadron prepared for war and cruisers were despatched to shadow the Russians, becoming particularly provocative as they passed down the coast of Spain, steaming close abreast the Russian ships at night and following them by day. The excitement faded as the Russian fleet steamed round Africa's west coast, coaling in French or German colonial ports from chartered German colliers.

When Rozhestvensky arrived at Madagascar he received news of the fall of Port Arthur, but other Russian ships were steaming to join him via the Suez Canal, and early in March he sailed for the Sunda Islands, coaling at sea in the Indian Ocean with barges carried by the colliers. The fleet coaled again off Indo-China, after passing Singapore, and met reinforcements led by the old 9,700-ton battleship *Nicholas I*, with three coast defence ships.

The Russian squadron steamed up the Chinese coast towards the Straits of Tsushima, where Rozhestvensky formed single line ahead with the *Suvoroff*, *Alexander III*, *Borodino* and *Oryol*, followed by the *Osliaba* and the older battleships, then the almost useless coast defence ships. He expected to meet Togo, who converged unseen with four battleships backed by eight, well-designed armoured cruisers; all able to steam at 18 knots to the Russian fleet's 9 or 10, after the long voyage.

Togo's fleet mounted sixteen 12-inch guns and one hundred and twelve 8- and 6-inch guns. The Russian squadron had twenty-six 12-inch, of which only sixteen were modern weapons, seventeen 10-inch and one hundred and twenty-one 8- and 6-inch. The Japanese fleet was enthusiastic and well tried; the 2nd Pacific squadron was weary of a long and extremely difficult voyage and most of its seamen sensed doom. As the fleets converged for action the Russians opened fire at 6,500 yards, with an accuracy which unsettled the Japanese. Fighting became general with the two fleets steaming on parallel courses and firing at 5,500 to 5,700 yards range. The larger Japanese ships concentrated on the *Suvoroff* which, although adroitly handled, was damaged and on fire when she fell out of line. Japanese cruisers attacked the *Osliaba* and sank her. Meanwhile the striken *Suvoroff* continued to fight and the other Russian ships were circling away from the Japanese which, in two lines, fired into them as guns would bear. The Russians replied spiritedly, though many were on fire. Battle raged into the afternoon and the new Russian flagship, the battleship *Borodino*, led surviving Russian ships which could steam adequately on a course for Vladivostok as mist and smoke veiled them from the enemy. But Togo soon overtook these remnants and shattered the *Alexander III* and *Borodino*. At dusk Japanese destroyers attacked the ships reforming astern of the *Nicholas I*, flagship of the little damaged third division.

Meanwhile Rozhestvensky and his staff had transferred from the still fighting *Suvoroff* to a destroyer, and when Japanese destroyers closed in to attack the *Suvoroff* the battleship's crew opened heavy fire, but the ship was sunk with three torpedoes. During the night torpedo attacks sank two old Russian battleships and a coast defence ship. Another old battleship had been sunk earlier by the gunfire of Japanese cruisers and at dawn only four Russian battleships were steaming for Vladivostok, with the *Oryol* the only remaining modern ship, but badly damaged. Togo again overhauled them and the Russian ships surrendered rather than be uselessly annihilated.

Rozhestvensky's destroyer was later captured by the Japanese and what came to be known as the Battle of Tsushima ended in disaster for Russia's fleet, relieved only by the tenacious heroism of its officers and men, who from the start had an impossible task. Japan had achieved command of the sea and her armies were victorious on land, giving her clear victory: a lesson and a warning to other fleets.

Throughout the battle superior Japanese speed enabled Togo to choose the range, and his gunners fired only when the guns would bear. The Russians were desperate to damage the Japanese and fired rapidly and constantly, whether they could see a target or not, though much of their shooting was more accurate than the Japanese expected. Tsushima was fought when all major fleets were fast changing their gunnery methods. These were quickly becoming more organised, with fire control from positions independent of the turrets (usually aloft in a new version of the old fighting top), from where the fall of shot could be spotted, ranges taken and deflection corrections made. By then battle practice firing in the British fleet was at 5,000–6,000 yards and long-range gunnery was developing under the general direction of Admiral Sir Percy Scott. Gunnery replaced smart paintwork as the fetish in navies, encouraged by an increasing rivalry and enthusiasm among not only the large powers but almost every nation with a fleet.

Everywhere, nations large and small were ordering warships. The Scandinavian coast defence navies were rivalling each other with new designs. In 1898 Norway ordered the 4,000-ton miniature battleships *Norge* and *Eidsvold* in Britain *(Plate 45)*. Demark embarked on a series of three 3,700-tonners including the *Olfert Fischer (Plate 56)* and Sweden built nine coast defence armoured ships between 1896 and 1906, when the 4,700-ton *Oscar II* was launched *(Plate 55)*. Although coast defence ships had very limited fighting value most were very long lived and many of the Scandinavian battleships were still serving during World War II.

Long-range gunnery continued to develop in major fleets, and as the spotting of falling shells around an enemy ship was best done if the shells were all of one size, this contributed to the desire of American, Italian and British naval architects to design battleships with the largest possible number of all big guns instead of the four 12-inch then generally fitted, backed perhaps by four 9.2-inch and ten 6-inch, as in the British "King Edward VII" class, or by eight 8-inch and twelve 7-inch in the American "Connecticut" type. The 12-inch gun was retained in the planning of the various projected ships as the best available weapon, firing perhaps two shots each minute and well proved in the recent

Japanese fleet actions against Russia.

During 1903 the Italian naval constructor Cuniberti writing in 'Jane's Fighting Ships', proposed an ideal battleship for the British fleet: a 17,000-ton ship armed with twelve 12-inch guns and capable of 24 knots. Early in 1905 the Americans authorised two battleships to mount eight 12-inch guns on a displacement of 16,000 tons, with a light secondary armament of twenty-two 3-inch guns. If Britain was to commission the first all big gun battleship she had to act quickly. Sir John Fisher was then First Lord of the Admiralty and this energetic personality had plans rushed out for a 17,900-ton ship with ten 12-inch guns in five paired turrets, not all on the centreline, as in the American ship. Design was directed by Philip Watts, who became Director of Naval Construction in 1903, and it was made more revolutionary by the choice of steam turbines for propulsion machinery, which had previously been tried in nothing larger than a cruiser, though it had been developed by Sir Charles Parsons' company since 1892, with increasing success. As this new battleship was experimental she was to be built as an individual ship then, if proved successful and when fully evaluated, classes of improved ships were to be built. She was built in a year and a day at Portsmouth dockyard, whose usually sedate progress was abandoned in the rush to build the *Dreadnought*, as she was to be named *(Plates 57 and 58)*. The keel was laid in October 1905 and building time was shortened by use of steel and armour intended for other ships, and the guns and turrets from the almost as large but more conventionally armed battleships *Lord Nelson* and *Agamemnon*, which had been begun in May 1905 and were temporarily stopped while the *Dreadnought* was building.

The all big gun *Dreadnought* proved a success and orders were given to go ahead with a "Dreadnought" class of battleship. Once again, all navies were now equal in effective battleship strength, apart from Britain's short-lived advantage of one ship.

The completion of the *Dreadnought* in 1906 opened a new phase in battleship design and international rivalry which ended in the 1914-18 war. Battleships built before her and after 1889 became generally known as "pre-Dreadnoughts" and were rendered obsolete in the battle line as the *Dreadnought*'s successors and rivals grew in numbers which are beyond the scope of this book.

Psara

GREEK 1892 *Plate 21*

Built	Granville, France
Laid down	1887
Launched	February 1890

21 PSARA, GREEK 1892

Completed	1892
Dimensions	Length overall 334ft 6in
	Length waterline 331ft
	Breadth 51ft 8in
	Draught 23ft 3in
Displacement	4,885 tons
Machinery	Twin screw
	Two 3-cylinder compound horizontal engines (later triple expansion)
	Four cylindrical type boilers by Forges & Chantiers de la Méditerranée
	IHP = 6,700 = 17 knots
	Speed 14.5 knots
Bunkers	Coal. 400 tons normal. 690 tons maximum
Armament	Two 10.6 inch. 36 calibre. Breech loading by Canet. In forward redoubt
	One 10.6-inch breech-loading gun by Canet. 30 calibre. In hooded barbette aft
	Five 5.9-inch quick-firers by Canet. One on centreline between 10.6-inch in redoubt. Remainder in armoured battery
	One 3.9-inch quick-firer. In bow
	Eight 9-pounder quick-firers. 50 calibre
	Twelve 1-pounders
	Four machine-guns
	Torpedo tubes. One 15-inch diameter torpedo tube in bow above water. Two 14-inch diameter torpedo tubes above water
Armour	Creusot. Steel
	Belt 11.8-inch – 4.7-inch
	Upper belt 3-inch
	Battery forward 13.7-inch
	Barbette aft 11.8-inch
	Barbette hood 6-inch
	Protective deck 2.3-inch
	Conning tower 12-inch
Complement	400

The *Psara*, and her sister ships *Spetsai* and *Hydra* were small battleships designed and built in France for Greek conditions. The disposition of armament was unusual: two of the 10.6-inch guns were mounted in an armoured redoubt forward, the other in a hooded barbette aft. Only two of these guns could fire ahead or on the beam at one time and only one astern. One of the secondary 5.9-inch guns was mounted on the centreline between the two 10.6-inch and the others were a deck lower, in the armoured battery under the redoubt. These ships were well sub-divided, having one hundred and eighteen watertight compartments. When built they had three masts of almost equal height, each having a fighting top.

The *Psara* had her masts altered in 1897 when she underwent a major refit at the French yard of La Seyne. The forward and after masts were lowered as shown in this photograph taken in 1902. The large rectangular side ports provided excellent light and ventilation but were vulnerable in a warship.

All three ships were reconstructed; the *Psara* in 1897 and the others during 1899-1900. They were the pride of the Greek fleet when war commenced between Greece and Turkey in April 1897. The Turkish fleet was superior in numbers and armament, but was almost totally laid up and disorganised. The Greeks controlled the sea but lost heavily on land and the war ended on 20th May with an armistice agreed when Russia applied pressure to Turkey.

During the Greek-Balkan league war against Turkey of October 1912 to May 1913, the *Psara*, *Spetsai* and *Hydra*, supported by the powerful armoured cruiser *Giorgios Averoff*, built in Italy in 1911, formed the backbone of a Greek fleet, including fourteen good destroyers and one small submarine, besides older and smaller ships. Her allies Bulgaria, Serbia and Montenegro had very limited naval forces and the seafaring Greeks faced the Turkish Navy alone.

On October 18th 1912 the *Psara* was part of a force, under Rear-Admiral Condouriotis, which included the *Spetsai*, *Hydra*, *Averoff*, fourteen destroyers, five modern torpedo boats, the submaine *Dolphin*, minelayer *Ares*, a hospital ship, troopships and auxiliaries which occupied the island of Lemnos and other islands in the approaches to the Dardanelles. During December 1912 Turkey signed an armistice with the allies of Greece, leaving her fighting on alone. The *Psara*, with her sisters and the *Averoff*, screened by destroyers, patrolled the approaches to the Dardanelles, and on December 16th a Turkish squadron sortied from anchorage. The squadron included the battleships *Torgut Reis* and *Heireddin Barbarossa (Plate 23)*, the armoured ships *Messudieh* and *Assar-I Tewfik*, the light cruiser *Medjidieh* and eight destroyers. After a short action in which the Greeks took the initiative, the Turks turned away and retired. The *Psara* was undamaged but her sisters and the *Averoff* were hit and damaged. The Turks came out again on January 18th 1913, with the four armoured ships, and another action ensued but with the Greeks showing boldness and inflicting much damage.

The fast Turkish cruiser *Hamidieh* escaped from the Dardanelles unobserved on January 14th, shelled the Greek island of Syra and fired on the Greek armed merchant cruiser *Macedonia*, which was severely damaged. The *Hamidieh* proceeded to Port Said and the Red Sea before returning to the Mediterranean where, after steaming to Beirut, she entered Malta due to stress of weather. The *Psara* and four destroyers were sent in pursuit, being the only Greek ships which could be spared from the blockade. However, the slow *Psara* had no hope of catching the Turkish cruiser and by March 11th the *Hamidieh* was shelling Serbian ports in the Adriatic. She afterwards steamed to the Red Sea where she remained until the end of the war rather than run the Dardanelles blockade.

Hostilities ended in May 1913.

Throughout this war the Greek fleet was principally dependent on the armoured cruiser *Averoff* as its main offensive weapon, the three old battleships having limited value. This caused the Greek government to purchase the old American "pre-Dreadnought" type battleships *Idaho* and *Mississippi* to counter Turkish acquisition of the similar ex-German battleships *Kurfürst Friedrich Wilhelm* and *Weissenburg* which were renamed *Heireddin Barbarossa* and *Torgut Reis*.

During 1913 it was proposed to refit the *Psara* and her sisters but this does not seem to have been done.

Greece entered World War I as an ally of Britain and France after July 1917, and once again the *Psara* was on active service. She and the *Hydra* were sold out of the Navy in 1920, but the *Spetsai* remained in service as a training ship until 1929 when she also was sold.

Brandenburg

GERMAN 1893 *Plate 22*

Built	A.G. Vulkan. Stettin
Laid down	1890
Launched	September 1891
Completed	1893
Dimensions	*Length overall* 380ft 6in
	Length waterline 354ft 3in
	Breadth 65ft 6in
	Draught 24ft 4in mean. 26ft 6in maximum
Displacement	10,062 tons
Machinery	Twin screw
	Two 3-cylinder vertical triple expansion engines
	Twelve cylindrical boilers
	IHP natural draught = 8,000
	IHP forced draught = 9,000 = 16 knots
Bunkers	Coal. 640 tons normal. 1,040 maximum
Endurance	4,500 miles at 10 knots
Armament	Four 11-inch Krupp guns. 40 calibre. Two forward and two aft in barbettes with shields
	Two 11-inch Krupp guns. 35 calibre. Two in barbettes amidships with shields
	Six 4.1-inch quick-firers. 30 calibre. In battery amidships. Two more 4.1-inch guns added 1903. Total eight
	Eight 3.4-inch quick-firers. 30 calibre. On after superstructure and in forward sponson
	Twelve 1-pounder quick-firers
	Eight machine-guns
	Five 18-inch torpedo tubes. One, stern. Two on each side
Armour	*Belt* 15.7-inch – 11.8-inch. Full length
	Barbettes 11.8-inch
	Barbette hoods 5-inch
	Casemates for 4.1-inch guns 3-inch
	Protective deck 3-inch
	Conning tower 11.8-inch
Complement	575

The *Kurfürst Friedrich Wilhelm, Brandenburg, Weissenburg (Plate 23)* and *Wörth* were laid down during 1890 as the first German battleships to be built since the "Baden" type, constructed between 1877-80. German designers thus avoided the low-freeboard type ships of the 1880's and the arrangements of their new ships were advanced and powerful. Contemporary ships in the British fleet were the "Royal Sovereign" class *(Plate 24)* mounting four 13.5-inch guns in barbettes forward and aft, compared to the "Kurfürst Friedrich Wilhelm" type with six 11-inch guns in three barbettes with armoured shields; better protected and with one and a half times the potential hitting power.

Although these ships did not attract much attention at the time, their main armament was a considerable advance on their contemporaries' and foreshadowed the "Dreadnought" type of fifteen years later. The amidship barbette, with its short guns, was only effective for firing abeam but was well placed for use at sea, being in the steadiest part of the ship, sheltered by the superstructures. Subsequent development of German battleships stemmed from these ships, which had a grim and businesslike appearance slightly relieved by the scrollwork at the stem. The heavy tubular masts and enclosed tops contrasted with the lighter ones of British ships, and the raised forecastle made them good sea boats, despite the mounting of the forward barbette closer to the stem than in most similar battleships. Unlike the "Royal Sovereign" class these were not elegant ships – the deckhouses, forward accommodation and gun sponsons destroyed their symmetry – but they were excellent fighting ships.

This photograph of the *Brandenburg* was taken in 1898 and shows among other features the cupola-shaped barbette shield amidships, the small-diameter ventilator cowls, the enclosed wheelhouse sunk into a comparatively small and screened bridge with conning position above, derrick stowage on each mast, and the stowage of boats on the after deckhouse which was connected to the forward superstructure by a flying bridge above the amidship barbette. A working party at the stem is painting the cable, while launches and boats lie at the booms and a dockyard craft noses alongside with stores.

These four battleships remained the principal force of the German fleet until the completion of the "Kaiser" class ships in 1898-1901, although, strangely, these reverted to a main armament of four 9.4-inch guns with a strong secondary armament *(Plate 40)*.

22 BRANDENBURG, GERMAN 1893

As the 1st division of the 1st squadron of "ships of the line", a term revived at that time in the German fleet, these four battleships were sent to reinforce the international forces in China during the Boxer rebellion of 1900.

During 1902-4 the *Brandenburg* and her sisters were reboilered and partially reconstructed. During 1910 the *Weissenburg* and *Kurfürst Friedrich Wilhelm* were sold to Turkey but the *Brandenburg* and *Wörth* remained in service with the German fleet, even though outdated. At the start of World War I the *Brandenburg* was used as a coast defence ship until 1915 but was disarmed during 1916 to become an accommodation and distillation ship at Libau. Later it was intended to use her as a target ship for the fleet but this was cancelled as the war developed. After Germany's surrender the *Brandenburg* was discarded in May 1919 and during 1920 was scrapped at Danzig, with her sister ship *Wörth*.

Weissenburg (later Torgut Reis)

GERMAN 1893 *Plate 23*

Built	A.G. Vulkan. Stettin
Laid down	1890
Launched	December 1891
Completed	1893
Dimensions	*Length overall* 380ft 6in
	Length waterline 354ft 3in
	Breadth 65ft 6in
	Draught 24ft 4in mean. 26ft 6in maximum
Displacement	10,062. tons
Machinery	Twin screw
	Two 3-cylinder vertical triple expansion engines
	Twelve cylindrical boilers
	IHP natural draught = 8,000
	IHP forced draught = 9,000 = 16 knots
Bunkers	Coal. 640 tons normal. 1,040 tons maximum
Endurance	4,500 miles at 10 knots
Armament	Four 11-inch Krupp guns. 40 calibre. Two forward and two aft in barbettes with shields
	Two 11-inch Krupp guns. 35 calibre. Two in barbette amidships with shield
	Six 4.1-inch quick-firers. 30 calibre. In battery amidships
	Two more 4.1-inch guns added 1903. Total eight
	Eight 3.4-inch quick-firers. 30 calibre. On after superstructure and forward sponson
	Twelve 1-pounder quick-firers
	Eight machine-guns
	Five 18-inch torpedo tubes. One, stern. Two each side. All submerged.
Armour	*Belt* 15.7-inch – 11.8-inch. Full length
	Barbettes 11.8-inch
	Barbette hoods 5-inch
	Casemates for 4.1-inch guns 3-inch
	Protective deck 3-inch
	Conning tower 11.8-inch
Complement	575

The *Weissenburg*, another of the "Kurfürst Friedrich Wilhelm" class battleships, was sister to the *Brandenburg* and *Wörth*. The *Weissenburg* served with the German fleet in the North Sea and the Baltic and was visiting England when this photograph was taken in 1898. She was refitted and reboilered at Wilhelmshaven during 1903-4, and continued serving with the fleet. In September 1910 she was sold to Turkey and renamed *Torgut Reis*. The *Kurfürst Friedrich Wilhelm* was also acquired by the Turks and renamed *Heireddin Barbarossa*. With the light cruisers *Hamidieh (Plate 110)* and *Medjidieh* and some good destroyers, these battleships formed the main force of the Turkish fleet until 1914.

The battleships sailed with five destroyers from Beirut on September 28th 1911, ignorant that war between Turkey and Italy was imminent as a result of Italy's intended annexing of Tripoli, then a Turkish possession. On 30th September the squadron was warned and retired into the Dardanelles, the narrow channel linking the eastern Mediterranean with the Sea of Marmora and the Black Sea, and subject of naval blockades, political manoeuvrings and intrigue for generations.

The war ended during September 1912, without the major Turkish ships being called to action. However, only a month later Turkey was at war with Greece, Serbia and Bulgaria, of which only Greece had a useful navy and that did not match the potential strength of the Turkish fleet, having only one modern armoured cruiser and three small old battleships. It was, however, far better organized.

On October 19th the *Torgut Reis* and *Heireddin Barbarossa*, accompanied by the old armoured ship *Messudieh*, the cruiser *Hamidieh* and four torpedo boats, bombarded the Black Sea port of Varna, firing on Bulgarian torpedo boats. Next day the Turks captured two torpedo boats and shelled the military depot at Kavarna. The squadron then moved to the Sea of Marmora to support the Turkish army falling back towards Constantinople before the Bulgarian advance. On November 21st four Bulgarian torpedo boats made a bold attack on Turkish ships off Varna. One torpedo struck the cruiser *Hamidieh*, which reached port with difficulty. The battleships continued to bombard Bulgarian army positions on the coast of the Sea of Marmora until an armistice was signed with Bulgaria and Serbia on 3rd December.

The *Torgut Reis* and other Turkish ships were freed to face the Greeks, who chose to fight on alone. On December 16th a Turkish cruiser and

23   WEISSENBURG, GERMAN 1893

eight destroyers sortied from the Dardanelles towards the fleet of Greek armoured ships and destroyers patrolling offshore. Shortly afterwards the Turkish flagship *Heireddin Barbarossa* led the *Torgut Reis, Messudieh* and *Assar-I-Tewfik* towards the Greek fleet, while the cruiser and destroyers retired within the range of coastal batteries.

The Turkish ships opened fire at 15.000 yards and the Greeks replied when this closed to 8,000 yards. After a five-minute engagement the Turkish ships turned and an hour later the incident ended with the Turks returning to the Dardanelles.

On December 22nd the *Torgut Reis* came out with the cruiser *Medjidieh* and three destroyers but returned on finding the Greek fleet awaiting her.

The *Torgut Reis* and the three other Turkish battleships came out on the morning of January 18th 1913 and steamed for the Greek naval base on the island of Lemnos, followed by the cruiser *Medjidieh* and thirteen destroyers and large torpedo boats. When about twelve miles from the island the Greek cruiser *Averoff* and the three Greek battleships appeared and the Turks turned and steamed for the Dardanelles, fighting a long-range action with the pursuing Greeks, which lasted about two hours. The *Averoff* hit the *Heireddin Barbarossa* several times until both she and the *Torgut Reis* were on fire and each had one barbette damaged by shell hits, but continued to steam and fight until well inside protected waters. They did not emerge after this affair and the war ended in April 1913.

Soon after, the Greeks purchased the old American "pre Dreadnought" battleships *Idaho* and *Mississippi*, and Turkey ordered a battleship to be built in Britain and a battlecruiser to be constructed in Germany.

The *Torgut Reis* and *Heireddin Barbarossa* saw no action during World War I when Turkey was allied to Germany and Austro-Hungary. However, the German battlecruiser *Goeben* and cruiser *Breslau* were acquired by Turkey in 1914 and posed a threat to the Black Sea and Mediterranean naval forces of Britain and her allies.

In 1920 the *Torgut Reis* was relegated to a depot ship with some or all guns removed. However, she was not sold until 1938 and was afterwards scrapped.

Royal Sovereign

BRITISH 1892 *Plate 24*

Built	Royal Naval dockyard, Portsmouth
Laid down	September 1889
Launched	February 1891 (from dock)
Completed	May 1892

Dimensions	*Length waterline* 380ft
	Breadth 75ft
	Draught 27ft 6in mean
Displacement	14,150 tons normal. 15,585 deep-loaded
Machinery	Twin screw
	Two 3-cylinder vertical triple expansion engines by Humphrys and Tennant
	Eight cylindrical single-ended boilers
	IHP natural draught = 9.000 = 15.5 knots
	IHP forced draught = 13,360 = 18 knots
Bunkers	Coal. 900 tons normal. 1,100/1,490 tons maximum
Endurance	4,720 miles at 10 knots. 2,780 miles at 14 knots
Armament	Four 13.5-inch breech-loading guns. Two forward and two aft barbettes
	Ten 6-inch quick-firers
	Sixteen 6-pounder quick-firers
	Twelve 3-pounder quick-firers
	Two machine-guns
	Seven 18-inch diameter torpedo tubes. Two submerged forward. Four above water broadside. One above water in stern. Later reduced to three tubes. Two submerged and one in stern
Armour	*Belt* 18-inch – 16-inch – 14-inch. 250ft long by 8ft 8in wide
	Bulkheads 16-inch – 14-inch
	Barbettes 17-inch – 16-inch – 11-inch
	Main deck casemates 6-inch
	Decks 3-inch – 2½-inch
	Side above belt 4-inch
	Screen bulkheads 3-inch
	Forward conning tower 14-inch
	After conning tower 3-inch
Complement	712

The *Royal Sovereign* gave her name to a class of eight battleships laid down under the Naval Defence Act of 1889. These were the first British battleships with high freeboard to carry all their main guns on the weather deck. They were the first to mount the secondary armament in casemates, to exceed 12,000 tons displacement and to have steel armour.

The class was designed under the direction of Sir William White, a noted naval constructor with a strong personality, who believed in the barbette system of heavy gun mounting. The *Royal Sovereign* carried two pairs of 13.5-inch guns mounted on turntables in pear-shaped armoured barbettes which projected slightly above the weather deck at each end of the superstructure. However, there were no barbette shields, which would have made them vulnerable in action.

The main deck secondary 6-inch guns were in casemates, which were frequently flooded in rough weather. Seven torpedo tubes were origi-

24   ROYAL SOVEREIGN, BRITISH 1892

nally fitted but these were later reduced to three.

These ships had a symmetry of design and an imposing appearance of well-balanced power which set a new standard of appearance and arrangement for many years.

On trials the *Royal Sovereign* was loaded to a mean draught of 27ft 6in and achieved 13,360 IHP under forced draft to reach 18 knots, making her the fastest battleship of the time. However, other ships of the class were restricted to 11,000 IHP to avoid straining their boilers, and consequently had lower speeds.

The ships were well sub-divided but were found to roll badly and were unsteady gun platforms.

The *Royal Sovereign* first commissioned in May 1892 as flagship of the Channel fleet and was the pride of the British Navy. With her sisters *Repulse*, *Resolution* and *Empress of India* she formed part of the British squadron under Sir Walter Kerr, attending the opening of the Kiel canal in June 1895. She became a private ship in the Channel fleet during December 1895 and was transferred to the Mediterranean fleet from June 1897 until August 1902. In November 1901 one of her 6-inch guns exploded, killing six and wounding nineteen. She returned home to become portguard ship at Portsmouth from autumn 1902 until May 1905, and refitted there during 1903 when casemates were fitted to the upper-deck 6-inch guns.

The *Royal Sovereign* lay in dockyard reserve at Devonport from May 1905 until February 1907 and then commissioned with a reduced crew. From April 1909 until 1913 she served in the 4th division, Home fleet, being relegated to material reserve during 1913. She was sold in October 1913 for £40,000, a high figure, to be broken up.

A small steam yacht lies alongside the starboard quarter and visitors prepare to leave at the gangway.

Resolution

BRITISH 1893 *Plate 25*

Built	Palmers, Jarrow-on-Tyne
Laid down	June 1890
Launched	May 1892
Completed	November 1893
Dimensions	*Length waterline* 380ft
	Breadth 75ft
	Draught 27ft 6in mean
Displacement	14,150 tons normal. 15,585 deep-loaded
Machinery	Twin screw
	Two 3-cylinder vertical triple expansion engines by Palmers

Eight cylindrical single-ended boilers
IHP natural draught = 9,000 = 15.5 knots
IHP forced draught = 11,000 = 16.5 knots

Bunkers	Coal. 900 tons normal. 1,100/1,490 tons maximum
Endurance	4,720 miles at 10 knots. 2,780 miles at 14 knots
Armament	Four 13.5-inch breech-loading guns. Two forward and two aft barbettes
	Ten 6-inch quick-firers
	Sixteen 6-pounder quick-firers
	Twelve 3-pounder quick-firers
	Two machine-guns
	Seven 18-inch diameter torpedo tubes. Two submerged forward. Four above water broadside. One above water in stern. Later reduced to three tubes. Two submerged and one in stern
Armour	*Belt* 18-inch – 16-inch – 14-inch. 250ft long by 8ft 8in wide
	Bulkheads 16-inch – 14-inch
	Barbettes 17-inch – 16-inch – 11-inch
	Main deck casemates 6-inch
	Decks 3-inch – 2½-inch
	Side above belt 4-inch
	Screen bulkheads 3-inch
	Forward conning tower 14-inch
	After conning tower 3-inch
Complement	712

One of the "Royal Sovereign" class, the *Resolution* was first commissioned at Portsmouth in December 1893 for the Channel fleet, with which she served until October 1901. The photograph, taken during this period, clearly shows the breeches of the 13.5-inch guns which are trained away to port. A 56ft steam pinnace capable of carrying 14-inch diameter torpedoes in dropping gear is being hoisted out by the derrick on the mainmast. The sternwalk is visible aft.

During December 1893 the *Resolution* was on passage from Plymouth to Gibraltar in company with the torpedo-gunboat *Gleaner*, when bad weather raised a short, steep sea. The battleship rolled so violently that she had to be put head to sea and eventually was forced to return to Queenstown to coal, while the little *Gleaner* was able to proceed. As a result in 1894 substantial bilge keels were fitted to reduce rolling. In July 1896 the *Resolution* collided with her sister ship *Repulse*, with little damage.

From November 1901 until February 1902 she was coastguard ship at Holyhead, then transferred as second flagship, reserve squadron. She refitted at Devonport during 1902-3 when casemates were installed for the secondary 6-inch guns. In February 1903, when on passage between Holyhead and Plymouth, she lost her rudder and suffered hull and steering gear damage. The *Resolution* commissioned in July 1904 as

25   RESOLUTION, BRITISH 1893

26   ROYAL OAK, BRITISH 1894

portguard ship at Sheerness, remaining there until June when she sailed for manoeuvres during July to September. Afterwards she paid off into the fleet reserve and recommissioned in July 1905 in the reserve at Chatham. She was in collision with her sister ship *Ramillies* during July 1906 and afterwards refitted at Chatham. From February 1907 to April 1909 she was at Devonport and then transferred to the 4th division, Home fleet.

Paid off in April 1911, the *Resolution* was towed to the Motherbank anchorage at Spithead and was laid up for sale, suffering damage from collision in March 1912. She was sold in 1914 to be broken up.

Royal Oak

BRITISH 1894 *Plate 26*

Built	Laird, Birkenhead
Laid down	May 1890
Launched	November 1892 (from dock)
Completed	June 1894
Dimensions	*Length waterline* 380ft
	Breadth 75ft
	Draught 27ft 6in mean
Displacement	14,150 tons normal. 15,585 tons deep-loaded
Machinery	Twin screw
	Two 3-cylinder vertical triple expansion engines by Laird
	Eight cylindrical single-ended boilers
	IHP natural draught = 15.5 knots
	IHP forced draught = 11,000 = 16.5 knots
	IHP trials = 11,608 = 18.27 knots (light condition)
Bunkers	Coal. 900 tons normal. 1,100/1,490 tons maximum
Endurance	4,720 miles at 10 knots. 2,780 miles at 14 knots
Armament	Four 13.5-inch breech-loading guns. Two forward and two aft barbettes
	Ten 6-inch quick-firers
	Sixteen 6-pounder quick-firers
	Twelve 3-pounder quick-firers
	Two machine-guns
	Seven 18-inch diameter torpedo tubes. Two submerged forward. Four above water broadside. One above water, stern
Armour	*Belt* 18-inch – 16-inch – 14-inch. 250ft long by 8ft 8in wide
	Bulkheads 16-inch – 14-inch
	Barbettes 17-inch – 16-inch – 11-inch
	Main deck casemates 6-inch
	Decks 3-inch – 2½-inch
	Side above belt 4-inch
	Screen bulkheads 3-inch
	Forward conning tower 14-inch
	After conning tower 3-inch
Complement	712

The *Royal Oak* was another of the "Royal Sovereign" class battleships. She cost £977,996 to build and was placed in reserve at Portsmouth from June 1894 until commissioned in July 1896 for the "particular service" squadron, created at the time of unrest in Europe preceding the South African war.

Beken's camera caught her that summer in the soft light of early morning, lying in Spithead with what became popularly known as the "flying squadron" – the trouble-shooting task force ready to steam anywhere in the world at any time to prove British naval supremacy. The unshielded mountings of the 13.5-inch guns are well shown.

The *Royal Oak* served with the squadron until November 1896, when she refitted at Portsmouth. From March 1897 until June 1902 she served in the Mediterranean fleet, returning to refit at Chatham, when casemates were fitted. During February 1903 she became second flagship, Home fleet, and later served in the Channel until March 1905 when she was transferred to the commissioned reserve at Chatham, where a minor magazine explosion occurred in May. Fire controls were installed during 1907 and in April 1909 she joined the Home fleet at Devonport. In January 1910 the *Royal Oak* became tender to the *Repulse* and passed into dockyard reserve during December 1911. In April 1913 she was towed to the Motherbank anchorage in Spithead and was offered for sale. During 1914 she was bought for £36,450 to be scrapped.

Re Umberto

ITALIAN 1893 *Plate 27*

Built	R.Cantiere di Castellammare di Stabia (Royal Naval Yard)
Laid down	July 1884
Launched	October 1888
Completed	February 1893
Dimensions	*Length overall* 418ft 6in
	Length between perpendiculars 400ft
	Breadth 76ft 9in
	Draught 28ft 6in mean
Displacement	13,893 tons
Machinery	Twin screw
	Four 2-cylinder vertical compound engines by Maudslay,

27   RE UMBERTO, ITALIAN 1893

Son and Field, London
Eighteen cylindrical boilers
IHP natural draught = 15,700 = 19.3 knots
IHP forced draught = 19,500 = 20.2 knots

Bunkers   Coal. 1,200 tons normal. Later, plus oil fuel. 3,000 tons maximum

Endurance   6,000 miles at 10 knots

Armament   Four 13.5-inch breech-loading guns. 30 calibre. Two in each barbette, forward and aft
Eight 5.9-inch quick-firers. 40 calibre
Sixteen 4.7-inch quick-firers
Sixteen 6-pounder quick-firers
Ten 1-pounder quick-firers
Two machine-guns
Five 17.7-inch diameter torpedo tubes

Armour   *Belt* 3.9-inch. 239ft long by extending from 3ft below water-line to upper deck
Bulkheads 2.7-inch
Barbettes 14.2-inch
Hoists to barbettes 11.8-inch
Deck 4.3-inch – 2-inch
Conning tower 11.8-inch

Complement   752

The *Re Umberto* was one of three almost sister battleships and was the first of the type to be laid down (during 1885), followed by the *Sardegna* and *Sicilia*. They cost an average of £1,050,000 each and were designed under the direction of Engineer Inspector Benedetto Brin. During construction it was decided to add side armour 3.9-in thick.

These ships could be compared with the British "Admiral" type (see the *Camperdown, Plate 13*) but had improved freeboard and carried the main guns much higher. However, the armour protection was comparatively poor. The disposition of three funnels and the single mast was unusual, even for that period. The engine-room was placed between the boiler-rooms.

Four 13.5-inch guns were mounted in pairs, in barbettes forward and aft. These were the first large naval guns to have central pivot mountings and were carried well above the waterline. The hulls had triple-bottom structure and for their time were effective battleships which steamed well and had a tactical turning diameter of about 1,000 yards.

They saw no action until the Italian-Turkish war of 1911-12 and the war service of the *Re Umberto* is described with that of her sister *Sardegna* (*Plate 28*). Afterwards the *Re Umberto* was laid up at Genoa and was later used as a depot ship. She was removed from the active list in May 1914 and was towed to La Spezia during June 1915 for use as a depot ship for the new battleship *Andrea Doria*, then completing. During December 1915 she was restored to the active fleet and was converted to a floating battery, serving defensively at the naval base of Brindisi before March 1916 until November 1917, and then until April 1918 as a floating battery at Valona. From April 1918 to October 1918 the *Re Umberto* was at the Taranto naval yard, at first being converted as a troop transport. However, this was abandoned as she was selected to be the attack ship for forcing the principal Austro-Hungarian naval base at Pola. For this service her 13.5-inch guns and barbettes were removed and eight 3-inch guns and many trench mortars were mounted. Special cutting gears were fitted forward for charging and clearing booms and harbour obstacles.

During October 1918 the *Re Umberto* arrived at Venice to prepare for the raid which was intended to open the harbour to about forty MAS motor torpedo boats which would attack the Austro-Hungarian ships inside. However, the war ended before the raid took place.

The *Re Umberto* was discarded by the Italian Navy in January 1920 and was subsequently scrapped.

Sardegna

ITALIAN 1895 *Plate 28*

Built   Royal Naval dockyard, Spezia

Laid down   November 1885

Launched   September 1890

Completed   February 1895

Dimensions   *Length between perpendiculars* 410ft
Breadth 77ft
Draught 28ft 6in mean. 29ft 3in maximum

Displacement   13,860 tons, normal. 15,674 tons, full load

Machinery   Twin screw
Four 3-cylinder triple expansion engines, two on each shaft. Designed by Maudslay, London, built at Naples by Hawthorn, Guppy and Co
Eighteen cylindrical boilers
IHP natural draught = 15,200
IHP forced draught = 22,800
IHP natural draught trials = 14,190 = 19.06 knots
IHP forced draught trials = 22,800 = 21.2 knots

Bunkers   Coal. 1,200 tons normal. Plus oil fuel. 3,000 tons maximum

Endurance   6,000 miles at 10 knots

Armament   Four 13.5-inch breech-loading guns. 30 calibre . Two in each barbette, forward and aft
Eight 5.9-inch quick-firers. 40 calibre
Sixteen 4.7-inch quick-firers. 40 calibre
Twenty 6-pounder quick-firers. 43 calibre

28 SARDEGNA, ITALIAN 1895

Ten 1 pounders
Two machine-guns
Five 17.7-inch diameter torpedo tubes. Two submerged.
Three above water

Armour Steel
Belt 4⅓-inch amidships. 249ft 3in long by 12ft 6in wide
Bulkheads at ends of belt 2¾-inch
Deck 4½-inch
Lower deck side 4-inch
Barbettes 14.2-inch
Hoods to barbettes 1-inch
Hoists to barbettes 12-inch
Conning tower 11.8-inch

Complement 752

The *Sardegna* was almost a sister ship to the *Re Umberto (Plate 27)* and *Sicilia*. She saw no action until the outbreak of war between Italy and Turkey on September 29th 1911 over the Italians' treaty right to occupy Tripoli. The *Sardegna* then formed part of the training division, which also included the *Re Umberto* and *Sicilia* and the armoured cruiser *Carlo Alberto (Plate 91)*. These ships, under Rear-Admiral B. Ricci, joined the 1st and 2nd squadrons which comprised the principal force of the Italian fleet.

On September 29th the *Sardegna* sailed from the Italian naval base at Augusta, Sicily, in company with the battleships *Benedetto Brin* and *Re Umberto,* to join the Italian fleet already blockading Tripoli. On October 3rd and 4th she participated with the *Re Umberto* and *Sicilia*, in the bombardment of Tripoli, firing on Fort Sultanieh and Fort "B", while other ships attacked elsewhere.

On October 5th the *Sardegna, Re Umberto* and *Sicilia* anchored off Fort Sultanieh to cover the landing of a naval brigade of 1,732 men, who occupied the fort and then Tripoli itself, while other ships bombarded Fort Hamidieh, which eventually exploded.

On April 10th 1912 the *Sardegna*, with the *Re Umberto, Sicilia*, the cruisers *Carlo Alberto* and *Marco Polo*, the gunboats *Agordat* and *Coatit*, two auxiliary cruisers and six torpedo boats, convoyed transports with 12,000 troops to Zuara, which was bombarded as a feint, before the force was successfully landed at Macabez, western Tripoli, despite a heavy sea.

With the Italian fleet in control of the Mediterranean, action moved to the Aegean. The *Sardegna* remained as part of the central Mediterranean force until the war ended on September 18th 1912.

By 1914 the *Sardegna* and her sisters were relegated to secondary duties but retained armament and still made good speed. Italy declared war on the side of Britain and France in July 1915 and her fleet's main task was to confine the efficient Austro-Hungarian fleet within the Adriatic.

Early in the war the *Sardegna* and the armoured cruiser *Carlo Alberto* covered the seaward flank of an inshore force of torpedo boats and small destroyers supporting Italian troops fighting the Austro-Hungarians on the Isonzo front, at the head of the Adriatic. By 1919 the *Sardegna's* armament had been reduced to four 13.5-inch guns and four 14-pounder anti-aircraft guns.

On July 4th 1923 the *Sardegna* was discarded by the Italian Navy and was subsequently broken up.

Barfleur

BRITISH 1894 *Plate 29*

Built Royal Naval dockyard, Chatham
Laid down October 1890
Launched August 1892
Completed June 1894
Dimensions *Length waterline* 360ft
Breadth 70ft
Draught 25ft 6in mean 26ft deep-loaded
Displacement 10,500 tons
Machinery Twin screw
Two vertical triple expansion engines by the Greenock Foundry Co
Cylindrical-type boilers
IHP natural draught trials = 9,934 = 17.1 knots
IHP forced draught trials = 13,163 = 18.5 knots
Bunkers Coal. 750 tons normal. 1,125 tons maximum
Endurance 6,500 miles at 10 knots. 9,750 miles at 10 knots
Armament *Original*
Four 10-inch 29-ton guns. 32 calibre. Two forward and two aft
Ten 4.7-inch quick-firers
Eight 6-pounder quick-firers
Twelve 3-pounder quick-firers
Four smaller
Torpedo tubes. Two submerged forward. Four above water broadside. One above water in stern
After refit 1904
Six 6-inch quick-firers replaced by 4.7-inch
Armour Compound and steel
Belt 12-inch 200ft long
Bulkheads 8-inch
Side above belt 4-inch
Barbettes 9-inch
Barbette shields 6-inch

29   BARFLEUR, BRITISH 1894

Deck 2-inch – 2½-inch
Main deck casemates 4-inch (removed 1902; 1904 reconstruction)
Casemates fitted during reconstruction 5-inch
Forward conning tower 12-inch
Aft conning tower 3-inch
Complement   620
Hull   Wood sheathed and coppered for tropical service

The *Barfleur* and her sister ship *Centurion* were second class battleships designed for the China and Pacific stations, with a draught of 26ft, enabling them to navigate the major Chinese rivers. The restriction on size resulted in a main armament of four 10-inch guns instead of the 13.5-inch and 12-inch of their contemporaries, but this was considered acceptable in view of the 10-inch and 8-inch gun armoured cruisers which the Russian fleet was then stationing in the Far East. The secondary armament was weak but it was envisaged that these two ships would act against ships of a potential enemy with a squadron of cruisers.

The *Barfleur* and *Centurion* resembled the "Royal Sovereign" class in general appearance. They were the first British battleships to have armoured shields over the barbettes to protect the gun crews, who worked above the mounting turntable, but the shields were open at the rear. The 10-inch guns were trained by steam or by hand and had all-round loading positions.

The *Barfleur* cost £533,666 to build and on completion in June 1894 went into reserve at Chatham, but commissioned for manoeuvres during July-September. She sailed for the Mediterranean during February 1895 to relieve the *Sanspareil* and served there until September 1898, being refitted at Malta during 1896-7 and 1897-8. She next served on the China station as rear-admiral's flagship and returned to Devonport in January 1902 to enter fleet reserve. Between August 1902 and July 1904 she was completely reconstructed; the 4.7-inch guns were removed and ten 6-inch substituted, allowing the removal of all superfluous weights.

The *Barfleur* commissioned for manoeuvres during July-September 1904, colliding with the battleship *Canopus* in Mount's Bay in August. She rejoined fleet reserve "A" and in January 1905 commissioned in the reserve. During February she sailed for the China station with a relief crew for the battleship *Vengeance*. She became flagship of the Portsmouth reserve from May 1905 and later in the year commenced a refit which continued into 1906. In March 1907 she was reduced to a nucleus crew and in April 1909 joined the 4th division, Home fleet, but during June was ordered to be laid up on the Motherbank. In July 1910 the *Barfleur* was sold for £26,550 to be scrapped.

This photograph was taken in 1905 when the *Barfleur* had completed her extensive reconstruction. She wore the flag of a rear-admiral, probably of the Portsmouth reserve. The secondary armament of ten 6-inch guns was mounted in a new system of casemates, the after bridge was

removed and the foremast was reduced to a signal mast. Windsails were used in place of the number of prominent ventilator cowls abaft the funnels, as built. The *Barfleur* was by then painted the uniform grey introduced into the Royal Navy during 1903.

Renown

BRITISH 1897 *Plates 30 and 31*

Built	Royal Naval dockyard, Pembroke
Laid down	February 1893
Launched	May 1895
Completed	January 1897
Dimensions	*Length* 380ft
	Breadth 72ft 4in
	Draught 26ft 9in mean
Displacement	12,350 tons
Machinery	Twin screw
	Two vertical triple expansion engines by Maudslay, Son and Field
	Eight cylindrical boilers
	IHP trials 8 hours natural draught = 10,708 = 17.9 knots
	IHP trials 4 hours forced draught = 12.901 = 19.75 knots
Bunkers	Coal. 800 tons normal. 1,760 tons maximum
Endurance	8,500 miles at 15 knots
Armament	Four 10-inch. 40 calibre. Two forward and two aft in turrets
	Ten 6-inch quick-firers
	Twelve 12-pounder quick-firers
	Twelve 3-pounder quick-firers
	Five 18-inch diameter torpedo tubes. Four submerged. One above water in stern
Armour	Harvey steel
	Belt 8-inch – 6-inch. 200ft long
	Bulkheads 10-inch – 6-inch
	Barbettes 10-inch
	Barbette shields 6-inch
	Main deck casemates 4-inch
	Upper deck casemates 4-inch
	Lower deck sides 6-inch
	Deck 3-inch
	Forward conning tower 9-inch
	Aft conning tower 3-inch
Complement	674
Hull	Wood sheathed and coppered for tropical service

30   *RENOWN, BRITISH 1897*

31   RENOWN, BRITISH 1897

The *Renown* was the only armoured ship ordered under the 1892-3 estimates of a Liberal government. She was an improvement on the "Barfleur" type, with a thinner but more effective belt of Harvey steel armour. In place of the usual flat deck above the belt, a sloping deck behind it was fitted and this innovation became used in subsequent British ships and those of other navies. The theory was that at whatever angle the belt might be hit and penetrated, the projectile then met further armour inclined at 45 degrees, which should deflect it. She was the first British ship to carry all secondary guns in casemates and was to have been the first of a class to mount 12-inch guns, but as these were not available, she was given similar armament to the earlier *Barfleur* and *Centurion*, making her a second class battleship – the last to be built for Britain. However, she was an important ship and set trends for many subsequent ones. Her appearance was admired throughout the fleet.

The *Renown* was four and a half years under construction and cost £746,247. She was completed at Devonport dockyard and passed into reserve in January 1897. In June she commissioned as flagship for the Jubilee naval review at Spithead, and *Plate 30* shows her here, with the old battleship *Thunderer* in the background. She afterwards sailed as flagship of the North American and West Indies station under Vice-Admiral Sir John Fisher. When he was transferred to the Mediterranean in 1899, the *Renown* was transferred with him, remaining there as flagship until February 1902. On return to England she was refitted to convey the Duke and Duchess of Connaught on their visit to India, and the main deck 6-inch guns were removed to provide increased accommodation and to reduce weight.

She returned to pass into fleet reserve at Portsmouth until July 1904, when she commissioned for naval manoeuvres. During 1904-5 she underwent major refitting and was commissioned in the reserve in February 1905. She was then prepared to act as a royal yacht to take the Prince and Princess of Wales (later King George V and Queen Mary) on a state visit to India during April to October 1905, and all 6-inch guns were removed. She was repainted with a white hull and was referred to as "the battleship yacht". She is shown in *Plate 31* getting up anchor at this time.

She commissioned in the reserve during May 1906 and joined the 4th division, Home fleet in 1907. Although outdated, she could still steam at 17.4 knots and with 12-inch guns would have been a useful ship. However, the *Renown* was relegated as tender to HMS *Victory* in October 1909 and later became a training ship for stokers at Portsmouth. She was placed under care and maintenance in January 1913 and laid up on the Motherbank in Spithead, and was sold during 1914 for breaking up.

Majestic

BRITISH 1895 *Plates 32 and 33*

Built	Royal Naval dockyard, Portsmouth
Laid down	February 1894
Launched	January 1895 (from dock)
Completed	December 1895
Dimensions	*Length overall* 413ft
	Length 390ft
	Breadth 75ft
	Draught 27ft 6in mean
Displacement	14,900 tons
Machinery	Twin screw
	Two 3-cylinder inverted triple expansion engines by the Naval Construction and Armaments Co
	Eight cylindrical boilers single-ended
	IHP trials 8 hours natural draught = 10,418 = 16.9 knots
	IHP trials 4 hours forced draught = 12,097 = 17.9 knots
Bunkers	Coal. 900 tons normal. 1,900 tons maximum. Plus 400 tons oil fuel added later
Endurance	3,500/7,600 miles at 10 knots. 1,700/4,000 miles at 15 knots
Armament	Four 12-inch 46-ton guns. 35 calibre. Two forward and two aft
	Twelve 6-inch quick-firers. 40 calibre
	Sixteen 12-pounder quick-firers
	Twelve 3-pounder quick-firers
	18-inch diameter torpedo tubes. Four submerged. One above water in stern
Armour	Harvey steel
	Belt 9-inch amidships. 220ft long by 16ft wide
	Bulkheads 14-inch forward. 12-inch aft
	Barbettes 14-inch
	Barbette shields 10-inch
	Casemates 6-inch
	Decks 4-inch – 3-inch – 2½-inch
	Conning tower forward 14-inch
	Conning tower aft 3-inch
Complement	672

The "Majestic" class battleships were ordered by a reluctant government in response to agitation for the need to maintain British naval supremacy over the navies of France and Russia, then considered the likeliest enemies.

Nine ships were laid down between 1893 and 1895, including the *Majestic*, *Magnificent*, *Hannibal*, *Prince George*, *Victorious*, *Jupiter*, *Mars*, *Caesar*, and *Illustrious*. They were essentially similar to the successful

32   MAJESTIC, BRITISH 1895

33   MAJESTIC, BRITISH 1895

Renown (Plate 31) but mounted four 12-inch guns in place of her 10-inch. The "Majestics" also had increased secondary armament, heavier armour, and were 10ft longer.

The *Majestic* and *Magnificent* were the first of the class to commission and were built in record time thanks to rivalry between the two dockyards – Portsmouth, where the *Majestic* was built, and Chatham, where the *Magnificent* was laid down.

The 12-inch guns superseded the 13.5-inch of the earlier "Royal Sovereign" ships and the "Majestics'" turrets had improved shell-handling arrangements and were hydraulically operated. However, eight of the twelve 6-inch secondary guns were mounted in main-deck casemates, which were of limited use in a seaway.

The concentration of protective armour over the central "citadel" in these battleships followed that of many preceding types. Beyond this, the hull was almost unprotected and an embarrassing damage occurred at Malta where the *Illustrious* was accidentally rammed by a steam picket boat which burst throught her stern plating.

The "Majestic" class were successful ships, steady gun platforms and could turn in a circle of 450 yards diameter at 15 knots speed. Not least, they were of imposing appearance; important for prestige and for the satisfaction of the British public whose money had been spent on these formidable-looking ships.

The *Majestic* cost £916,382 to build and commissioned at Portsmouth in December 1895 as flagship of the Channel fleet, where she served until February 1904; a remarkably long commission. These photographs were taken during this period *(Plates 32 and 33)*. She paid off at Portsmouth and in July again commissioned in the Channel fleet. During December an explosion of coal gas in a bunker killed one man and injured two others. She transferred to the Atlantic fleet in August 1906 and commissioned in the reserve during October, joining the Home fleet at the Nore in February 1907. The *Majestic* refitted at Chatham during 1907-8 when fire control and wireless transmitting equipment were fitted.

During January 1908 she was with the Devonport division of the Home fleet but between February to June was temporarily attached to the Nore division of the Home fleet. She rejoined the Devonport division, Home fleet, between June 1908 and August 1909, with a nucleus crew, and from August 1910 until May 1912 acted as a parent ship for battleships. Afterwards she joined the 3rd fleet at Devonport and during July 1912 collided with the battleship *Victorious*, without sustaining damage. Later she formed part of the 4th division at Devonport until August 1914, when she commissioned there with the 7th battle squadron for war service. During October she escorted a convoy of Canadian troops bound for France and afterwards operated in the Channel on patrol duty and bombarded the Belgian coast with the Dover patrol.

In 1915 the *Majestic* was equipped with bow gear for "mine bumping" in the Dardanelles operations and also participated in the bombardments there.

She became the flagship of Admiral Nicholson on 26th May and was sunk next day off Gaba Tepe by the German *U 21*. The *Majestic* was anchored with torpedo nets out, surrounded by transports discharging stores and equipment and protected by patrolling destroyers and trawlers. Nevertheless, the submarine penetrated the screen and fired two torpedoes which sliced through the nets. Forty of her crew were killed or drowned but excellent discipline saved the remainder. She capsized in 9 fathoms and rested upside down on her masts until a gale at the end of the year collapsed the foremast and she disappeared.

Magnificent

BRITISH 1895 *Plate 34*

Built	Royal Naval dockyard, Chatham
Laid down	December 1893
Launched	December 1894 (from dock)
Completed	December 1895
Dimensions	*Length overall* 413ft
	Length 390ft
	Breadth 75ft
	Draught 27ft 6in mean
Displacement	14,900 tons
Machinery	Twin screw
	Two 3 cylinder inverted triple expansion engines by Penn
	Eight cylindrical boilers single-ended
	IHP trials 8 hours natural draught = 10,301 = 16.5 knots
	IHP trials 4 hours forced draught = 12,157 = 17.6 knots
Bunkers	Coal. 900 tons normal. 1,900 tons maximum. Plus 400 tons oil fuel added later
Endurance	3,500/7,600 miles at 10 knots. 1,700/4,000 miles at 15 knots
Armament	Four 12-inch 46-ton guns. 35 calibre. Two forward and two aft
	Twelve 6-inch quick-firers. 40 calibre
	Sixteen 12-pounder quick-firers
	Twelve 3-pounder quick-firers
	18-inch diameter torpedo tubes. Four submerged. One above water in stern
Armour	Harvey steel
	Belt 9-inch amidships. 220ft long by 16ft wide
	Bulkheads 14-inch forward and 12-inch aft
	Barbettes 14-inch
	Barbette shields 10-inch
	Casemates 6-inch
	Decks 4-inch – 3-inch – 2½-inch

34 MAGNIFICENT, BRITISH 1895

Conning tower forward 14-inch
Conning tower aft 3-inch
Complement   672

The *Magnificent* cost £909,789 to build and commissioned at Chatham in December 1895 as second flagship of the Channel fleet, serving as such until February 1904, when she paid off for refitting at Devonport. This photograph was taken about 1897 and shows the casemate guns of the 6-inch secondary armament trained on the broadside, illustrating how difficult it was to work the main-deck guns in a seaway. The white painted canvas dodgers rigged around the guardwires gave the effect of bulwarks.

The *Magnificent* commissioned in July 1904 with the Channel fleet and during December transferred to the Atlantic fleet. In June 1905 one of her guns exploded on firing, causing eighteen casualties. In November 1906 she commissioned in the reserve at Chatham and transferred to the Home fleet at the Nore in February 1907. She was temporarily flagship of the commander-in-chief during November and refitted during 1907-8 when oil-fuel burning and fire control equipment was fitted. She became second flagship, Home fleet, from August 1908 until January 1909 and during February became flagship of the Nore division of the Home fleet with a nucleus crew. During 1910 the *Magnificent* became flagship of the vice-admiral, Home fleet, 3rd and 4th divisions, and in February 1911 was transferred as tender to HMS *Vivid*, as turret drill ship. In May 1912 she was sent to Devonport as a seagoing gunnery training ship but again became an independent command in September 1912. In June 1913 she grounded, with slight damage, off Cawsand and the following month joined the 3rd fleet at Devonport.

In August 1914 the *Magnificent* commissioned for service with the 9th battle squadron, based on the Humber, but was transferred to Scapa Flow defence. During 1915 her 12-inch guns and turrets were removed, as were those of the *Mars*, *Illustrious* and *Victorious*. The guns were re-mounted in the new monitors of the "Lord Clive" type, vitally needed to bombard the Belgian coast and for similar shallow water duties where big-gun range was required but battleships were unable to float.

The *Magnificent* was converted to a troopship for Mediterranean service by September 1915 when she took part in the Sulva landing. Afterwards she was relegated to secondary duties and became an ammunition store at Rosyth until 1919, being sold in 1921 to be broken up at Inverkeithing.

Caesar

BRITISH 1898 *Plate 35*

Built	Royal Naval dockyard, Portsmouth
Laid down	March 1895
Launched	September 1896
Completed	January 1898
Dimensions	*Length overall* 413ft
	Length between perpendiculars 390ft
	Breadth 75ft
	Draught 27ft 6in mean
Displacement	14,560 tons 15,730 fully loaded
Machinery	Twin screw
	Two 3-cylinder inverted triple expansion engines by Maudslay, Son and Field
	Eight cylindrical boilers
	IHP trials 8 hours natural draught = 10,630 = 16.7 knots
	IHP trials 4 hours forced draught = 12,652 = 18.7 knots
Bunkers	Coal. 900 tons normal. 1,900 tons 2,200 tons. Later also oil fuel
Endurance	3,500 miles at 10 knots. 7,600 miles at 10 knots
Armament	Four 12-inch 46-ton wire-wound guns. 35 calibre. 860-pound weight projectile. Two forward and two aft
	Twelve 6-inch quick-firers. 40 calibre. In casemates
	Sixteen 12-pounder quick-firers
	Twelve 3-pounder quick-firers
	Two maxims
	Five 18-inch diameter torpedo tubes. Four submerged. One above water in stern
Armour	Harvey
	Belt 9-inch. 220ft long by 16ft wide
	Bulkheads 14-inch – 12-inch
	Barbettes 14-inch
	Barbette shields 10-inch
	Casemates 6-inch
	Decks 4-inch – 3-inch – 2½-inch
	Conning towers 14-inch – 3-inch
Complement	672 (later 757)

The *Caesar*, another of the "Majestic" class battleships, cost £872,474 to build. She had an active career and first commissioned at Portsmouth in January 1898 for the Mediterranean, but was temporarily attached to the Channel fleet and did not arrive at Malta until May. She remained in the Mediterranean until October 1903 and was refitted at Malta during 1900-1.

Returning to Portsmouth for further refitting, she commissioned in

35 CAESAR, BRITISH 1898

February 1904 as flagship of the vice-admiral, Channel fleet, joined the Atlantic fleet in December and in March 1905 became flagship of the rear-admiral, Channel fleet. In June she ran down the barque *Afghanistan* off Dungeness, suffered damage and was repaired at Devonport, afterwards resuming her flagship duties. In February 1907 the *Caesar* temporarily became flagship of the Atlantic fleet and in May joined the Devonport-based division of the Home fleet. Fire controls were fitted to her at various times between 1905-7 and she refitted at Devonport during 1907-8. In May 1909 she joined the Nore division of the Home fleet and in May-June became temporarily the flagship of the vice-admiral, 3rd and 4th divisions, Home fleet. By April 1911 she was a unit of the Devonport 3rd division, Home fleet, and in March 1912 was in the 4th division with a nucleus crew. After May 1912 she was in the 3rd and later 4th divisions, Home fleet.

In 1914 the *Caesar* was commissioned at the outbreak of war in the 7th battle squadron for service in the Channel and with the Southern fleet. During 1915-18 she served on the North American and West Indies station and in the Atlantic. In 1918-19 the *Caesar* was transferred to the Mediterranean and later to the Black Sea. She was sold in 1921 to be broken up in Germany.

This photograph, perhaps more than any other in this book, typifies the power and pomp of the Victorian Navy. It shows the *Caesar* steaming at about 14 knots and wearing the flag of vice-admiral of the Channel fleet in 1903 or early 1904.

By then communications at sea were becoming more important as fleet speeds increased and manoeuvres became more complicated. As well as flags, major warships were by now using searchlight and semaphore for signalling. The *Caesar* had searchlights mounted on each wing of the forward bridge and semaphores on the wings of the after bridge, with another at the head of the main topmast. Searchlights for scanning were fitted at each lower masthead.

The torpedo net booms were prominent on her sides. Torpedo nets were carried by British battleships for many years and when the "Majestic" class were built the technique of their use in forming a steel mesh curtain around a warship while at anchor or steaming slowly was still developing, though other navies regarded nets as of doubtful value and the American fleet never adopted them. "Out nets" became an important evolution in the British fleet and some of the "Majestic" class had a net shelf fitted at main deck level instead of at the upper deck, reducing time for swinging out nets to ten seconds and stowing them to one minute; excellent performances in view of the weight and bulk of the nets. They were suspended from 30ft long steel tubular booms which stowed diagonally along the ship's side, as in this photograph. When lowered the nets formed a curtain about 25ft deep and a ship could steam at about 6 knots, protected against torpedo attack at sea. However, the net-penetrating torpedo made the nets largely obsolete though they were retained in the British fleet until World War I when they were principally used for protection at anchor.

Hannibal

BRITISH 1898 *Plate 36*

Built	Royal Naval dockyard, Pembroke
Laid down	May 1894
Launched	April 1896
Completed	April 1898
Dimensions	*Length overall* 413ft
	Length 390ft
	Breadth 75ft
	Draught 27ft 6in
Displacement	14,900 tons
Machinery	Twin screw
	Two 3-cylinder inverted triple expansion engines by Harland and Wolff
	Eight cylindrical boilers. Single-ended
	IHP trials 8 hours natural draught = 10,357 = 16.3 knots
	IHP trials 4 hours forced draught = 12,253 = 18 knots
Bunkers	Coal. 900 tons normal. 1,900 tons maximum. Plus 400 tons oil fuel added later
Endurance	3,500/7,600 miles at 10 knots. 1,700/4000 miles at 15 knots
Armament	Four 12-inch 46-ton guns. 35 calibre. Two forward and two aft
	Twelve 6-inch quick-firers. 40 calibre
	Sixteen 12-pounder quick-firers
	Twelve 3-pounder quick-firers
	18-inch diameter torpedo tubes. Four submerged. One above water in stern
Armour	Harvey steel
	Belt 9-inch amidships. 220ft long by 16ft wide
	Bulkheads 14-inch forward and 12-inch aft
	Barbettes 14-inch
	Barbette shields 10-inch
	Casemates 6-inch
	Decks 4-inch – 3-inch – 2½-inch
	Conning tower forward 14-inch
	Conning tower aft 3-inch
Complement	672

The *Hannibal* cost £906,799 to build. Her completion was delayed by strikes and labour unrest. She first commissioned at Portsmouth in April 1898, to go into fleet reserve. In May she commissioned for the Channel

36   HANNIBAL, BRITISH 1898

37   BATTLESHIPS AT THE CORONATION NAVAL REVIEW SPITHEAD, 1902

fleet. This photograph was taken in 1902 and shows boat activity around the anchored *Hannibal*. Like most contemporary British battleships, the "Majestic" class carried 14-inch diameter torpedoes to be used by the two steam picket boats which were carried on board. These were equipped with dropping gear. There was no intention to use them at sea but they were considered as potentially useful when patrolling the anchored parent ship against enemy attack, in a sortie against an enemy ship or port, or possibly during inshore blockade duties.

In October 1903 the *Hannibal* collided with her sister ship the *Prince George,* without sustaining damage. During December 1904 she transferred to the Atlantic fleet but returned to the Channel fleet in February 1905 and paid off at Devonport in August. She refitted between June and November 1906, receiving oil burning equipment and fire controls, and was recommissioned during October in the reserve. Oil-fuel burning equipment was first fitted to a large ship in the *Mars,* but it produced a lot of smoke, annoying her boiler-room staff who were rightly jealous of their reputation a efficient stokers. The *Hannibal* was the most economical steamer of her class so far as oil consumption was concerned.

From January to June 1907 the *Hannibal* served with the Channel fleet and transferred to the Devonport division, Home fleet, in July, serving there until 1914. In August 1909 she struck rocks off Babbacombe, Devon, and was seriously damaged. During October she collided with Torpedo Boat *105* but sustained no damage. She became temporary guard ship at Devonport in June 1910 and refitted there from November 1911 until March 1912. When war commenced in August 1914 it was intended she should join the 9th battle squadron, but she was ordered to the Humber river, on the east coast, as guard ship, later proceeding to Scapa Flow defence.

In September 1915 the four 12-inch guns and their turrets were removed from the *Hannibal* for installation in new monitors being built for bombardment work, and she was converted to a troopship, serving in the Mediterranean until 1916. Afterwards she carried troops to the East Indies and to Egypt. The *Hannibal* was sold in 1920 to be broken up in Italy.

Battleships at the Coronation Naval Review, Spithead, 1902

Plate 37

Six "Majestic" class battleships lying in line. Ships in review generally anchored two cables (400 yards) apart and precision of anchoring was important where scores of large vessels would be brought up in a confined area.

Despite efficient stoking, the smoke haze from the numbers of coal fired ships was inevitable and here emphasised the sun glitter on a Spithead alive with sailing and steam yachts. Crews are busy with ships' boats at the booms and the scene colourful with the varied liveries of an international gathering of warships paying respect to the newly crowned King Edward VII.

Fuji

JAPANESE 1897 *Plate 38*

Built	Thames Ironworks, Poplar, London
Laid down	August 1894
Launched	March 1896
Completed	August 1897
Dimensions	*Length overall* 412ft
	Length waterline 390ft
	Breadth 73ft
	Draught 26ft 6in
Displacement	12,533 tons normal
Machinery	Twin screw
	Two 4-cylinder reciprocating triple expansion engines by Humphrys and Tennant
	Ten cylindrical boilers
	IHP trials natural draught = 10,200 = 16.8 knots
	IHP trials forced draught = 14,100 = 18 knots
Bunkers	Coal. 700 tons normal. 1,300 tons maximum
Armament	Four 12-inch Elswick guns. 40 calibre. Two forward and two aft
	Ten 6-inch quick-firers. 40 calibre
	Twenty 3-pounders
	Four 2½-pounders
	Five 18-inch torpedo tubes. One above water bow. Four submerged broadside
Armour	*Main belt* 18-inch – 14-inch
	Bulkheads 14-inch
	12-inch gun shields 6-inch
	Barbettes 14-inch upper. 9-inch lower
	Casemates 6-inch face. 2-inch rear
	Deck 2½-inch over belt
Complement	600

In 1892 the Japanese were on the verge of war with China but had few armoured ships, so the naval programme for that year included the sister battleships *Fuji* and *Yashima*, to counter the two German built battleships in the Chinese fleet. However, the war ended before these ships

38   FUJI, JAPANESE 1897

were built.

The *Fuji* and *Yashima* were constructed in Britain to designs by G.C. Macrow, naval architect of the Thames Ironworks and still remembered by generations of shipbuilders for his invaluable technical pocket book for the industry. These ships were an improvement on the "Royal Sovereign" design but were armed with 12-inch instead of 13.5-inch guns and had improved armour protection of the barbettes. The 12-inch guns were a new Elswick pattern which proved equally effective as the larger weapon, could fire an 850-pound shell every 80 seconds with end-on loading, and could be trained through 240 degrees. However, only four of the secondary 6-inch guns were in casemates, the others being mounted on the upper deck, foreshadowing the re-positioning of such guns in British battleships during World War I to avoid casemates being flooded at sea and rendering the guns ineffective. The 2½-pounder guns then regarded as anti-torpedo boat armament were mounted on the shelter deck.

During 1901 the ships were refitted and the 2½-pounders replaced by sixteen 12-pounder guns, though four 3-pounders were retained in the fighting tops, which were removed during a refit in Japan in 1905.

At the outbreak of the Russo-Japanese war in 1904 the *Fuji* was one of six battleships in the 1st division of the 1st squadron of the fleet and was active throughout. On February 9th 1904 she was in a fleet action against Russian warships off their base at Port Arthur, particularly engaging the cruiser *Bayan* and suffering damage and casualties. On March 22nd 1904 she and the battleship *Yashima* bombarded the base with their big guns and later participated in the inconclusive actions off the coast.

On August 10th Russian warships sailed from Port Arthur and were engaged by a Japanese force including the *Fuji*, which concentrated her fire on the battleship *Tsarevitch*.

At the decisive battle of Tsushima, which destroyed the Russian 2nd Pacific squadron, the *Fuji* fired a last 12-inch shell as the Japanese fleet turned away in the evening and this exploded the magazines of the Russian battleship *Borodino*, which capsized and sank with loss of all but one of her crew. The *Fuji* suffered few casualties and little damage in this bitter battle.

In 1910 she was reclassified as a coast defence ship. New "Miyabara" type water tube boilers were installed and her funnels were lowered.

During World War I the *Fuji* could steam at only 15 knots. Later she became a training ship for stokers, gunners and navigators. In 1922-3, under the Washington treaty of naval reductions, she was disarmed and her propellers were removed. Eventually she became a naval barracks training ship for seamen and pilots. By 1945 she was tender to the navigation school and later capsized. In 1948 the *Fuji* was scrapped at Yokosuka.

Masséna

FRENCH 1898 *Plate 39*

Built	St Nazaire
Laid down	1892
Launched	July 1895
Completed	1898
Dimensions	*Length overall* 384ft 8in
	Length waterline 380ft 6in
	Breadth 66ft 3in
	Draught 26ft 3in normal mean. 27ft maximum
Displacement	11,924 tons
Machinery	Triple screw
	Three vertical triple expansion engines
	Twenty-four Lagrafel d'Allest type boilers
	IHP natural draught. Sixteen boilers. 24 hours' trial 1898 = 9,650 = 15.49 knots
	IHP natural draught. Twenty-four boilers. 24 hours' trial 1898 = 13,460 = 17 knots
Bunkers	Coal. 635 tons normal. 800 tons maximum. (later included some oil)
Armament	Two 12-inch. 40 calibre. In single turrets forward and aft
	Two 10.8-inch. 40 calibre. In single turrets on each beam
	Eight 5.5-inch quick-firers. 45 calibre. In separate turrets
	Eight 3.9-inch quick-firers
	Twelve 3-pounder quick-firers
	Eight 1-pounders
	Four 18-inch diameter torpedo tubes. Two submerged. One on each quarter.
Armour	Creusot Harvey steel
	Belt 17.7-inch – 9.7-inch. 350ft by 7ft 6in
	Side above belt 4-inch
	Bulkhead 9½-inch
	12-inch turrets 15.7-inch – 13.7-inch
	Secondary turrets 3.9-inch
	Protective deck 2.7-inch
	Splinter deck below protective deck 1.5-inch (2ft 4in lower)
	Conning tower 13.7-inch
Complement	610 – 642

The *Masséna*, like many French battleships, was of unusual arrangement and mixed armament, weak in comparison to the British "Majestic" class *(Plate 32)*. The arrangement of the principal guns may be compared with the American armoured cruiser *Brooklyn (Plate 85)*, which had French influence in her design, and there was some similarity to the Russian battleship *Pobieda (Plate 46)*. She was developed from the earlier

39   MASSENA, FRENCH 1898

French battleship *Carnot*.

The position of the single forward 12-inch gun turret placed a heavy weight far forward and high, badly exaggerating pitching despite the buoyancy of the ram, made accurate shooting in a seaway difficult. The large and secondary turrets were turned electrically or by hand gear. The guns mounted at upper deck level were difficult to work in a sea, when the low freeboard allowed waves to sweep the after deck.

The *Masséna* cost over £1,100,000 but failed to achieve her designed speed of 18 knots. However, she averaged 17 knots for twenty-four hours, which was a good practical demonstration of her potential. She retained this speed for about ten years.

The curved deck edges and sides and circular turrets and barbettes were intended to resist and deflect shell hits. The pronounced ram bow was used in the design of many contemporary French battleships and cruisers, the intention being that any damage to the long ram would leave intact the watertight forward bulkheads of the hull proper. The tubular masts were similar to those fitted in German battleships of the time *(Plate 23)* and resisted risk of masts failing by damage in action. The large profile, flat-sided funnels reduced the number needed by combining uptakes, but added considerably to the target silhouette.

The rectangular side ports for light and air were often fitted in French, Italian and Greek warships intended principally for Mediterranean service, but constituted a structural weakness in the hull. The cumbersome stocked anchors were still widely used in most navies at the beginning of the twentieth century, although stockless anchors stowing in hawse pipes were already in use in many merchant ships.

French warships have always seemed to carry much larger ensigns than those of other navies, as shown in this photograph of the *Masséna* taken about 1905.

She was one of eight individual battleships built for the French fleet between 1891 and 1899, only another three being sister ships in a class. Thereafter French battleships were laid down in classes. The strengthening alliance between Britain and France after 1902 enabled the previous naval rivalry between the countries to end and offset the increasing naval building competition between Britain and Germany until the clash of World War I.

The *Masséna* remained an effective battleship until 1913, but was sunk to form a breakwater at Gallipoli in 1915.

Kaiser Friedrich III

GERMAN 1898 *Plate 40*

Built	Naval dockyard, Wilhelmshaven
Laid down	May 1895
Launched	July 1896
Completed	September 1898
Dimensions	*Length overall* 410ft
	Length waterline 384ft
	Breadth 65ft 6in
	Draught 27ft 6in maximum
Displacement	11,150 tons
Machinery	Triple screw
	Three 3-cylinder vertical triple expansion engines by builders
	Eight cylindrical boilers. Four Thornycroft (later four Schultz)
	IHP = 13,500 = 18 knots
Bunkers	Coal. 650 tons normal. 1,050 tons maximum
Endurance	5,000 miles at 10 knots
Armament	Four 9.4-inch. 40 calibre. In turrets. Two forward and two aft
	Eighteen 5.9-inch quick-firers. Single mounts. Casemates and turrets
	Twelve 3.4-inch quick-firers. Single mounts
	Twelve 1-pounders
	Twelve machine-guns
	Six 18-inch diameter torpedo tubes. One bow. One stern. Two each broadside. All submerged
	During reconstruction four 5.9-inch guns removed
Armour	Krupp steel
	Belt 11¾-inch – 4-inch. 294ft long by 6ft 6in wide
	Barbettes 10-inch
	Turrets 10-inch
	Small turrets 6-inch
	Casemates 6-inch
	Bulkhead aft 8-inch
	Protective deck 3-inch – 2½-inch
	Forward conning tower 10-inch
	After conning tower 4-inch
Complement	655

The *Kaiser Friedrich III* was the name ship of a class of five sister battleships, the others being the *Kaiser Wilhelm II, Kaiser Wilhelm der Grosse, Kaiser Karl der Grosse* and the *Kaiser Barbarossa*, completed between 1898-1901. They cost an average of £962,500 to build and were designed as part of a striking force which in the event of war with Britain could attack the east coast of England, covering an invasion fleet and engaging in North Sea operations.

The armament of these ships was light for their size, the heaviest guns being only four 9.4-inch, compared with the four 12-inch usual in similar British ships. However, these 9.4-inch were capable of rapid fire and the

40   KAISER FRIEDRICH III, GERMAN 1898

strong secondary armament of eighteen 5.9-inch guns was powerful against the usual British twelve 6-inch and was further strengthened by twelve 3.4-inch guns. The disposition of armament was also unusual; the two forward 9.4-inch guns were mounted 30ft above the waterline in a turret mounted on a barbette surrounded by a deckhouse. The forward end of this had two casemates for 5.9-inch guns. Two more 5.9-inch guns were similarly mounted in the after deckhouse, firing above the twin after 9.4-inch turret which was mounted a deck lower. Four more casemates with 5.9-inch guns were disposed at the break of the raised deck and at the bow quarter position, with six other 5.9s mounted in small turrets, three on each beam, sponsoned out.

This photograph of the *Kaiser Friedrich III* was taken in 1902 and shows the large boat cranes which were a distinctive feature of German warships at the time. The tubular masts were low but topmasts were carried, with semaphores on both. Although these ships were good steamers, they had high coal consumption and the 9.4-inch guns were slow in rate of fire. Generally they were unsatisfactory battleships but were followed by the slightly larger but very similar "Wittelsbach" class of five ships.

The *Kaiser Friedrich III* and her sisters were the pride of the German fleet for a few years but by 1906 she was docked for reconstruction and reboilering. Four 5.9-inch guns were removed, with a considerable amount of deckhouses and superstructure. However, this reduction in weight so reduced draught that the lower edge of the armour belt was brought close to the waterline and this, with the poor armament, caused the class to be relegated to subsidiary service or reserve. The strong tubular masts were removed and replaced by pole masts, with topmasts for wireless aerials stayed to wide spreaders in the current German fashion.

She underwent a further refit at Wilhelmshaven during 1908-9 but was almost obsolete and remained in reserve until 1916 when, like many older major German warships, she was disarmed to release munitions and crew for the growing numbers of submarines and destroyers being built for the fleet. She subsequently served at Kiel as a detention ship and during 1918 became an accommodation ship at Flensburg. After the surrender of the German fleet she was discarded in December 1919 and was scrapped at Kiel during 1920. All her sister ships survived the war and were scrapped at that time.

Albion

BRITISH 1901 *Plate 41*

Built	Thames Ironworks, Blackwall, London
Laid down	December 1896
Launched	June 1898
Completed	June 1901
Dimensions	*Length overall* 418ft
	Length 390ft
	Breadth 74ft
	Draught 25ft 10in mean. 26ft 6in maximum
Displacement	13,150 tons. 14,320 tons deep-loaded
Machinery	Twin screw
	Two 3-cylinder vertical inverted triple expansion engines by Maudslay, Sons and Field
	Twenty Belleville type water tube boilers
	IHP trials 8 hours natural draught = 13,885 = 17.8 knots (trial carried out in gale conditions)
Bunkers	Coal. 800 tons normal. 1,800 tons maximum
Armament	Four 12-inch. 35 calibre. Two forward and two aft
	Twelve 6-inch quick-firers
	Ten 12-pounder quick-firers
	Six 3-pounders
	Two machine-guns
	Four 18-inch diameter submerged torpedo tubes
Armour	Krupp and Harvey steel
	Belt 6-inch amidships. 2-inch bow. 195ft long by 14ft wide
	Forward bulkhead 10-inch – 8-inch – 6-inch
	After bulkhead 12-inch – 10-inch – 6-inch
	Barbettes 12-inch – 6-inch
	Barbette shields 8-inch
	Casemates 6-inch
	Protective decks 3-inch – 2-inch
	Main deck 1-inch
	Forward conning tower 12-inch
	After conning tower 3-inch
Complement	682 – 750. As a flagship 780

The *Albion* was one of the "Canopus" class battleships which were laid down between 1896-98 and included the *Glory, Albion, Goliath, Ocean, Vengeance* and *Canopus*. They were designed for service in the Far East, to counter Japanese naval expansion after their victorious war against China during 1894-5, when the Japanese fleet proved superior to the ill-equipped Chinese Navy. Draught of the *Canopus* type was limited for passage of the Suez canal and they were the first British battleships to have water tube boilers, which had only previously been used in small craft and were to be fitted in the large cruisers *Terrible* and *Powerful*, then building. Distribution of the boilers enabled a fore and aft placing of the funnels, the after one being largest in diameter.

In the "Canopus" type Krupp side armour was fitted for the first time in British warships, and its relative thinness caused the battleships to be regarded as inferior to their predecessors, even though its power of resistance was superior to twice the thickness of compound armour.

41 ALBION, BRITISH 1901

Improvements in armament enabled the *Albion*'s four 12-inch guns to fire one round in 32 seconds. The secondary 6-inch guns in the main deck end casemates were sponsored out to improve ahead and astern fire, giving an unusual appearance for a British ship.

The *Albion* cost £858,745 to build and her launch at the Thames Ironworks yard was disastrous; the wash as she left the ways carried away spectator stands and drowned thirty people, mainly women and children.

She commissioned in June 1901 for the China station, serving there until 1905. The "Canopus" class were the principal force of the British China squadron during that period, which ended when the alliance between Britain and Japan enabled them to return for service in British waters.

The *Albion* joined the Channel fleet in August 1905 and collided with the battleship *Duncan* off Lerwick, Shetland Isles, during September, without sustaining damage. During April 1906 she commissioned in the reserve at Chatham for refitting of machinery and boilers which lasted until December 1906. In February 1907 she was temporarily with the Home fleet at Portsmouth and in March joined the Atlantic fleet. The *Albion* refitted at Gibraltar during 1908-9, when fire control equipment was installed. She became the parent ship for the 4th division of the Home fleet at the Nore in August 1909 and in May 1912 transferred to the 3rd fleet at the Nore and refitted at Chatham. During 1913 she lay at Pembroke dockyard.

The *Albion* and her sisters saw varied service during World War I, in areas as far apart as the Falklands and Archangel. In August 1914 the *Albion* was a unit of the 8th battle squadron in the Channel and later that year sailed for the Cape and East African station. In February 1915 she was sent to the Dardanelles and participated in the bombardment of the Turkish forts and shore positions. On 25th April she was part of a force covering the landing at Helles and suffered shell damage on 25th April and 2nd May. During October 1915 the *Albion* transported troops to Salonika and afterwards returned to England to be based on the east coast from 1916-18 as part of a force guarding against the repetition of German naval raids. She became an accommodation ship at Devonport in 1918 and was sold during 1919 to be broken up at Morecambe, Lancashire.

This photograph was taken at the Spithead naval review of 1911, in honour of the coronation of King George V. The *Albion*, in the foreground, had been equipped with fire control arrangements housed in the upper fore top and the mizzen top platforms. The layout of the secondary armament and the net shelf at main deck level are clearly shown. Although wireless had been fitted, battleships retained long yards and fidded topmasts.

Irresistible

BRITISH 1902 *Plate 42*

Built	Royal Naval dockyard, Chatham
Laid down	April 1898
Launched	December 1898
Completed	February 1902
Dimensions	*Length overall* 431ft 8in
	Length 400ft
	Breadth 75ft
	Draught 25ft – 26ft mean. 27ft 9in maximum
Displacement	15,000 tons
Machinery	Twin screw
	Two 3-cylinder vertical triple expansion engines by Maudslay, Son and Field
	Twenty Belleville type water-tube boilers
	IHP full power trial 8 hours = 15,500 = 18.2 knots
Bunkers	Coal. 900 tons normal. 2,200 tons maximum
Endurance	3,000/8,000 miles at 10 knots
Armament	Four 12-inch 50-ton guns. 40 calibre. 850 pounds shell. Two forward and two aft
	Twelve 6-inch quick-firers. 45 calibre
	Sixteen 12-pounder quick-firers
	Six 3-pounders
	Two machine-guns
	18-inch diameter torpedo tubes. Four submerged broadside
Armour	*Belt and lower deck sides* 9-inch. 216ft long by 15ft wide
	Bulkheads 12-inch – 10-inch – 9-inch
	Forward side plating 3-inch
	Aft side plating 1½-inch
	Barbettes 12-inch – 6-inch
	Barbette shields 10-inch – 8-inch
	Casemates 6-inch
	Deck 3-inch – 2-inch
	Main deck 1-inch
	Conning tower forward 14-inch
	Conning tower aft 3-inch
Complement	780. 810 as flagship

The three "Formidable" class battleships were laid down under the 1897 naval programme and were to be of greater displacement than the preceding "Canopus" type, particularly as the Japanese and French Navies were adding ships of about 15,000 tons to their battle fleets. The class comprised the *Formidable*, *Irresistible* and *Implacable*. They were

42   IRRESISTIBLE, BRITISH *1902*

based on the "Majestic" type and were superior to the "Canopus" class. The four 12-inch, 40-calibre guns had improved shell-handling equipment and protection, and the armour was generally heavier. Water tube boilers were then established in British naval engineering and their efficiency increased power and speed. The inward-turning propellers of these ships made them difficult to manoeuvre at slow speeds.

Completion of the *Irresistible* was delayed because her engines were being constructed by Maudslay, Son and Field, the notable London engineers, who were sliding into liquidation at the time. The *Irresistible* cost £1,048,136 to build and commissioned at Chatham in February 1902, for the Mediterranean fleet. During March she collided with the Norwegian steamship *Clive* and sustained considerable damage. In October 1905 she grounded at Malta and was repaired, and the opportunity was taken to fit fire controls. She was again refitted at Malta between October 1907-January 1908 and then returned to England to join the Channel fleet. Later in the month she collided with a merchant schooner in fog, without damage. She joined the 1st division, Home fleet in 1909 when this photograph was taken of her steaming through the Solent, between the Isle of Wight and the Hampshire shore, with a fleet of similar ships and cruisers.

She was reduced to nucleus crew in May 1910 and refitted at Chatham between June and February 1911, when she became part of the Nore division, Home fleet. She went to the Portsmouth sub-division, Home fleet, in August 1911 and during November was sent to the Tyne where her crew were transferred temporarily to the new battleship *Monarch* for her trials. In March 1912 the *Irresistible* joined the Devonport division of the Home fleet, later joining the 5th battle squadron during 1912-14, serving on Channel patrol at the commencement of World War I.

She was ordered to the Dardanelles in February 1915 and was in the 2nd division bombarding the Turkish positions on the 25th, and on the 1st March the action continued in a gale, with the ships suffering heavy fire.

During an attempt to force the Dardanelles on March 18th, the *Irresistible* was heavily struck by shell fire from the Turkish forts and her two turrets put out of action. Shortly afterwards she struck one of the many mines the Turks had laid and her crew were taken off, twenty being killed. The current set the abandoned battleship within range of the narrows forts and she was sunk by their guns about three hours after being mined. It was a disastrous day for the Allies; the French battleship *Bouvet* had blown up shortly before and the British battleship *Ocean* was sunk by mine and gunfire afterwards, while the British battlecruiser *Inflexible* and the French battleships *Gaulois* and *Suffren* were badly damaged.

Implacable

BRITISH 1901 *Plate 43*

Built	Royal Naval dockyard, Devonport
Laid down	July 1898
Launched	March 1899
Completed	September 1901
Dimensions	*Length overall* 431ft 8in
	Length 400ft
	Breadth 75ft
	Draught 25ft – 26ft mean. 27ft 9in maximum
Displacement	14,480 tons at 25ft draught. 15,805 tons at full draught
Machinery	Twin screw
	Two 3-cylinder vertical triple expansion engines by Laird
	Twenty Belleville type water tube boilers
	IHP full power trial 8 hours = 15,500 = 18 knots
Bunkers	Coal. 900 tons normal. 2,200 tons maximum
Endurance	3,000/8,000 miles at 10 knots
Armament	*Original*
	Four 12-inch 50-ton guns. 40 calibre. 850 pounds shell. Two forward and two aft
	Twelve 6-inch quick-firers. 45 calibre
	Sixteen 12-pounder quick-firers
	Six 3-pounders
	Two machine-guns
	18-inch diameter torpedo tubes. Four submerged broadside
	Alterations 1918
	Eight 6-inch quick-firers redisposed on upper deck
	Eight 12-pounder quick-firers redisposed
Armour	*Belt and lower deck sides* 9-inch. 216ft long by 15ft wide
	Bulkheads 12-inch – 10-inch – 9-inch
	Forward side plating 3-inch
	Aft side plating 1½-inch
	Barbettes 12-inch – 6-inch
	Barbette shields 10-inch – 8-inch
	Casemates 6-inch
	Deck 3-inch – 2-inch
	Main deck 1-inch
	Conning tower forward 14-inch
	Conning tower aft 3-inch
Complement	780

The *Implacable* cost £989,116 to build and commissioned at Devonport in September 1901 for service with the Mediterranean fleet. Fire controls were fitted at Malta between 1904-6. Two boiler explosions occurred on

43 *IMPLACABLE,*
BRITISH 1901

board – in July 1905 and August 1906 – the first killing two and injuring others. She returned to refit at Chatham during 1908-9 and joined the Channel fleet in February 1909. During April she transferred to the 1st division, Home fleet and joined the Atlantic fleet in June. Later she was with the 3rd battle squadron, 1st fleet and in May 1912 transferred to the 2nd fleet at the Nore, with a nucleus crew. Later in 1912 until 1914 the *Implacable* was a unit of the 5th battle squadron and at the commencement of World War I was engaged in Channel patrols.

The *Implacable* was sent to the Dardanelles in March 1915 and participated in the bombardment covering the landing at Helles during April, and in subsequent operations. In May she was one of several British "pre-Dreadnought" battleships sent to the Adriatic to stiffen the Italian fleet against the possibility of the Austro-Hungarian fleet breaking out into the Mediterranean. Later that year and early in 1916 she served in the Indian Ocean, between the Red Sea and the East Indies. The *Implacable* returned to the Mediterranean, where her armament was altered at Malta, the main-deck 6-inch gun casemates being plated-in and four of the guns remounted on each side on the deck above; the displaced 12-pounders being remounted and some deleted. This was completed in 1918 when she returned to England and joined the northern patrol between Scotland and Norway until 1919. She was sold to be broken up in Germany during 1921.

This photograph was taken during the Coronation naval review at Spithead in 1911. The ship's company are manning the side and are drawn up in review order, with marines on the bridge, ready to salute the sovereign with three cheers as he steams through the lines of British and foreign warships. King George V had been trained and had served as an active naval officer and the occasion must have filled him with more than usual pride of review. The guns of the secondary armament are trained outboard, above the torpedo net shelf at main deck height. Fire controls had been fitted in the upper fore top. The strake of 3-inch armour plating carried forward to the stem is clearly visible against the thinner ordinary shell plating.

Illinois

UNITED STATES 1901 *Plate 44*

Official	
number	BB7
Built	Newport News Shipbuilding Co
Laid down	February 1897
Launched	October 1898
Completed	1901
Dimensions	*Length overall* 375ft 3in
	Length waterline 368ft
	Breadth 72ft 3in
	Draught 23ft 6in mean. 26ft maximum
Displacement	11,565 tons normal
Machinery	Twin screw
	Reciprocating triple expansion engines
	Eight single-ended Mosher type boilers
	IHP = 10,000 normal. 11,920 maximum
	Speed = 16 knots nominal. 16.2 knots maximum
Bunkers	Coal. 850 tons normal. 1,450 tons maximum
Armament	*Original*
	Four 13-inch. 35 calibre. Two forward and two aft
	Fourteen 6-inch quick-firers. 40 calibre. In casemates
	Seventeen 6-pounders
	Sixteen 1-pounders
	Four 18-inch torpedo tubes above water
	Alterations in 1918
	Secondary armament reduced to eight 6-inch
	Two 3-inch anti-aircraft added
Armour	Harvey
	Main belt 16-inch – 9¼-inch. Bow 4-inch
	Turrets 14-inch
	Barbettes 15-inch – 10-inch
	Deck 4-inch
	Conning tower 10-inch
Complement	711

The *Illinois* and her sister ships *Alabama* and *Wisconsin* were ordered during 1896 and were completed between 1900 and 1901. There was some British and German influence in the design and the funnel arrangement was reminiscent of the British "Royal Sovereign" class. They cost about £950,000 in contemporary values.

The *Illinois* participated in the circumnavigation of the world by the "Great White fleet", to show the strength of the new United States Navy around the world. This squadron of sixteen battleships and three auxiliaries sailed from Hampton Roads, Virginia, on December 16th 1906 and returned on February 22nd 1909. At that time American warships retained the white hulls and buff funnels of the fleet's late-19th-century livery, but in 1910 a light grey-green colour was introduced, similar to that in many other fighting fleets.

The *Illinois* underwent reconstruction during 1909. The fore military mast was replaced by a circular lattice "cage mast" and the mainmast was similarly replaced in 1911, when four 3-inch guns replaced the 6-pounders. The torpedo tubes were removed. Refitting cost about £130,000 in contemporary value but by 1913 the *Illinois* was regarded as a second class battleship. Two 3-inch anti-aircraft guns were added to the armament by 1918, for aircraft attack had become a positive threat to warships by the end of World War I.

44   ILLINOIS, UNITED STATES 1901

45   NORGE, NORWEGIAN ARMOURED COAST DEFENCE SHIP 1901

The *Illinois* remained a fleet unit until about 1921 and during 1924 became a training ship for engineering personel, numbered *IX15*. In January 1941 she was renamed *Prairie State* and was scrapped at Baltimore, Maryland, during 1956.

The *Alabama* was sunk as a target in September 1921 and the *Wisconsin* scrapped during 1922.

Norge

NORWEGIAN ARMOURED COAST DEFENCE SHIP 1901 *Plate 45*

Built	Armstrong and Co., Elswick
Laid down	1899
Launched	March 1900
Completed	1901
Dimensions	*Length overall* 301ft 3in
	Length between perpendiculars 290ft
	Breadth 50ft 6in
	Draught 16ft 6in normal. 17ft 8in maximum
Displacement	3,847 tons normal. 4,166 tons maximum
Machinery	Twin screw
	Two 4-cylinder triple expansion engines by Hawthorn, Leslie and Co
	Eight Yarrow type boilers
	IHP = 4,800 = 16.5 knots
Bunkers	Coal. 250 tons (later 440 tons) normal. 400 tons (later 550 tons) maximum
Armament	Two 8.2-inch quick-firers. 44 calibre. One in turret forward and one in turret aft
	Six 5.9-inch quick-firers. 46 calibre. Four in casemates. Two in shields
	Eight 12-pounder quick-firers
	Six 3-pounder quick-firers
	Two 18-inch diameter torpedo tubes submerged
	Two 3-pounder anti-aircraft guns added by 1920
Armour	Krupp steel
	Belt 6-inch – 4-inch
	Turrets 8-inch
	Slopes of protective deck 2-inch
	Casemates 5-inch
	Conning tower 6-inch
Complement	248 (later 261)

The *Norge* and her sister ship *Eidsvold* were designed and built at Elswick by Armstrong, Whitworth and Co Ltd for the Royal Norwegian Navy as armoured coast defence ships of moderate cost and maximum effectiveness on limited dimensions. They were a miniature version of "pre-Dreadnought" battleships, with an arrangement and profile satisfying to national pride, and followed the slightly smaller, Tyne-built coast defence ships *Harald Haarfagre* and *Tordenskjold*, completed in 1898 and 1899. At that time the Norwegian, Swedish and Danish Navies were being expanded, probably due to the rise of nearby Germany as an ambitious power and to counter any threat to the expected neutrality of their coastal waters by German or Russian warships.

The *Norge* and *Eidsvold* cost £350,000 each to build and may be compared with the Danish *Olfert Fischer (Plate 56)* or Sweden's *Dristigheten*.

This photograph of the *Norge*, taken in 1902, shows the handsome and well-balanced appearance. The weak main armament of two 8.2-inch guns was backed by the relatively strong secondary six 5.9-inch in single mounts, disposed in casemates at each end of the superstructure and two in shields on the upper deck amidships. The unusual choice of 8.2-inch guns followed the armament of the *Harald Haarfagre* and *Tordenskjold* and of several contemporary Swedish coast defence ships.

For a period around 1905 the navies of Sweden and Norway were combined under a political union. Both services were efficient, their ships constantly drilled in navigating the difficult channels of the coasts and fjords and in manoeuvres against supposed blockading fleets. Three-quarters of Norwegian personnel were conscripts. Gunnery and torpedo drills were regular and frequent and navigation excellent. The engineering was good but many Scandinavian warships had heavy coal consumption. The *Norge* and *Eidsvold* remained coal-fired and unaltered in arrangement and appearance throughout their peaceful existence – Norway was neutral during World War I.

When the Germans invaded neutral Norway in the spring of 1940, their reception varied from collaboration to fierce resistance. The small and outdated Norwegian fleet fought bravely. The *Norge* and *Eidsvold* were sent north, probably to preserve the ships as long as possible and in hope of a ceasfire. Both were torpedoed at Narvik by German destroyers on 9th April 1940. They went down fighting.

Pobieda

RUSSIAN 1902 *Plate 46*

Built	New Admiralty Yard, St Petersburg
Laid down	August 1898
Launched	May 1900
Completed	1902
Dimensions	*Length overall* 435ft

46   POBIEDA, RUSSIAN 1902

Length between perpendiculars 411ft
Length waterline 424ft
Breadth 71ft 6in
Draught 27ft 3in at 12,674 tons displacement

Displacement	12,674 tons
Machinery	Triple screw
	Three reciprocating 3-cylinder triple expansion engines
	Thirty Belville type boilers
	Designed continuous sea speed = 16 knots
	Speed at 13,500 tons displacement = 18 knots
	IHP trials = 15,492 = 18.51 knots
Bunkers	Coal. 1,063 tons normal. 2,058 tons maximum. Plus 120 tons oil fuel
Endurance	10,000 miles at 10 knots
Armament	*Original*
	Four 10-inch Obukhoff guns. 45 calibre. Two forward and two aft
	Eleven 6-inch. In casemates
	Twenty 3-inch. At sides
	Twenty-six smaller guns
	Six torpedo tubes. Two submerged. Four above water
	Electric hoists to all guns. Large guns electrically controlled
	Modified as Japanese "Suwo"
	Four 10-inch Obukhoff guns. 45 calibre (2 x 2)
	Sixteen 3-inch. 40 calibre
	Two 18-inch diameter torpedo tubes
Armour	Krupp and Harvey
	Main belt 9-inch – 4-inch at ends
	Lower belt 5-inch
	Deck 2¾-inch on slopes. 2-inch on flat
	Turrets 10-inch
	Turret bases 9-inch
	Casemates 5-inch
	Conning towers 10-inch
Complement	732

The *Pobieda* and her sister ships *Peresviet* and *Osliabia* were intermediate between battleships and armoured cruisers. Although their 10-inch guns were capable of long-range action, they were not so effective as the 12-inch carried by most contemporary battleships and the armour protection was comparatively light. The considerable freeboard of these ships was principally due to improved living accomodation, but provided a large target. Each cost the equivalent of £1,000,000.

The mounting of the 3-inch gun battery on two decks at the sides was unusual. In arrangement she could be compared with the French *Massena* (Plate 39).

The *Pobieda* arrived at Port Arthur, Russia's Far East naval base, during July 1903 to join the fleet which at the outbreak of war with Japan in February 1904 included seven battleships, six large cruisers and twenty-five destroyers.

On April 13th 1904 the *Pobieda* was with a squadron of major Russian ships which engaged Japanese cruisers off Port Arthur. Shortly after the loss by mine of the battleship *Petropavlosk*, the *Pobieda* struck a mine near the Tiger Peninsular but remained afloat and the squadron returned to Port Arthur where repairs were commenced, and completed in June. On 22nd of June the *Pobieda*'s captain was taken ill and was relieved on the eve of a sortie by the fleet to attack the Japanese base in the Elliot Islands. They retired on meeting a Japanese force attempting to entice them seaward.

On August 10th the Russian fleet again sortied and the *Pobieda* had engine-trouble which slowed the ships. They engaged a Japanese force but again retired to Port Arthur to await Russia's 2nd Pacific squadron which was steaming out from the Baltic as reinforcement.

This ill-fated force was however defeated by the Japanese at the battle of Tsushiba where the *Pobieda*'s sister ship *Osliabia* was the first Russian ship to be sunk. As the Japanese advanced on land to besiege Port Arthur the *Pobieda* and *Peresviet* were scuttled. The *Pobieda* was the most heavily damaged but both were raised and refitted at Yokosuka for service in the Japanese fleet. *Pobieda*'s forward military mast was removed during the refit, together with four 3-inch guns, the bow 6-inch gun, three torpedo tubes and all the 3- and 1-pounder guns. About 800 tons of ballast were shipped to improve stability.

Commissioned into the Japanese fleet in October 1908 as the *Suwo*, she rated as a second class battleship until 1920, later being reclassed as a first class coast defence ship. Afterwards she served as a training ship for engineers and cadets. The *Suwo* was discarded in April 1922. She capsized during removal of the armour, was raised and moored at Kure until the end of World War II, being broken up in 1945.

London

BRITISH 1902 *Plates 47 and 48*

Built	Royal Naval dockyard, Portsmouth
Laid down	December 1898
Launched	September 1899
Completed	June 1902
Dimensions	*Length overall* 431ft 8in
	Length 400ft
	Breadth 75ft
	Draught 26ft 6in normal

47 *LONDON, BRITISH 1902*

48 *LONDON, BRITISH 1902*

Displacement	14,420 tons normal. 15,640 tons deep load
Machinery	Twin screw
	Two vertical triple expansion engines by Earle
	Twenty Belleville type water-tube boilers
	IHP = 15,000 = 18 knots
Bunkers	Coal. 900/2,100 tons
Endurance	3,000/7,000 miles at 10 knots
Armament	*Original*
	Four 12-inch 50-ton. 40 calibre. Two forward and two aft
	Twelve 6-inch quick-firers. 45 calibre
	Sixteen 12-pounder quick-firers
	Six 3-pounders
	Two machine-guns
	18-inch diameter torpedo tubes submerged broadside. Two forward. Two aft
	Secondary armament altered 1916
	Eight 6-inch quick-firers redisposed on upper deck
	Eight 12-pounder quick-firers redisposed
Armour	Krupp steel
	Belt 9-inch – 3-inch. 250ft long by 15ft wide
	Aft bulkhead only 12-inch – 10-inch – 9-inch
	Barbettes 12-inch – 8-inch – 6-inch
	Barbette shields 10-inch – 8-inch
	Casemates 6-inch
	Lower deck 2½-inch
	Middle deck 2-inch – 1-inch
	Main deck 2-inch – 1½-inch
	Forward conning tower 14-inch
	After conning tower 3-inch
Complement	733. 789 as flagship

Three battleships of the "London" class were authorised under the 1898 British naval programme. They were a transitional design between the "Formidable" type *(Plate 42 and 43)* and the "Duncan" class. The *London*, *Bulwark* and *Venerable* were laid down in 1898 and 1899, the sister ships *Queen* and *Prince of Wales* following in 1900. Appearance was similar to the "Formidable" type but the armour protection was rearranged.

The *London* cost £1,036,393, to build and commissioned in June 1902 at Portsmouth as flagship for the Coronation naval review of King Edward VII. Afterwards she sailed to join the Mediterranean fleet, serving there until April 1907 and suffering engine defects and other machinery troubles. She returned in June 1907 to join the Home fleet at the Nore. A year later she was transferred to the Channel fleet as rear-admiral's flagship, then moved to Chatham for a major refit. In 1910 she commissioned as rear-admiral's flagship, Atlantic fleet, and in May 1912 joined the 3rd battle squadron, 1st fleet, with a nucleus crew. Later that month she transferred to the 2nd fleet, 5th battle squadron, at the Nore, where she was fitted with a temporary runway extending from the forward side of the bridge to the stemhead, from which experiments in launching seaplanes were successfully made, similar trials being carried out from the battleship *Hibernia*. Soon after, the *London* collided with the merchant ship *Don Benito* off Hythe, and later in 1912 joined the 5th battle squadron.

At the commencement of World War I the *London* participated in Channel patrols before being ordered to the Mediterranean in March 1915 to replace losses in the fleet attacking the Dardanelles. During May she, with the battleships *Implacable*, *Prince of Wales* and *Queen*, was ordered to the Adriatic to reinforce the Italian fleet and prevent the breaking out of the Austro-Hungarian fleet into the Mediterranean.

In 1916 the *London*'s secondary armament was altered similarly to that of the *Implacable* and during 1917 she was converted to a minelayer, the after barbette being removed along with the secondary armament. A 6-inch gun was mounted on the after deck. During 1919 she became a reserve depot ship and was sold during 1920 to be broken up in Germany.

Plate 47 shows the *London* as flagship of the 1902 Coronation naval review at Spithead with a line of four-funnelled cruisers beyond, possibly ships of the "Diadem" class. *Plate 48* was taken in 1911 and the *London* has undergone modernisation; fire controls are fitted to the fore top and wireless equipment is spread at the mastheads. Although outdated by the "Dreadnought" type ships, the large number of earlier battleships in all major fleets remained a substantial part of the backbone for several years and were included in the foremost battle squadrons.

Prince of Wales

BRITISH 1904 *Plate 49*

Built	Royal Naval dockyard, Chatham
Laid down	March 1901
Launched	March 1902
Completed	March 1904
Dimensions	*Length overall* 431ft 8in
	Length 400ft
	Breadth 75ft
	Draught 26ft 6in normal
Displacement	14,140 tons normal. 15,380 tons deep load
Machinery	Twin screw
	Two vertical triple expansion engines by Greenock Foundry Co
	Twenty Belleville type water-tube boilers
	IHP = 15,000 = 18 knots

49   PRINCE OF WALES, BRITISH 1904

Bunkers	Coal. 900/2,100 tons
Endurance	3,000/7,000 miles at 10 knots
Armament	Four 12-inch 50-ton. 40 calibre. Two forward and two aft
	Twelve 6-inch quick-firers. 45 calibre
	Sixteen 12-pounder quick-firers
	Six 3-pounders
	Two machine-guns
	18-inch diameter torpedo tubes submerged broadside. Two forward. Two aft
Armour	Krupp steel
	Belt 9-inch – 3-inch. 250ft long by 15ft wide
	Aft bulkhead only 12-inch – 10-inch – 9-inch
	Barbettes 12-inch – 8-inch – 6-inch
	Barbette shields 10-inch – 8-inch
	Casemates 6-inch
	Lower deck 2½-inch
	Middle deck 2-inch – 1-inch
	Main deck 2-inch – 1½-inch
	Forward conning tower 14-inch
	After conning tower 3-inch
Complement	733. 789 as flagship

The *Prince of Wales* was named for the heir to the throne, Prince George, later King George V. She cost £1,193,308 to build and on completion in March 1904 went into fleet reserve at Chatham and commissioned for service with the Mediterranean fleet in May. In July 1905 she collided with the merchant ship *Enidween* off Oran and suffered damage. The *Prince of Wales* returned to England in May 1906 and commissioned in the reserve at Portsmouth, refitting there during June-November before proceeding to the Mediterranean where she became rear-admiral's flagship until August 1907. She became Atlantic fleet flagship of the commander-in-chief from November 1908 until December 1910. This photograph was taken in 1909 and shows the *Prince of Wales* wearing the flag of a vice-admiral. Fire controls had been fitted in the tops and she carries extensive wireless aerials. Between February 1911 and May she refitted at Gibraltar and in May 1912 transferred to the 3rd battle squadron, 1st fleet, being briefly flagship of the vice-admiral. She then joined the 2nd fleet at Portsmouth and during the autumn the 5th battle squadron. She was an unlucky ship; in April 1906 an engine-room accident killed three and injured four, a stokehold explosion in July 1909 caused damage, and in June 1913 she was run into by the submarine *C 32* during exercises and again sustained damage.

At the start of World War I the *Prince of Wales* was engaged in Channel patrols but was sent to the Dardanelles in March 1915 and provided support for the ANZAC landing in April. During May she went to the Adriatic in company with the *London, Implacable* and *Queen*. She was sold in 1920 to be broken up at Milford Haven.

Bulwark

BRITISH 1902 *Plate 50*

Built	Royal Naval dockyard, Devonport
Laid down	March 1899
Launched	October 1899
Completed	March 1902
Dimensions	*Length overall* 431ft 8in
	Length 400ft
	Breadth 75ft
	Draught 26ft 6in normal
Displacement	14,490 tons normal. 15,700 tons deep load
Machinery	Twin screw
	Two vertical triple expansion engines by Hawthorn Leslie
	Twenty Belleville type water-tube boilers
	IHP = 15,000 = 18 knots
Bunkers	Coal. 900/2,100 tons
Endurance	3,000/7,000 miles at 10 knots
Armament	Four 12-inch 50-ton. 40 calibre. Two forward and two aft
	Twelve 6-inch quick-firers. 45 calibre
	Sixteen 12-pounder quick-firers
	Six 3-pounders
	Two machine-guns
	18-inch diameter torpedo tubes submerged broadside. Two forward and two aft
Armour	Krupp steel
	Belt 9-inch – 3-inch. 250ft long by 15ft wide
	Aft bulkhead only 12-inch – 10-inch – 9-inch
	Barbettes 12-inch – 8-inch – 6-inch
	Barbette shields 10-inch – 8-inch
	Casemates 6-inch
	Lower deck 2½-inch
	Middle deck 2-inch – 1-inch
	Main deck 2-inch – 1½-inch
	Forward conning tower 14-inch
	After conning tower 3-inch
Complement	733. 789 as flagship

The *Bulwark* was another of the "London" class battleships. She cost £997,846 to build and first commissioned in March 1902 as flagship of the Mediterranean fleet. Fire controls were fitted during 1904-6 and she returned to England to become flagship of the Home fleet in February 1907 and refitted at the end of the year. In August 1908 she joined the Channel fleet and in April 1909 the 1st division, Home fleet. In March 1910 the *Bulwark* transferred to the Home fleet at the Nore with a nucleus crew as vice-admiral's flagship, 3rd and 4th divisions. In April 1911 she

112   *50*   *BULWARK, BRITISH 1902*

became a private ship and this photograph was taken in June 1911. It shows her fire control installations completed in the upper fore and the after tops. The mounting of the 12-pounder, quick-firer batteries behind light armour on the upper deck amidships was questionable, as war experience in the Sino-Japanese war of 1894-5 had shown that light guns were better left exposed, allowing all but direct hits to pass them, as the shields or light protection only caused the shells to burst, resulting in heavy casualties.

In June 1912 she joined the 5th battle squadron and was 2nd fleet flagship of the rear-admiral in August and September. Later in the year she was a unit of the 5th battle squadron and was serving with it when she was destroyed by an explosion on November 26th 1914, while lying in the river Medway. She had shipped some ammunition the day before and at 7.50 am a spurt of flame emerged near her after turret and ran forward as the ship exploded with great violence, the report being heard in London. Of a crew of almost eight hundred, only fourteen survived and two of these died soon afterwards. At first sabotage was suspected but later it was thought that a defective lyddite shell had caused the accident. The accident came at a time of increasing pessimism as the war showed signs of proving a harder struggle than the British public had at first envisaged and the loss of a battleship, old and outdated though she was, was a serious blow to morale.

Albemarle

BRITISH 1903 *Plate 51*

Built	Royal Naval dockyard, Chatham
Laid down	January 1900
Launched	March 1901
Completed	November 1903
Dimensions	Length overall 432ft
	Length 405ft
	Breadth 75ft 6in
	Draught 25ft 3in mean. 26ft 4in maximum
Displacement	13,440 tons normal. 14,930 tons deep load
Machinery	Twin screw
	Two 4-cylinder vertical inverted triple expansion engines by Thames Ironworks
	Twenty-four Belleville type boilers
	IHP natural draught = 18,000 = 19 knots. 8 hours trial = 18.6 knots
Bunkers	Coal. 900 tons normal. 2,240 tons maximum
Endurance	7,200 miles at 10 knots
Armament	Four 12-inch 50-ton. 40 calibre. Two forward and two aft

Twelve 6-inch quick-firers. 45 calibre
Ten 12-pounder quick-firers
Six 3-pounders
Two machine-guns
Four 18-inch diameter torpedo tubes submerged

Armour	*Belt* 7-inch – 3-inch. 286ft long by 14ft wide
	Bulkhead aft only 11-inch – 7-inch
	Barbettes 11-inch – 4-inch
	Barbette shields 12-inch – 3-inch
	Casemates 6-inch – 2-inch
	Protected deck 2½-inch slopes. 1-inch on flat
	Maindeck where armoured 2-inch
	Conning tower 12-inch
Complement	750 778 as flagship

During the late 1890's Russia was building several battleships with a continuous sea speed of 16 knots. The *Pobieda (Plate 46)* was one of this type, which carried only 10-inch guns. To counter this design the Admiralty ordered six battleships of the "Duncan" class, which included the *Cornwallis, Albemarle, Exmouth, Russell, Montagu,* and *Duncan,* laid down between 1899 and 1900 and completed by 1904.

Their design was based on the "Formidable" type but a speed of 19 knots was intended, with a continuous sea speed of 18 knots. On trials the *Cornwallis* proved fastest at 19.56 knots but the *Albemarle* was the most reliable fast ship of the class.

The armour protection was a subject of controversy and was limited to save weight and achieve the desired speed. The prominent ventilator cowls of earlier ships were discarded in favour of wind sails – the first complete installation of this sort in British battleships. This was the last class of battleship to be painted in the smart black, white and buff of the British fleet.

The *Albemarle* and *Montagu* were ordered last, in 1899, and all were delayed by strikes and labour unrest in the shipbuilding and engineering industries.

The *Albemarle* cost £1,100,000 and first commissioned at Chatham for the Mediterranean fleet in November 1903, serving as third flagship until July 1905 when she joined the Channel fleet. In February 1907 she became rear-admiral's flagship, Atlantic fleet, and during that month collided with the sister ship *Commonwealth,* with slight damage. From January until May 1909 she was rear-admiral's flagship, Gibraltar, but in February 1910 was part of the 3rd division, Home fleet, at the Nore, reduced to a nucleus crew. She transferred to Portsmouth as rear-admiral's flagship during June to October 1910. This photograph was taken at that time. She lies at the head of four sister ships. Fire controls have been fitted and extensive wireless aerials, but the style and arrangement of the "Duncan" class remained related to the "Royal Sovereign" type of battleship of ten years earlier.

51 *ALBEMARLE, BRITISH 1903*

The *Albemarle* refitted throughout 1912, then joined the 4th battle squadron, Home fleet. In May 1913 she became a gunnery tender at Portsmouth but retained a place in the 6th battle squadron.

In August 1914 the *Albemarle*, with the *Russell* and *Exmouth*, joined the Grand fleet at Scapa Flow, and served in the northern patrol between Scotland and Norway. These ships of the 6th battle squadron were placed ahead of the more valuable "Dreadnought" type battleships of the Grand fleet when proceeding to sea through waters unswept for mines, and became known as the "mine bumpers", until moved in November 1914 to other duties. During February 1915 the *Albemarle* was serving in the 6th battle squadron in the Channel fleet, later transferring to the 3rd battle squadron, both comprised of her sister ships. In November 1915 she was damaged by heavy weather in the Pentland Firth when deep loaded. She shipped a big sea which smashed her bridge. After refitting she joined the squadron at Scapa in December.

During the Allied campaign in support of the Russian war effort, the *Albermarle* was at Archangel as guardship and occasional ice-breaker with the old battleship *Glory* and the cruisers *Intrepid* and *Iphigenia*. During 1917 the *Albemarle*'s main deck battery of 6-inch guns was removed and four 6-inch guns were remounted on the deck above. She remained in reserve at Devonport until sold in 1920 for breaking up, but stranded on passage to Swansea and did not arrive there until 1922.

Dominion

BRITISH 1905 *Plate 52*

Built	Vickers
Laid down	May 1902
Launched	August 1903
Completed	July 1905
Dimensions	*Length overall* 453ft 8in
	Length 425ft
	Breadth 78ft
	Draught 24ft 6in mean. 26ft 8in maximum
Displacement	16,350 tons normal. 17,020 tons deep load
Machinery	Twin screw
	Two 4-cylinder vertical triple expansion engines by Vickers
	Sixteen Babcock and Wilcox type water-tube boilers
	IHP trials 8 hours = 18,438 = 19.3 knots
Bunkers	Coal. 950 tons normal. 2,200 tons maximum. Plus 380 tons oil fuel
Endurance	3,150 miles at 17 knots. 7,000 miles at 10 knots
Armament	Four 12-inch 50-ton guns. 40 calibre. Two forward and two aft

Four 9.2-inch. 45 calibre. In single turrets two on each side
Ten 6-inch quick-firers. 50 calibre
Fourteen 12-pounder quick-firers
Fourteen 3-pounders
Two machine-guns
18-inch diameter torpedo tubes. Four submerged. Two forward and two aft. A stern tube was removed soon after completion

Armour	Krupp steel
	Belt 9-inch – 2-inch
	Bulkheads aft only 12-inch – 8-inch
	Barbettes 12-inch – 6-inch
	Barbette shields 12-inch – 8-inch
	9.2-inch gun barbettes 4-inch
	9.2-inch gun barbette shields 9-inch – 5-inch
	Battery amidships 7-inch
	Lower deck 2½-inch – 2-inch – 1-inch
	Middle deck 2-inch – 1-inch
	Main deck 2-inch – 1½-inch
	Conning tower 12-inch
Complement	777. As flagship 800

The "King Edward VII" class battleships were ordered under the 1901 naval estimates and included the *Dominion, Commonwealth, Hibernia, Hindustan, New Zealand, Africa, Britannia* and *King Edward VII*. They were begun between March 1902 and July 1904 and were completed between February 1905 and January 1907. They were the last numerous class of British battleship to be built with only four main guns, but the nominal displacement was increased to about 15,700 tons.

A secondary battery of four 9.2-inch guns was added, mounted in single turrets at the corners of the superstructure, besides ten 6-inch. With the lesser guns, this resulted in six different types of ammunition being carried, which posed magazine stowage problems. When fired longitudinally the 9.2-inch guns caused a blast effect on the 12-inch turrets. They fired a shell of 380-pounds weight, capable of piercing 14-inch thick steel plate at 3,000 yards with a rate of fire of four shells each minute. However, fire control spotting became difficult since the splashes of 12-inch and 9.2-inch shells appeared similar. The 6-inch guns were mounted on the broadside only 12ft 9in above water, and were difficult to work in a seaway. A total of twenty-eight 12- and 3-pounder guns were mounted on the superstructure and the turret tops, some ships having four on a turret without shields, a practice which persisted in British battleships for some years. Bunker capacity remained as in previous classes but some oil fuel was carried, though these ships were criticised for their endurance compared with ships of foreign construction.

Having only moderate freeboard the "King Edward VII" type were

52 *DOMINION, BRITISH 1905*

wet in a seaway and had a quick roll but could turn in about 350 yards diameter at 15 knots.

They were completed with only searchlight platforms aloft, fighting tops being considered inefficient, but fire control platforms were fitted before they were completed.

The *Dominion* cost £1,364,318 to build and was commissioned in August 1905 with the Atlantic fleet. She grounded in Chalon Bay, St Lawrence River, during August 1906 and was repaired at Bermuda between September and January 1907, proceeding to Chatham for permanent repairs lasting from February until June 1907. During April 1909 she joined the 2nd division, Home fleet and in May 1912 transferred to the 2nd battle squadron, 1st fleet. The *Dominion* sailed for the Mediterranean fleet in October 1913 with the 3rd battle squadron, which had been sent there temporarily. By August 1914 the squadron was with the Grand fleet based on Scapa Flow and the *Dominion* became vice-admiral's flagship during August-September 1915. She then refitted at Devonport and was afterwards attacked by a German submarine in May 1916, but avoided the torpedoes. She remained with the 3rd battle squadron, Grand fleet until 1918 when she was relegated to a depot ship in the Swin, off the Essex coast, for the operations to block Zeebrugge on the Belgian coast. During 1921 the *Dominion* was sold to be broken up but was temporarily laid up at Belfast, being dismantled at Preston during 1924-5.

Commonwealth

BRITISH 1905 *Plate 53*

Built	Fairfield Shipbuilding and Engineering Company, Glasgow
Laid down	June 1902
Launched	May 1903
Completed	March 1905
Dimensions	*Length overall* 453ft 8in
	Length 425ft
	Breadth 78ft
	Draught 24ft 6in/26ft 8in
Displacement	15,610 tons normal. 17,040 tons deep load
Machinery	Twin screw
	Two 4-cylinder vertical triple expansion engines by Fairfield
	Sixteen Babcock and Wilcox type water-tube boilers
	IHP trials 8 hours = 18,538 = 19.01 knots
Bunkers	Coal. 950 tons normal. 2,200 tons maximum. Plus 380 tons oil fuel
Endurance	3,150 miles at 17 knots. 7,000 miles at 10 knots
Armament	*Original*
	12-inch 50-ton guns. 40 calibre. Two forward and two aft
	Four 9.2-inch. 45 calibre. In single turrets, two on each side
	Ten 6-inch quick-firers. 50 calibre
	Fourteen 12-pounder quick-firers
	Fourteen 3-pounders
	Two machine-guns
	18-inch diameter torpedo tubes. Four submerged. Two forward and two aft. A stern tube was suppressed after completion
	Alterations 1918
	Ten 6-inch guns removed
	Two 6-inch guns remounted on each side, behind shields on upper deck
Armour	Krupp steel
	Belt 9-inch – 2-inch
	Bulkhead aft only 12-inch – 8-inch
	Barbettes 12-inch – 6-inch
	Barbette shields 12-inch – 8-inch
	9.2-inch gun barbettes 4-inch
	9.2-inch gun barbette shields 9-inch – 5-inch
	Battery amidships 7-inch
	Lower deck 2½-inch – 2-inch – 1-inch
	Middle deck 2-inch – 1-inch
	Main deck 2-inch – 1½-inch
	Conning tower 12-inch
Complement	777. As flagship 800

The *Commonwealth* cost £1,320,127 to build and commissioned at Devonport in April 1905 for service with the Atlantic fleet. During February 1907 she collided with the battleship *Albemarle* off Lagos, sustaining severe damage. After repairs she joined the Channel fleet in May and during August grounded in the Clyde, without damage. In 1908 the *Commonwealth* became temporarily the flagship of the rear-admiral and in April 1909 was transferred to the 2nd division, Home fleet. In June 1911, when this photograph was taken, she became a unit of the 3rd division, Home fleet, stationed at the Nore, and refitted during 1912. In May 1913 she joined the 3rd battle squadron, 1st fleet, serving temporarily in the Mediterranean. In December 1914 she commenced a refit which lasted until February 1915, then rejoined her sister ships in the 3rd battle squadron, attached to the Grand fleet, based on Scapa Flow in the Orkney Islands. Before April 1915 the Grand fleet battle squadrons were a mixture of old battleships carrying only four 12-inch guns, and "Dreadnought" type battleships with upwards of ten 12-inch guns.

The eight "King Edward VII" class ships were 3 knots inferior in speed to the "Dreadnought" type ships and this complicated deploy-

53 COMMONWEALTH, BRITISH 1905

ment of the fleet for action. When cruising, the 3rd battle squadron were stationed astern of the "Dreadnought" squadrons with orders to take station in their rear when coming into action. During their Grand fleet service the "King Edward VII" class became known as "the wobbly eight" because of their short period of roll. Throughout the war these ships were never in a position to get a shot at the enemy, though the *Dominion, Commonwealth, Hindustan* and *Zealandia* (the renamed *New Zealand*) formed the 3rd battle squadron, Grand fleet until January 1918, led by the then equally outclassed *Dreadnought*.

During 1918 the *Commonwealth* was altered, the 6-inch guns were removed, the most advanced gunnery controls were fitted and a tripod replaced the pole foremast. Her hull was fitted with anti-torpedo bulges but she saw no action before the war ended and between 1919-21 was used as a sea-going gunnery training ship at Invergordon. The *Commonwealth* was sold in November 1921 to be broken up in Germany.

New Zealand

BRITISH 1905 *Plate 54*

Built	Royal Naval dockyard, Portsmouth
Laid down	February 1903
Launched	February 1904
Completed	June 1905
Dimensions	*Length overall* 453ft 8in
	Length 425ft
	Breadth 78ft
	Draught 24ft 6in mean. 26ft 8in maximum
Displacement	15,585 tons normal. 17,060 deep load
Machinery	Twin screw
	Two 4-cylinder vertical triple expansion engines by Humphreys, Tennant and Co
	Twelve Niclausse type boilers plus three cylindrical type
	IHP = 18,400 = 18.6 knots
Bunkers	Coal. 950 tons normal. 2,200 tons maximum
Endurance	3,150 miles at 17 knots. 7,000 miles at 10 knots
Armament	*Original*
	Four 12-inch 50-ton guns. 40 calibre. Two forward and two aft
	Four 9.2-inch. 45 calibre. In single turrets, two on each side
	Ten 6-inch quick-firers. 50 calibre
	Fourteen 12-pounder quick-firers
	Fourteen 3-pounders
	Two machine-guns
	18-inch diameter torpedo tubes. Four submerged. Two

forward and two aft. A stern tube was suppressed after completion

	Alterations 1918
	Ten 6-inch guns removed
	Two 6-inch guns remounted on each side, behind shields on upper deck
Armour	Krupp steel
	Belt 9-inch – 2-inch
	Bulkhead aft only 12-inch – 8-inch
	Barbettes 12-inch – 6-inch
	Barbette shields 12-inch – 8-inch
	9.2-inch gun barbettes 4-inch
	9.2-inch gun barbette shields 9-inch – 5-inch
	Battery amidships 7-inch
	Lower deck 2½-inch – 2-inch – 1-inch
	Middle deck 2-inch – 1-inch
	Main deck 2-inch – 1½-inch
	Conning tower 12-inch
Complement	777. As flagship 800

The *New Zealand* differed from her sister ships of the "King Edward VII" class in being the only ship not originally fitted to burn oil fuel. She cost £1,335,975 to build and commissioned with the Atlantic fleet in July 1905. From October to December 1906 she was at Gibraltar refitting and in June 1907 joined the Channel fleet, refitting at Devonport during August to November 1908. In March 1909 the *New Zealand* transferred to the 2nd division, Home fleet and was temporarily the flagship of the rear-admiral. In August, when this photograph was taken, she had reverted to a private ship.

During August 1911 she joined the Portsmouth sub-division of the Home fleet and in December was renamed *Zealandia* as her name was required for the new battle cruiser *New Zealand*. In May 1912 she transferred to the 3rd battle squadron, 1st fleet, serving in the Mediterranean and afterwards was thoroughly refitted.

At the commencement of World War I she was with the 3rd battle squadron, Grand fleet, based on Scapa Flow. In November 1915 she was sent to the Dardanelles. By January 1917 she had returned to the Grand fleet and the 3rd battle squadron composed of her sister ships, remaining there until after January 1918. Later that year the *Zealandia* was altered and refitted for shore bombardment purposes in a similar manner to her sister ship *Commonwealth (Plate 53)*. The 6-inch guns were removed from the main deck and four of them were remounted on the upper deck. A tripod mast was stepped forward, but the war ended almost before she was ready and the *Zealandia* became an accommodation ship at Portsmouth.

She was sold during 1921 to be scrapped, then resold to be broken up in Germany.

54 *NEW ZEALAND, BRITISH 1905*

55   OSCAR II, SWEDISH ARMOURED COAST DEFENCE SHIP 1907

Oscar II

SWEDISH ARMOURED COAST DEFENCE SHIP 1907 *Plate 55*

Built	A.B. Lindholmen, Gothenburg
Laid down	1903
Launched	June 1905
Completed	1907
Dimensions	*Length* 313ft 4in
	Breadth 49ft 6in
	Draught 18ft maximum
Displacement	4,270 tons
Machinery	Twin screw
	Two triple expansion engines
	Twelve Yarrow type boilers
	IHP trials = 9,400 = 18.96 knots
Bunkers	Coal. 350 tons normal. 500 tons maximum
Endurance	2,950 miles at 10 knots
Armament	Two 8.3-inch. 45 calibre. In single turrets forward and aft
	Eight 6-inch. 50 calibre. In paired turrets port and starboard
	Ten 6-pounders
	Three 1-pounders
	Two 18-inch diameter torpedo tubes
Armour	*Amidship belt* 6-inch
	Deck 2-inch
	Bulkheads 6-inch
	8.3-inch gun-turrets 7½-inch – 5-inch
	Hoists 7-inch
	6-inch gun-turrets 5-inch – 3-inch
	Conning tower 7-inch
Complement	326

The Royal Swedish Navy was a coast defence force with a total personnel of 4,000 in 1906. The minister of sea defence was often a general and the ministry suffered from political interference in a traditionally pacifist country.

Sweden too was affected by the general wave of naval enthusiasm and expansion of trade and merchant shipping throughout Europe at the beginning of the present century, and was influenced as well by the rise of German militarism and her proximity to Russia. Though Swedish armed forces could not expect to counter a major power, the neutrality of coastal waters could best be confirmed by a show of naval force.

The *Oscar II* was one of a developing series of small armoured coast defence ships designed for the Swedish Navy, which rated them as first class *pansarbatar*. The series commenced with the 258ft *Gota*, *Thule* and *Svea* of 1895, mounting one 8.3-inch and seven 6-inch guns, through the 3,715-ton *Oden* of 1896 and the similar *Thor* and *Niord* of 1899 armed with two 10-inch and six 4.7-inch guns, to the more distinguished looking *Dristighenten*, a 3,600-tonner completed in 1902 with two 8.3-inch and six 6-inch guns. The *Aran* , *Vasa*, *Tapperheten* and *Manligheten* of 1901-3 were similar, but reverted to single turret mounts for the 6-inch guns.

The *Oscar II* was a good example of a well-designed, compact, coast defence ship with arrangement probably influenced by contemporary "pre-Dreadnought" battleships in major navies. A single 8.3-inch gun was mounted forward and aft and the 6-inch were in turret-mounted pairs, with the casings recessed in way of the traverses. Her length of 316ft improved speed to about 19 knots and she was a good sea boat.

No further Swedish coast defence ships were ordered until 1911 when the *Sverige*, *Drottning*, *Victoria* and *Gustav den Femta* were projected, but the orders were cancelled after Liberal Party agitation in Parliament. This angered many Swedes and a fund to build some of these ships raised the equivalent of £970,000 by the end of April 1912 and the orders were finally placed during 1912 and 1915, for the first two ships.

Swedish warships rarely left the Baltic as the country had few colonies or international obligations. The fleet exercised and patrolled in home waters or refitted at the naval dockyards of Karlskrona and Stockholm.

The *Oscar II* was present at the British naval review for the coronation of King George V in 1911, when the photo (frontispiece) was taken.

In 1920 her official name was *Oscar den Anrdra*, but armament and appearance remained unchanged for many years.

The *Oscar II* saw no action throughout her existence as Sweden remained neutral during the two world wars; the fleet vigilant but at peace. In 1939 the torpedo tubes were removed and four 57-mm guns and two 25-mm anti-aircraft guns were added to the ship during a programme of reconstruction. During 1950 the *Oscar II* was removed from the active fleet, the armament was unshipped and she was berthed at the quay of Berga naval school as a damage-control training hulk. She continued to serve until sold in September 1974, to be scrapped at Gothenburg.

Olfert Fischer

DANISH ARMOURED COAST DEFENCE SHIP 1905 *Plate 56*

Built	Royal Naval dockyard, Copenhagen
Laid down	1901
Launched	May 1903
Completed	1903
Dimensions	*Length between perpendiculars* 271ft 8in
	Breadth 50ft 6in

123   *56   OLFERT FISCHER, DANISH ARMOURED COAST DEFENCE SHIP 1905*

	Draught 16ft 9in maximum
Displacement	3,700 tons
Machinery	Twin screw
	Two triple expansion engines
	Six Thornycroft boilers
	IHP trials = 4,600 = 15.8 knots
Bunkers	Coal. 255 tons maximum
Endurance	Approx 2,000 miles at 10 knots. 1,050 miles at 14¾ knots
Armament	*Original*
	Two 9.4-inch Bofors guns. 43 calibre. In single turrets one forward and one aft
	Four 5.9-inch Bofors quick-firers. 43 calibre. In casemates
	Ten 6-pounder quick-firers
	Six smaller guns
	Two machine-guns
	Three 18-inch diameter torpedo tubes. One bow. Two broadside. All submerged
	Modified by 1920
	Two 9.4-inch
	Four 5.9-inch
	Six 14-pounders
	Two 6-pounder anti-aircraft guns
	Two 1-pounders
	Two machine-guns
	Three 18-inch torpedo tubes
Armour	Creusot steel
	Belt 7-inch amidships. 4-inch aft. 7ft wide
	Bulkhead 7-inch
	Turrets 7-inch
	Casemates 5.9-inch
	Protective deck 3-inch forward
	Conning tower 7-inch
Complement	250 – 255

The *Olfert Fischer* was one of a class of Danish armoured coastal defence ships which commenced with the *Herluf Trolle*, laid down in 1896, and included the *Olfert Fischer* and the later *Peder Skram*, completed in 1909. Although very similar they were not identical. These ships were smaller and lighter versions of the various coast defence ships built for Norway and Sweden at the end of the 19th century and early in the 20th. The role of the Royal Danish Navy was defensive and although small it was of high standard.

These three armoured ships, with the older ship *Skjold* and the larger *Niels Juel* completed in 1922, formed the backbone of the Danish Navy for thirty years. They were wet sea boats, having a freeboard of only three feet. The *Olfert Fischer* failed to attain her designed speed of 16 knots with 4,200 IHP.

This photograph, taken in 1911, shows her circular turrets and the monitor-like hull. The tall topmasts were fitted to carry wireless equipment.

The *Olfert Fischer* was paid off in October 1936. On the 5th, 6th and 7th of October she was used as an aerial bombing target by the Danish Air Force, steaming at 9 knots. Three hundred and eight-six bombs were dropped, of which only twelve hit the ship. She returned to harbour and the hull was sold to a firm of Danish ship-breakers. The armour was sold to Sweden but her guns had been retained and were stored until 1948, when they were sold for scrap.

Dreadnought

BRITISH 1906 *Plates 57 and 58*

Built	Royal Naval dockyard, Portsmouth
Laid down	October 1905
Launched	February 1906
Completed	October 1906
Dimensions	*Length overall* 527ft
	Length between perpendiculars 490ft
	Breadth 82ft
	Draught 26ft 6in normal
Displacement	17,110 tons normal. 21,845 tons deep-loaded
Machinery	Four screws
	Four steam turbine engines by the Parsons Steam Turbine Co
	Eighteen Babcox and Wilcox boilers
	HP 23,000 = 21 knots
	HP trials 26,350 = 21.6 knots
	Continuous sea speed = 18.5 knots
Bunkers	Coal. 900 tons normal. 2,900 tons maximum. Plus 1,120 tons oil fuel and 120 tons patent fuel
Endurance	6,620 miles at 10 knots
	4,910 miles at 18.4 knots
Armament	*Original*
	Ten 12-inch guns. 45 calibre. Five paired turrets. Three on middle line and one on each beam
	Twenty-four 12-pounder quick-firers
	Five 18-inch diameter torpedo tubes submerged. Four broadside. One stern
	Alterations in 1916
	Only ten 12-pounder guns were mounted
Armour	*Belt* 11-inch – 8-inch – 6-inch – 4-inch
	Bulkheads 8-inch

57 DREADNOUGHT, BRITISH 1906

126   *58* *DREADNOUGHT, BRITISH 1906*

Barbettes 11-inch – 4-inch
Turrets 11-inch
Conning towers 11-inch – 8-inch
Main deck ¾-inch
Middle decks 3-inch – 1¾-inch
Lower decks 4-inch – 1½-inch
Complement 695. 773 as flagship

The *Dreadnought* was the first large warship propelled by turbines and the first British battleship to steam at 21 knots. She carried a revolutionary "all big gun" armament for long range firing and was unique in arrangement by having officers' accommodation forward and crew accommodation aft.

The 1903 edition of *Fighting Ships*, edited by F.T. Jane, contained an article by the distinguished Italian naval constructor V. Cuniberti, advocating an ideal battleship for the British fleet: a 17,000-ton ship with twelve 12-inch guns, well protected, and capable of 24 knots. The outline design was intended to attack an enemy ship at moderate or close range with concentrated fire. However, increasing accuracy and range of guns, improved shells and need for salvo-firing to assist gunnery control at longer ranges, combined with results of gunnery tests, proved that a uniform main armament of ten heavy guns could be most effective. Threat of torpedo attack also tended to increase battleship range from the 3,000 yards common in 1903 to a possible 6,000 yards with advanced gunnery techniques, with probable hits at 8,000 yards.

Many considered the mixed-armament, 18-knot *Lord Nelson* and *Agamemnon*, then building, to be the best type of battleship for Britain; others feared that Germany would produce an "all big gun" ship capable of accurate fire at extreme range and of high speed.

During 1904 and 1905 British naval authorities pondered the construction of such a ship and early in 1905 the Americans authorised the sister battleships *Michigan* and *North Carolina*, to carry eight 12-inch guns and twenty-two 3-inch, on a displacement of 16,000 tons and with a speed of 18.5 knots. Some naval board members had pressed for 19,000-ton ships with ten 12-inch guns.

Britain could no longer delay if she wished to be able to claim she was the first to commission an "all big gun" battleship. A quick decision was made by Sir John Fisher, who had become First Sea Lord in October 1904. He claimed to have first considered the type during 1900 and later to have discussed it with Mr Gard of the Royal Corps of Naval Constructors. In 1904 he instituted a committee of naval officers, constructors and shipbuilders to examine the need for and construction of the new type of battleship, which many held to be a mistaken policy which would put British naval supremacy in hazard by rendering obsolete all other existing battleships and reducing Britain's considerable lead over the battleship forces of other nations to only one ship.

The decision made, great care was taken to ensure she would be successful; she was strongly constructed to withstand the effects of salvo-firing of eight 12-inch guns simultaneously, compared with the four 12-inch of earlier battleships. A speed of 21 knots was desired, and to achieve it and to lower the centre of gravity of the machinery weights to compensate for the increased weight of armament, Fisher agreed to the use of steam turbines in place of the usual reciprocating steam engines which, although capable of propelling contemporary battleships at 18 knots on trials, broke down if full power was imposed for any length of time, reducing the effective sea speed of battle fleets to about 14 knots. Turbines had previously only been fitted in destroyers and one cruiser was building which would have them. To choose such untried machinery for Britain's most advanced and experimental warship was dangerous but characteristic of the whole "Dreadnought" scheme. Parsons, the marine turbine manufacturer, assured the committee of the efficiency of their machinery, which was to drive four instead of the usual two screws of earlier battleships and had an astern turbine on each propeller shaft. The *Dreadnought*'s turbine installation was as revolutionary as the "all big gun" armament, and as successful.

When completed the *Dreadnought* outclassed all other battleships. The advantage was short-lived but she achieved renewed respect for the British Navy and the speed and secrecy of her construction took other nations by surprise. Her construction created a dilemma about the future of the battleships *Lord Nelson* and *Agamemnon*, which were still building at the time. It was decided eventually to complete these ships as designed, with four 12-inch guns, but to appropriate their already manufactured 12-inch guns for use in the *Dreadnought*, to speed her completion, which was of paramount importance. It was also decided that no other British battleship would be commenced until the *Dreadnought* had undergone trials.

The *Dreadnought* was laid down at Portsmouth dockyard on 2nd October 1905 and was launched on 10th February 1906. She was completed for trials on 3rd October 1906; an unprecedented speed for a large and experimental capital ship and only made possible by the suspension of much other construction. To speed building, much of the work of drawing office and mould loft was combined, resulting in rapid laying-off and material template making. She cost £1,783,883.

The *Dreadnought* was first commissioned, in reserve, on 1st September 1906. Her trials, which occupied October, November and December, were held in the West Indies as being the area most secluded from rival observation. The engines proved reliable and after a month's steaming she returned on a 7,000-mile passage back to England at an average speed of 17½ knots, without defects.

She joined the Home fleet for special service and became flagship of the commander-in-chief during April 1907. This photograph was taken a few months later and shows the positioning of her turrets which enabled eight of her ten 12-inch guns to fire abeam. The tripod masts were an innovation but the after mast was too low to be effective and the foremast fire-control top suffered from funnel fumes and heat.

During May 1912 the *Dreadnought* was relieved by the battleship *Neptune*. She then joined the 1st division, Home fleet and became flagship of the 4th battle squadron from December 1912 until May 1916. On March 18th 1915 she rammed and sank the German submarine *U 29* during a North Sea sweep.

The *Dreadnought* was refitted in the spring of 1916 and in May transferred to the 3rd battle squadron as flagship, based on Sheerness as protection against a repetition of the German naval raids on the English east coast. She rejoined the Grand fleet in March 1918, serving with the 4th battle squadron until July 1918, when she was paid off. In February 1919 she went into reserve at Rosyth and was offered for sale by March 1920. A year later she was sold, to be scrapped at Inverkeithing during 1923.

The *Dreadnought* remains perhaps the best-remembered British battleship and was followed by numbers of "improved Dreadnoughts", as the type became known, then by "super Dreadnoughts" and even "hyper-super Dreadnoughts". Until 1918 navies measured their power by possession of a greater number of "Dreadnought" type battleships than their rivals. Afterwards the term fell into disuse.

CRUISERS

The cruiser type descended from the frigates, corvettes and sloops of the sailing fleets, emerging through the wooden, fully-rigged steam frigates and corvettes which were built for many navies and carried the guns broadside on one deck in traditional frigate fashion. Steam and sail paddle frigates were built but proved unsuccessful hybrids, with paddle-boxes vulnerable to damage in action. Many existing swift wooden sailing frigates were fitted with an auxiliary screw, and specially-designed and fully-rigged screw steam frigates were built for many fleets.

In 1854 the United States commenced construction of five large rigged steam frigates armed with shell-firing guns. The 275ft waterline *Merrimac* mounted twenty-four 9-inch, fourteen 8-inch and two 10-inch guns and steamed at 8.8 knots in smooth water. She sailed well. In response to these powerfully armed ships capable of ocean cruising, Britain built three pairs of fast steam frigates of which the best were the *Mersey* and the *Orlando,* completed in 1858. These were 336ft long, steamed at a maximum of 13.2 knots and mounted twenty 10-inch and twelve 68-pounder guns.

Second class steam and sail frigates continued to be built, with lighter armament. The functions of a frigate continued to be those either of independent cruising or as supplements to a battle fleet. Ocean cruising was a frequent duty and most passages were made under sail for strict economy in coal and pride in seamanship.

Britain needed large numbers of frigates to serve on the many naval stations of her Empire, to show the flag around the world and to protect her vital ocean shipping. By 1860 the introduction of large, ironclad steam frigates mounting a heavy armament and acting as major warships of a battle fleet led to a delay in construction of unarmoured steam frigates under construction for the British fleet. Traditionally a frigate was not expected to engage a line of battleship, but the new ironclad steam frigates were more powerful than any existing line of battleship and had the steam speed of a fast frigate. Preoccupation with ironclad building and uncertainty about the future trend of frigate development held up British unarmoured frigate-building for several years, though

France built numbers of *corvettes rapides,* and wooden frigate construction continued for other navies.

Proof of the potential of commerce-raiding cruisers came from America where during the Civil War of 1861-5 the Southern States seriously damaged Northern commerce with cruiser attacks on ocean trade. The iron, screw, steam and sail cruiser *Alabama* was the most noted of these raiders. She was built in England by Laird of Birkenhead for the Confederate States Navy under conditions of secrecy, then surveillance, and slipped out of the Mersey on pretext of a trial ship. She was armed in the Atlantic from a Southern ship, to commission as the Confederate ship *Alabama* under Captain Raphael Semmes. The *Alabama* captured large numbers of Northern States merchant and whaling ships. From one, Semmes learned of the Northern blockade of Galveston and steamed there to lure away the blockading ship *Hatteras* and engage and sink her, before continuing to capture about seventy merchant ships and prove the destructive effects of commerce raiding under steam. In June 1864 the *Alabama* entered Cherbourg to refit and was brought to action off there by the Northern States steam sloop *Kearsarge,* which finally sank the voyage-worn cruiser. Together with the Confederate cruisers *Florida* and *Shenandoah,* the *Alabama* had almost cleared the seas of Northern merchant ships, for those that had evaded capture feared to leave port.

Towards the end of the American Civil War the Northern States Navy commenced construction of six fast cruisers, partly to discourage intervention by France or Britain. The ships were designed to become commerce raiders, or to be used for hunting down Southern States cruisers such as the *Alabama.*

The *Wampanoag* was typical of these ships, with a 335ft wooden hull displacing 4,200 tons. A two-cylinder engine drove a single propeller through wooden gear wheels and there were eight tubular boilers with superheaters. Despite this advanced machinery, she was designed with a barque rig, later reduced to three pole masts, which blended better with the two pairs of rakish funnels, flush deck and straight stem. The *Wampanoag* sailed satisfactorily as a barque and under steam achieved the then astonishing speed of 17¼ knots and maintained it for almost forty hours on trial. At the time most sail and steam frigates were lucky to achieve 15 for a short spurt but this American cruiser could maintain 16¾ knots and had the ability to overtake any warship afloat, or run from her if outgunned.

In Britain the *Alabama*'s example led the Admiralty to order a large unarmoured frigate which was to achieve high speed under steam. She was to have a single screw, good seakeeping ability and a full rig to conserve coal. She had an iron hull of 5,780 tons displacement, which overcame the longitudinal weakness of earlier wooden fast frigates. The bottom was sheathed with wood so it could be coppered to minimise fouling by marine growth during long distance cruising away from docking facilities. A 7,360 horsepower engine drove her at 16.5 knots and when completed in 1866 she was second only to the *Wampanoag* in speed but was well armed and a good sea boat which survived the Biscay gale which overwhelmed the ironclad *Captain* in 1870.

The *Inconstant*, as she was named, also sailed well, which was important as her bunker capacity only allowed 54 hours steaming at full power, or about 2,000 miles at 10 knots. She was considered large for an unarmoured frigate and was followed by the 3,300-ton *Active* and *Volage* (*Plate 59*), completed in 1869 with iron hulls. These steamed at 15 knots and were able ships, but used sail for ocean work.

During 1870-1 the wooden steam frigate *Raleigh* of 5,200 tons barely managed 14 knots but the 4,130-ton *Euralyas* and *Bacchante*, with 5,250 horsepower steamed at 15. In 1873 the 6,250-ton wooden steam frigate *Shah* was built with 7,840 horsepower to achieve 16 knots, but remained an inferior ship to the *Inconstant*. All were unarmoured and almost useless as fighting ships.

Then, for several years, Britain built only smaller, comparatively slow cruisers of wood and iron construction, around 2,000 tons displacement and 12-13 knots speed. These were lightly armed with broadside-mounted, muzzle-loading guns and had counterparts in most navies. The German steam corvette *Stosch* (*Plates 61 and 62*) was typical. These obsolete ships were in contrast to the fast iron-hulled French cruisers *Tourville* and *Duquesne* – 5,800-tonners steaming at 17 knots and mounting big guns with hull recesses for ahead and astern fire. The smaller *Duguay Trouin* at 3,660 tons and 16 knots speed was superior to contemporary British cruisers.

In 1870 the Russian Navy ordered the 4,600-ton *General Admiral* as an "armoured cruiser", though the term originated later. Her sides were protected along the waterline by a complete armour belt. Four 8-inch and two 6-inch guns were carried in a central battery and she was fully rigged when completed in 1874. The *Gerzog Edinburgski*, a similar ship, was launched in 1875.

These Russian cruisers prompted the design of the 5,390-ton British armoured cruiser *Shannon*, laid down in 1873 and completed four years later. She was partially successful in having a strong armament, but the armour belt was only 9 inches thick and extended over ¾ of the waterline. However, above it she had an armoured deck 1½-inches thick, which shielded the magazines, machinery, boilers and steering gear from plunging fire, and the hull was well sub-divided. Two 10-inch muzzle-loading guns fired ahead, six 9-inch were broadside-mounted and one fired as a stern chaser. The *Shannon* was ship-rigged and had a single screw, but carried only 280 tons of coal and steamed at only 12 knots maximum speed. As a result much use was made of sail and she was useless for overhauling another cruiser or fighting a second class battleship likely to be encountered in distant seas. A curious feature of her design was a triangular ram which was carried on board to be fitted to her stem in time of war.

The British Admiralty were convinced that armoured cruising ships were needed by the Royal Navy and the *Nelson* and the *Northampton* (*Plate 60*) were built in 1878, of 7,630 tons displacement, heavily armed with four 10-inch and eight 9-inch guns. Although at first classed as "second class battleships", these ships were in fact armoured cruisers with an armour belt at the waterline and an armoured deck. Theoretically they were capable of fighting a ship-to-ship action with a second class battleship or of pursuing a cruiser and overwhelming her with superior gun power, but the heavy rig and displacement offset the twin screws and length, so top speed was only 13 knots. These ships also proved unsatisfactory and served mainly as flagships on colonial stations.

The French built some comparable ships, termed *cuirassés de croisers*, of the "Duguesclin" type of around 6,000 tons, protected by an armour belt 10-6½-inches thick and mounting between four and six 9.4-inch and six 5.5-inch guns. These ships were primarily intended for coast defence.

After the cumbersome armoured cruisers, the Admiralty swung to the other extreme with the first steel-hulled fast unarmoured cruisers *Iris* and *Mercury* of 3,700 tons and 7,300 horsepower, very lightly built and armed but with twin screws and a speed of 18 knots. These too were of little practical use and became rated as "despatch vessels". Armament was thirteen 5-inch guns, showing the variety of weapons then mounted in British cruising ships.

The era of unarmoured cruisers relying for effectiveness on gun power, high speed, and a combination of steam and sail for ocean endurance, waned during the late 1870's with the development of lighter guns with increasing range and improved shells. Some protection of the engine and boiler spaces was necessary and as great weight of armour was irreconcilable with good speed, the thin steel protective deck was increasingly incorporated in British and other cruisers and the "protected cruiser" emerged as a type built in numbers.

Britain still had insufficient ships to police her world Empire and between 1878-84 three classes of small cruisers were built with partial protective decks: the "*Pylades*", "Calliope" and "Comus" types of which the *Calliope* (*Plate 65*) is best remembered. The nine "Comus" type built between 1878 and 1881 were ship-rigged steel screw corvettes (*Plates*

63 and 64), later rated as third class cruisers of 2,380 tons displacement and mounting various armaments from ten 6-inch breech-loaders to two 4½-ton and twelve 64-pounder muzzle-loaders. Low speed was offset by good coal endurance and these ships were much used on foreign service. The 2,770-ton "Calliope" class completed in 1884 were still fully rigged, despite having four 6-inch and twelve 5-inch breech-loading guns, but they steamed at 14.6 knots. The *"Pylades"* type were only 1,420 tons and had a speed of 14 knots but mounted fourteen 5-inch guns. These overcrowded ships were built with composite hulls of wood on steel frames and were outdated before building commenced.

Because of their work in remote seas cruisers of colonial powers retained a full sailing rig, but the use of sail in warships of any type was criticised by increasing numbers of experienced naval officers and the two-year cruise of the cruisers *Inconstant* and *Bacchante* with a squadron of steam and sail corvettes, emphasised this. The ships sailed for nine-tenths of the time under way, but the majority of the crews regarded sail drill as a useless exercise for war, though sail did steady the ships under steam in a seaway, and of course conserved coal.

Sail began to be discarded in the early 1880's when the four 4,300-ton "Amphion" type British second class protected cruisers were given only a barquentine rig for fuel saving. Twin screws drove these ships at 17 knots and the 315ft hull had a protective deck and bunkers for 1,000 tons of coal, which enabled 10 knots to be maintained for 11,000 miles. Ten 6-inch guns made the ships suitable for fleet work or for ocean trade route protection. They served mainly in the Pacific.

By then the frigate and corvette classes of the British Navy were reclassed as cruisers, divided into the protected and armoured types, with the protected ships being further sub-divided into first, second and third class.

In 1880 France increased the number of battleships under construction and an economy-minded British government decided to build two armoured ships for overseas service, of limited size and with full sailing rig to reduce coal consumption. These had to be large enough to fight enemy cruisers or an armoured ship of equal strength and for the design the Admiralty copied the layout of the French "Marceau" type battleships in mounting a heavy gun forward and aft and one on each side amidships. The new ships emerged as armoured cruisers of 8,500 tons named *Impérieuse* and *Warspite*, mounting four 9.2-inch and ten 6-inch guns. The big guns were in barbettes with shields and an armoured deck and side armour was fitted. Speed was 16 knots with twin screws but they were rigged as brigs with a large sail area, long topmast and bowsprit – ridiculous in a fully-powered warship. After trials, in 1886, the rigs were removed and a pole mast fitted as both ships were 1,000 tons overweight. When completed the armour belt was usually below water and they relied on the side coal bunkers for protection. However, these were steady ships, which made for good gunnery, but both steered wildly. These ineffective cruisers served as flagships on the Pacific

station and spent much time in reserve.

While naval authorities were producing cruisers which were usually expensive failures, the Tyne shipbuilders Sir Robert Armstrong were building the Chilean protected cruiser *Esmeralda* to the design of their naval architect William White, afterwards a noted Director of Naval Construction. The 2,950-ton *Esmeralda* was 270ft long and steamed at 18 knots with twin screws. She was not rigged and the flush-deck, clean-looking hull had the bridge between the funnels for good visibility in action. The heavy armament of one 10-inch gun forward, one aft and three 6-inch on each side amidships, made her a powerful ship and there was a 1-inch steel deck below the waterline. She was so successful and purposeful that more were built and attracted buyers in many navies. Similar cruisers were sold to Argentina and Brazil. Italy purchased the *Giovanni Bausan* from Armstrong's in 1885 and built further ships of the type in the "Etna" class. In 1888 Armstrong's designed and built the cruiser *Piemonte* for Italy as the first warship with a principal armament of all quick-firing guns; six 6-inch and six 4.7-inch. The Admiralty copied the *Esmeralda* arrangement in the four "Mersey" type second class cruisers of 1886 which made 18 knots on a displacement of 4,000 tons.

In 1887 the seven armoured cruisers of the "Aurora" class *(Plates 68 and 69)* followed the same basic arrangement with two 9.2-inch and ten 6-inch guns. Displacement was 5,600 tons and speed 18 knots. 10-inch side armour gave protection, and endurance was 5,000 miles at 10 knots, but the large number of guns, limited displacement and poor protection for gun crews made them indifferent fighting ships.

French cruiser design was almost as diverse and the ships were more lightly armed than their British counterparts but were faster in a seaway. Many remained fully rigged. The protected cruisers *Alger, Isly* and *Jean Bart* were typical with a displacement of 4,160 tons. Eight 16- and 14-cm guns were singly mounted on side sponsons, a stern chaser protruded from a port in the counter stern and two bow chasers poked above a bulbous ram bow. The two squat funnels contrasted with a barque rig, with machine-guns in the fighting tops.

Sail lingered. In the 1889 British naval manoeuvres the ship-rigged protected cruiser *Calypso* was chased by two cruisers of the "enemy" fleet at night. Under steam alone, against wind, she made 11.8 knots but, altering course, she made "all plain sail" (less royals) and under steam and sail escaped at 15 knots in misty weather. Such incidents continued the sail and steam controversy. The same summer the American cruisers *Chicago, Boston, Atlanta* and *Yorktown* steamed from Boston to Lisbon, then visited the Mediterranean, England and Northern Europe. The transatlantic passage demonstrated their coal endurance, for they steamed 200 miles a day and arrived with fuel to spare. Sail was used whenever possible on passage.

The *Blenheim* and *Blake* were the first cruisers of uncompromising appearance in the British fleet and formed the pattern for subsequent protected cruisers for many years. 375 feet long by 65 feet beam, they displaced 9,000 tons and steamed at 22 knots, with 20 knots sustained sea speed and a range of 15,000 miles at 10 knots or 3,000 at 20. These were fine ships for the time, well armed with two 9.2-inch and ten 6-inch guns, and capable of steaming across the Atlantic at the speed of a contemporary liner without coaling.

Cruisers were the principal British naval force in colonial seas and an example of their preparedness and of contemporary communications occurred during 1889 when Britain seemed likely to be involved in war with Portugal in East Africa. On Christmas Day the Admiralty telegraphed to Indian Ocean stations for all available ships in the Indian Ocean to concentrate at Zanzibar as a show of strength. Seven ships were there already and fifteen days later there were two second class cruisers, eight third class, two sloops, one gun vessel, one gunboat and one survey ship; a force manned by 3,300 sailors and reckoned strong enough to "occupy and hold every Portuguese military station on the coast". Many were ships stationed at the Cape, others had been on passage across the Indian Ocean.

Nine 2,500-ton cruisers of the "Pelorus" class were built principally for foreign service but the eight 4.7-inch guns were too many for the 265ft long hulls and the larger "Medea" type had only six 6-inch.

An advance in the cruiser concept occurred when French naval constructor Bertin directed design of the 6,300-ton armoured cruiser *Dupuy de Lôme*, completed in 1890. The 374ft hull had a long ram bow and a similarly shaped stern profile. The ram provided buoyancy forward, instead of a long forecastle which would have been affected by blast from the forward 6.4-inch gun. Six 6.4-inch guns in single turret mounts were disposed forward and aft, and a 7.6-inch gun-turret was placed on each side amidships. These guns had great range for the time and the hull was designed to withstand explosive shell hits. The entire side was armoured and an armoured deck gave further protection. The long profile, short funnels and two tubular masts with circular tops made her modern-looking, with a strangely German appearance.

As with British battleships, the Naval Defence Act of 1889 was a turning point from sporadic British cruiser construction to classes of cruisers intended for certain duties. The 3,400-ton "Apollo" class of elven protected cruisers and the ten similar "Aeolus" type of 3,600 tons (*Plates 73, 74 and 75*) mounted two 6-inch and six 4.7-inch guns. Trial speed was 20 knots, but this soon diminished.

The six "Astraea" class of 4,360 tons mounted only two more 4.7-inch guns but were improved ships with greater length, making them better sea boats (*Plate 76*). The 7,700-ton *Crescent* and *Royal Arthur* were completed in 1893 with a 9.2-inch bow chaser and twelve 6-inch quick-firers. These were the first British cruisers designed to be used as flagships on foreign stations, and were imposing and successful ships (*Plates 79, 80 and 81*).

Seven almost similar "Edgar" class cruisers followed, mounting a second 9.2-inch gun aft (*Plates 77 and 78*). A large bow and stern chaser was considered essential armament for a cruiser of any size, though heavy guns such as the 9.2 or 10-inch, which were often fitted, would have punished the ship in a sustained action, and the weight at the ends detracted from seaworthiness.

Until the introduction of wireless, cruisers were vital scouts for a battle fleet, probing enemy strength and deployment and parrying enemy cruisers as a screen for battleships. After about 1892, cruisers became an essential complementary force to major battle fleets. In 1894 Britain had thirty-one first class armoured and protected cruisers to France's fourteen and Russia's eleven. The figures for second and third class protected cruisers were fifty-four, twenty-two and three; emphasising Britain's awareness of the need for protection of her ocean trade.

The nine "Eclipse" class cruisers of 1896-8 were 5,600 tons and had five 6-inch and six 4.7-inch guns, but only made 19½ knots. These ships spent much time overseas (*Plates 87, 88 and 89*). The four "Arrogant" class of 1897 were unique in being designed with a bow specially strengthened for ramming and eventually mounted ten 6-inch guns (*Plate 90*). The "Hermes" type which followed had one more 6-inch gun (*Plate 101*).

The large protected cruiser reached a peak with the 14,440-ton *Powerful* and *Terrible* of 1898, armed with two 9.2-inch, twelve 6-inch and sixteen 12-pounder guns (*Plates 95 and 96*), designed as long-range ships for protecting trade routes against the Russian *Rurik* and similar cruisers. However, these large ships were vulnerable with only a 6-inch protective deck and although a speed of 22 knots was satisfactory, the expense of building and maintenance limited their usefulness. The Admiralty did not learn the lesson of limiting size and four 11,000-ton cruisers of the "Diadem" class were built, quickly followed by four more of the "Ariadne" class; all ships which presented huge targets in action and had a light armament for their size (*Plates 97 and 98*).

French protected cruisers developed from ships of about 1,700 tons, suh as the *Milan* of 1884, which mounted five 4-inch guns and steamed at 18½ knots, through the "Surcouf" and "Cosmao" classes, with exaggerated ram bows, three masts and four 5.5-inch guns in side casemates, to much larger cruisers of the 1890's, culminating in the 440ft long *Jurien de la Gravière* of 1900, with high freeboard, four funnels and 21.7 knots speed, carrying eight 6.4-inch guns in single shield mountings and side casemates.

Occasionally attempts were made to evolve a cruiser which would carry both a defensive armament and several torpedo boats to sea, in hope of launching them in a surprise attack on an enemy fleet. In 1889 Britain completed the 350ft-long torpedo cruiser *Vulcan* of this type, which also had workshops to maintain her torpedo flotilla and was capable of carrying mines.

France developed the type with the 6,000-ton *Foudre*, completed in 1897, having a flush decked hull with three short funnels amidships and the bridge well forward. There were two lifting gantries amidships and aft for eight torpedo boats and four torpedo-carrying launches, which could be hoisted on board and stowed in chocks on deck. Her function was to approach an enemy coast in darkness or fog, lower the torpedo boats to attack an enemy anchorage or fleet before hopefully escaping under cover of the *Foudre*'s eight 4-inch guns. She was an ingenious ship with a speed of 19½ knots, but was not copied.

The 8,000-ton *Châteaurenault* was an unusual French protected cruiser, completed in 1901 as a commerce raider and designed to resemble a contemporary four-funnelled ocean liner, with plumb stem, counter stern, light pole masts, flush sheer and boats along the rail amidships. Normal speed was 21 knots but she could make 24½ for an hour or so, to overhaul a prize. A 6.4-inch gun was mounted forward and aft, and six 5.5-inch in side casemates. The *Châteaurenault* was an isolated ship, not repeated in other fleets which built numbers of high-speed commerce-raiding cruisers as potential attackers of British merchant ships in war.

By the end of the nineteenth century the cruiser epitomised dash in action. Fast by contemporary standards, often long-ranging, well-armed and rakish in appearance, command of these ships was often a step to senior promotion in major fleets. The new breed of cruiser also seemed useful to nations with limited overseas colonies. Holland, with islands to rule in the Caribbean and East Indies, built 3,900-ton protected cruisers of the "Holland" class, completed between 1897-1900. They were compact ships about 320ft long mounting two 6-inch and six 4.7-inch guns and four torpedo tubes. Speed was about 20 knots and the construction was reputedly the best of any comparable cruisers. These were good sea boats, smart looking with two large funnels.

Construction of warships by builders in leading naval countries such as Britain, France, and later Italy and Germany, accelerated and the market became so assured that during the 1880-1900 period, protected cruisers were laid down in Britain as speculations, to be completed on the berth to a purchaser's requirements. The Tyneside yard of Armstrong continued to specialise in foreign cruisers and produced well-designed ships such as the Argentine *Buenos Aires* of 1895 *(Plate 83)*, the Japanese *Takasago* of 1898 *(Plate 92)* the Chinese *Hai Chi* of 1899 *(Plate 99)* and the Chilean *Chacabuco* of 1902 *(Plate 106)*.

As Germany possessed few colonies and her fleet expansion did not commence until national ambitions were aroused in the late 1890's, she had few classes of cruisers until then. The *Prinzess Wilhelm* and *Irene* of 1888 *(Plate 66)* were the first twin-screw ships in the German fleet and the first unrigged German cruisers. These were efficient if unusual ships, which were rearmed several times in the search for ideal guns for cruisers.

The 3,765-ton *Gefion* of 1894 *(Plate 82)* and the 2,000-ton *Hela* of 1896 were individual ships designed in the search for the best cruiser qualities, but the 5,600-ton "Freya" and "Hertha" class of five ships were completed in 1898 as a force of well-armed cruisers mounting two 8.2-inch and six 5.9-inch guns, and steaming at 19 knots.

Ten "Gazelle" type ships averaging 2,700 tons followed in 1899-1901,

setting a pattern for light, fast German cruisers by mounting ten 4.1-inch guns and steaming at 21.5 knots. The many "Town" classes of light cruisers which followed, started with the five "Bremen" type of 3,250 tons, capable of 23 knots and again mounting ten 4.1-inch guns. All had the exaggerated ram bow then typical of German cruisers, but were fast and hard hitting. The type evolved into the notable ocean-ranging cruisers of World War I, such as the *Emden*, *Königsberg* and *Nürnberg*.

Contemporary British small cruisers were the 3,000-ton "Topaze" class of four ships, armed with twelve 4-inch guns and steaming at 22 knots, and completed during 1904-5. By then the British "River" class destroyers had become seagoing ships able to escort a fleet at sea, or carry out a sea "sweep", and to work with these as leaders, a new type of fast, light "scout" cruiser was developed, having a sea speed of about 25 knots. The two "Sentinel" class, completed in 1905, were the first; well armed with nine 4-inch guns. The *Forward* and *Foresight*, *Pathfinder* and *Patrol*, *Adventure* and *Attentive* followed; all completed during 1905 and of similar size and armament to the *Sentinel*.

By then the Japanese had more experience with fast protected cruisers armed with quick-firing guns than any other navy and the *Takasago (Plate 92)* was typical of the type of cruiser which they had proved in action during the wars with China (1894-5) and Russia (1904-5). The Japanese also made good use of armoured cruisers, including the *Asama (Plate 105)*.

Britain completed no armoured cruisers for thirteen years after the "Orlando" class in 1888, but other navies persevered with the type, which were capable of many of the duties of the battleship at much less cost. The American Navy was typical. It had become a minor fleet for twenty years after the Civil War, materially inferior to many small navies, and as the nation had little ocean trade, governments were reluctant to spend much on warships, particularly during such an experimental era. The armoured cruiser type offered advantages when fleet expansion commenced at the end of the 1880's and the 6,600-ton *Maine* was commissioned for the American fleet in 1891 as a hybrid type of armoured cruiser with two turrets amidships mounting four 10-inch guns, causing her to be sometimes rated as a second class battleship.

In 1892 the armoured cruiser *New York* was completed as a much improved design displacing 8,500 tons and having a 6-inch thick armoured deck. The four 8-inch guns were mounted in single turrets forward and aft, and one on each beam in shields; an unusual arrangement.

The 9,250-ton *Brooklyn (Plate 85)*, completed in 1896, was a successful armoured cruiser with similar armament to the *New York* and a speed of 22 knots. Both ships were well tried at the battle of Santiago, off Cuba in 1898, as part of the American fleet which fought the Spanish armoured cruisers *Almirante Oquendo*, *Infanta Maria Teresa* and *Vizcaya*; 7,000-ton ships built in Spain and completed during 1892 with two 11-inch and ten 5.5-inch guns of Spanish manufacture, good armour protection and a speed of 20 knots. Three sister ships were building in Spain at the outbreak of war, but were not involved in it.

France continued to develop armoured cruisers as a secondary battle force and as potential commerce raiders capable of fighting most British cruisers. Seventeen were built between 1891-1903. The 5,365-ton *Pothuau* of 1896 *(Plate 84)* was typical of the smaller ships, ranging to the 12,400-ton "Jules Ferry" type. The 9,500-ton *Montcalm (Plate 107)* of 1901 was a useful size, armed with two 7.6-inch and eight 6.4-inch guns and steaming at 21 knots.

The gradual challenge of these French ships seemed to give the British Admiralty little concern, but the Russian armoured cruiser *Rurik*, completed in 1897, attracted considerable attention in Britain and elsewhere because of her size and seagoing endurance. At 11,000 tons she was as large as a second class battleship, 435ft long and mounting four 8-inch, sixteen 6-inch and six 4.7-inch guns, besides five torpedo tubes and many smaller guns. Four engines drove twin screws to give 18 knots speed and she could steam 18,000 miles without rebunkering – the equivalent of a passage from Kronstadt to Vladivostok. The large protected cruisers *Powerful* and *Terrible* were built in reply to this ship but would probably have had difficulty in fighting her.

The German Navy built the largely experimental armoured cruiser *Fürst Bismarck* in 1897; a fine ship of 10,700 tons, capable of steaming with a fleet and of giving useful support in action with a battle squadron. She was followed by the *Prinz Heinrich* of 1900 and by then the Admiralty had ordered the six armoured cruisers of the "Cressy" class, 12,000-tonners with two 9.2-inch and twelve 6-inch guns, steaming at 21 knots *(Plates 102 and 104)*. These ships had very large crews, which were wasteful of manpower for fighting efficiency, and were vulnerable to torpedo attack, which was proved when the *Aboukir, Hogue* and *Cressy* were all torpedoed and sunk within an hour in 1914 by the small German submarine *U 9*.

Four "Drake" class ships which followed were 14,100 tons, steamed at 23 knots and had a 9.2-inch gun in barbettes forward and aft, with sixteen 6-inch quick-firers in paired casemates along the topsides; a bad arrangement as the lower guns could not be fought in a seaway.

The comparable American "California" class of armoured cruisers, completed in 1903, had 13,400 tons displacement and 22 knots speed, and mounted four 8-inch guns in twin turrets and fourteen 6-inch, while the Russian *Gromoboi*, completed in 1901, was 12,300 tons, had 20 knots speed and had four 8.4-inch and sixteen 6-inch guns. She was an improved version of the *Rossia (Plates 93 and 94)*.

France continued to develop individual armoured cruisers of similar appearance and usually having many funnels arranged in two groups at the ends of the ship; the *Montcalm (Plate 107)* was typical.

The 11,300-ton *Jeanne d'Arc*, completed in 1901, was designed to achieve 23 knots but obtained only 18 on trials, with 28,000 horsepower from thirty-six boilers, five of which overheated. This was typical of the then frequent mechanical breakdown in French warships. During 1903

France commissioned the *Victor Hugo* of 12,500 tons with 22 knots speed and four 7.6-inch and sixteen 6.4-inch guns in twin turrets.

Germany continued to build armoured cruisers in small numbers but they were generally good ships. The 9,000-ton *Prinz Albert* and *Friedrich Karl* of 1903 were heavily armed with four 8.2-inch and ten 5.9-inch guns, but only 21 knots speed. Two years later the similar *Roon* and *Yorck* were completed.

Italy had also developed the armoured cruiser from the *Marco Polo* of 1894 through the "Carlo Alberto" class of 1898 *(Plate 91)*, to the powerful "Garibaldi" type, which were also built for the Spanish, Japanese and Argentine fleets *(Plate 111)*.

The 5,000-ton Swedish *Fylgia (Plate 112)* of 1906 was the most interesting small armoured cruiser, having light armour and eight 5.9-inch guns in paired turrets of advanced concept.

Major navies regarded the renaissance of the armoured cruiser as a serious addition to the battle fleets as well as isolated commerce raiders.

As France ordered further ships, Britain built new classes of armoured cruisers. The "Monmouth" or "County" class of ten ships of 9,800 tons were lightly armed with fourteen 6-inch guns but had a speed of 23 knots and did much work in World War I, when the *Kent* particularly distinguished herself at the battle of the Falklands by sinking the German cruiser *Nürnberg* and reaching a speed of 25 knots during the exciting chase *(Plate 108)*.

Six "Devonshire" class armoured cruisers followed, completing in 1904-5 and having the mixed armament of four 7.5-inch and six 6-inch guns.

The two "Black Prince" and four "Warrior" class armoured cruisers which were completed during 1906-7 are outside the scope of this book and were the last of the type built for Britain. All participated in World War I and some, such as the *Achilles, Warrior* and *Cochrane*, participated in fierce action.

Armoured cruisers were made obsolete by the building of fast battle-cruisers – really lightly armoured battleships – for the British Navy in 1907.

Volage

BRITISH CORVETTE 1870 *Plate 59*

Built	Thames Shipbuilding Co, Blackwall, London
Laid down	1867
Launched	February 1869
Completed	1870
Dimensions	*Length between perpendiculars* 270ft
	Breadth 42ft

135   *59   VOLAGE, BRITISH CORVETTE 1870*

	Draught 18ft forward. 12ft aft. Later increased to 21ft 8in
Displacement	3,320 tons full load
Machinery	Single screw (hoisting type)
	Trunk type engine by Penn
	Five rectangular boilers
	Speed. 15 knots, mean, on trials
Bunkers	Coal. 420 tons
Armament	*Original*
	Six 7-inch rifled muzzle-loaders. Three port. Three starboard on slide mountings
	Two 6-inch 64-pounder muzzle-loading rifled guns. One port. One starboard. Truck mountings
	Two 6-inch 64-pounder muzzle-loading rifled guns. One poop. One forecastle. Traversing mountings
	Rearmed 1872
	Sixteen 6-inch 64-pounder muzzle-loaders. Truck mountings
	Two 6-inch 64-pounder muzzle-loaders. Slide mountings
	Further rearmed 1880
	Ten 6-inch 80-pounder breech-loaders. Slide mountings
	Two 6-inch 64-pounder muzzle-loaders. Slide mountings
	Two 14-inch torpedo tubes installed
Complement	340

The *Volage* was representative of the steam and sail corvettes constructed for many navies between 1860-80. She was sister to the *Active* and similar to the *Rover*, having an all upper-deck broadside armament when built.

These ships were intended for cruising duties, though the cruiser did not emerge as a type name until the 1880's. They were equal in size to many of the immediately preceeding wooden frigates.

In 1866 the British Admiralty decided to build the world's first iron-hulled cruising craft, commencing with the *Inconstant* and *Volage*. The design of the *Volage*, *Active* and *Rover* attempted to combine seaworthiness and speed for cruising efficiency, and the proportions of length to beam were the highest then designed in warships of that size. They were built side by side on the Thames, the *Volage* having a complete iron hull sheathed externally with oak planking and copper sheathed over that below the waterline – a system of anti-fouling protection which persisted in iron- and steel-hulled warships, particularly cruisers likely to serve on foreign stations, for several decades.

The *Volage* had a clipper bow and rounded, upswept stern profile with a long poop and a topgallant forecastle. There were two complete decks. Officers and men lived on the main deck, the captain's quarters being in the poop. As the armament was mounted on the upper deck, quarters were spacious but badly lit and ventilated by hinged side ports which could not be opened at sea except in fine weather.

Although heavily rigged the sail area was modest, but the form and proportions enabled her to sail well, 13 knots being her highest speed under canvas. The trunk engines had a heavy coal consumption and she spent much time under sail with the telescopic funnel lowered. There was a steam anchor capstan but steering was by hand wheels. As built, the *Volage* and *Active* rolled badly and pitched considerably, making them unsteady gun platforms, but they were able sea boats.

The *Volage*'s armament reflected changes in contemporary thought. She was built with an armament of a few rifled, muzzle-loading guns. By 1872 these were changed to a larger number of smaller muzzle-loading guns and in 1880 were replaced by the general adoption of breech-loaders in that size of armament. Two torpedo tubes were also installed in the early enthusiasm for that weapon.

The *Volage* was first commissioned in March 1870 with the Channel fleet under Captain Culme Seymour. Later that year she was transferred to the detached or "flying squadron" – a group of warships which had no permanent station and sailed the world almost continuously. The *Volage* sailed many thousands of ocean miles with the flying squadron, returning to Britain to pay off at the end of 1872.

After armament changes she recommissioned during mid-1874 and was ordered to take a scientific expedition to observe a transit of the planet Venus from the Kerguelen Islands, near the Antarctic circle. Her next commission was to Rio de Janiero under Captain Fairfax, senior naval officer South America, which was then an Atlantic station. This was the only period of her thirty years' service when the *Volage* was attached, all her other voyaging being in moving squadrons. She was relieved in 1879 to return to England for re-arming, reboilering and refitting.

Soon afterwards the *Volage* was engaged in sailing trials against the steam frigate *Shah*, completed in 1875, which left her astern, particularly in strong winds.

The *Volage* was then transferred to the training squadron, the last mast-and-sail organisation in the British Navy, in which she served five commissions, only ending when the training squadron was dissolved during 1899, thirty years after she was launched. She had probably steamed and sailed more miles than any contemporary British warship, and after being placed in reserve was sold to be broken up in 1904.

Northampton

BRITISH ARMOURED CRUISER 1878 *Plate 60*

Built	Napier, Glasgow
Laid down	October 1874
Launched	November 1876
Completed	December 1878

60 *NORTHAMPTON, BRITISH ARMOURED CRUISER 1878*

Dimensions	Length 280ft
	Breadth 60ft
	Draught 25ft 10in
Displacement	7,630 tons
Machinery	Twin screw
	Two 3-cylinder vertical inverted compound (or single expansion) engines by Penn
	Ten oval type boilers
	IHP = 6,073 = 13.17 knots
Bunkers	Coal. 540 tons normal. 1,150 tons maximum
Endurance	3,500 miles at 12½ knots. 5,000 miles at 10½ knots
Sail area	24,766 sq ft
Armament	Four 10-inch 18-ton muzzle-loading rifled guns
	Eight 9-inch 12-ton muzzle-loading rifled guns
	Six 20-pounders
	Sixteen machine- and light guns
	Two 60ft torpedo boats carried
Armour	Iron
	Belt 9-inch – 6-inch. 181ft long by 9ft wide
	Bulkheads 9-inch – 8-inch – 6-inch
	Decks 3-inch – 2-inch
	Conning tower 9-inch
Complement	560

The *Northampton* and her sister ship *Nelson* were developed from the armoured cruiser *Shannon*, completed in 1877. They were sometimes regarded as second class battleships but were never seriously considered as effective fighting ships. These were the last major warships to carry the main armament on the broadside and between decks. They were the first armoured ships to have a protective deck at the ends and the first in which heavy belt armour and large guns were considered more important than gun protection. These ships were intended as ocean-cruising commerce protectors, capable of fighting foreign cruisers in ship-to-ship actions. However, they were in reality too slow to do this effectively. The armament was intended for salvo-firing, the guns being loaded and trained behind protective armour and then fired electrically without exposing the crews. Having fired, the ship was to turn bow on to the enemy while reloading and then manoeuvre for a further broadside salvo.

The engines, by Penn, had three cylinders of equal capacity, capable of working as a single-expansion high-pressure engine at full power or as a compound for economical steaming, the forward cylinder operating at high pressure. At reduced power the engine could also work as a simple expansion with low pressure steam.

The *Northampton* was a knot slower than the *Nelson*, despite propeller changes, and she eventually reduced to about 10 knots sea speed. Both ships, with their twin screws, were sluggish sailers and only came to life in strong winds.

The *Northampton* cost £414,441 to build and commissioned at Chatham in September 1879 as flagship of the North American and West Indies station, where she served until 1886. She then became temporary reserve ship at Portsmouth and during November passed into third reserve at Chatham. She commissioned for manoeuvres in 1888 and in March 1889 went to Sheerness as flagship, participating in the naval manoeuvres of 1890, 1891, and 1892. In August 1893 the *Northampton* again went into reserve at Sheerness and the following February passed to the fleet reserve.

In June 1894 the *Northampton* was commissioned as a seagoing training ship for boys and this photograph taken in 1901 shows her in company with two brigs of the training squadron. This work seems to have been the *Northampton*'s most successful service and she trained many hundreds of youngsters for the Navy. In November 1904 she went into fleet reserve until she was sold at Chatham during April 1905 to be broken up.

Stosch

GERMAN, LATER CADET TRAINING SHIP 1879 *Plates 61 and 62*

Built	Vulkanwerft, Stettin
Launched	October 1877
Completed	September 1879
Dimensions	Length 244ft 4in
	Breadth 44ft 10in
	Draught 19ft 8in mean
Displacement	2,856 tons
Machinery	Single screw
	IHP = 2,581 = 13 knots
Bunkers	Coal. 365 tons
Endurance under steam	2,000 miles
Armament	Ten 5.9-inch Krupp breech-loading guns
	Two 8.8-cm quick-firers
	Six machine-guns
	One torpedo tube
Armour	None
Complement	404. As training ship 450
Hull bottom	Sheathed with copper
Ship-rigged	

The *Stosch* was one of a series of protected cruiser-corvettes launched from various German yards after the mid-1870's. These included the *Bismarck, Blücher, Moltke, Gneisenau* and *Stein*. All were built during 1877-

61 STOSCH, GERMAN LATER CADET TRAINING SHIP 1879

62   STOSCH, GERMAN LATER CADET TRAINING SHIP 1879

9, of composite construction with wood planking over iron frames and deck beams. Each had a triple-expansion engine and were ship-rigged to conserve coal when cruising.

They set 23,000 square feet under all plain sail, whose smartness of handling was still the delight of all navies. The funnel was telescopic to improve appearance when not under steam.

The main armament was carried broadside, firing through ports in the hull. When built, these ships compared well with cruisers of other navies and were rated as "frigate-built cruisers" or as "third rates".

After completion in 1877 the *Stosch* served overseas until 1886, principally in the Zanzibar operations which led to the annexation of German East Africa. After 1888 she became a "Schuleschiff" to train cadets. This photograph was taken about 1902. In 1907 she was withdrawn from service to be broken up. Despite her bulky appearance, the *Stosch* was fine-lined below water and spent much time at sea under sail. She could be compared with the British *Volage (Plate 59)* and the *Calliope (Plate 65)*.

Plate 62 is of the *Stosch* lying in Cowes Roads in 1893 and preparing to get under weigh.

Champion

BRITISH SCREW CORVETTE, LATER THIRD CLASS PROTECTED CRUISER 1879 *Plates 63 and 64*

Built	Elder and Co, Glasgow
Launched	1878
Completed	1879
Dimensions	*Length* 225ft
	Breadth 44ft 6in
	Draught 19ft 3in
Displacement	2,380 tons
Machinery	Single screw
	Compound engines by builders
	Boilers
	IHP = 2,340 = 12.75 knots
Bunkers	Coal. 470 tons maximum
Endurance	3,840 miles at 10 knots under steam
Armament	(1890)
	Four 6-inch breech-loading rifled guns. Single mounts port and starboard
	Eight 5-inch breech-loading rifled guns. Single mounts port and starboard
	Four 3-pounder quick-firers
	Six machine-guns
	Two torpedo launching carriages
Armour	Protective deck 1½-inch
Complement	265
Hull	Wood sheathed and coppered

The *Champion* was one of the ten ships of the "Comus" type, which also included the *Calypso, Carysfort, Cleopatra, Conquest, Constance, Cordelia, Curaçoa, Champion* and *Calliope (See plate 65)*. These were not exact sister ships but the *Champion* and *Cleopatra* were very similar. All were completed between 1878-84. When built they were classed as screw corvettes but were later rated as third class cruisers. They were designed under the direction of Nathaniel Barnaby for foreign service, were the earliest steel warships built for the British fleet and incorporated the then new steel protective deck over boiler- and engine-rooms and magazines.

The *Champion* cost £113,983 to build and although a well-armed steel steamship, was given a full ship rig, then still considered necessary to supplement a cruiser's bunker capacity on distant stations. As late as 1890 authorities were still arguing the desirability of retaining masts and sails in cruisers, despite the rapidly improving reliability of propelling engines.

Originally the "C" type ships were fitted with muzzle-loading rifled guns but these were replaced with 6- and 5-inch breech-loaders when that type of gun returned to favour in the fleet.

One of the class was described as being "as self-contained as a ship could possible be. Well armed, she could carry and lay mines and land nearly two hundred armed men with a field gun. She held six months' provisions and used only salt water in her boilers. Her 470 tons of coal were used only when necessary. It would be hard to imagine a ship more scientifically equipped for . . . trade protection and Empire policing."

Plate 63 shows the *Champion* under steam. The sponson mounts of the four 6-inch guns and the side ports for the 5-inch are prominent. Her appearance and arrangement can be compared with the German *Stosch (Plate 61)*.

Plate 64 shows the *Champion* being conned under steam from the bridge immediately forward of the mizzen, above the wheelhouse – an inefficient position for visibility when steaming, but essential under sail and therefore considered more seamanlike. The scrubbed hammocks drying in the fore and main shrouds are an interesting sidelight on contemporary crew conditions. The party on the foredeck and the lead-man on his platform amidships, busy recovering the lead for another cast, suggest that the *Champion* is about to anchor.

Like several of her class, the *Champion* served on the Pacific station and during 1890 was the largest ship there, supported by seven smaller sloops and gunboats. Her service was in the middle of a long period when the British Navy kept world peace and was respected in the remotest places. An instance illustrating this occurred in Guatemala during 1874. Mr Magee, the British vice-consul at the port of San Jose, who was also a merchant, offended the local military governor who ordered him to be

63   CHAMPION, BRITISH SCREW CORVETTE, LATER THIRD CLASS PROTECTED CRUISER 1879

143   *64   CHAMPION, BRITISH SCREW CORVETTE, LATER THIRD CLASS PROTECTED CRUISER 1879*

seized and flogged in public. After a hundred lashes, Magee's punishment was ended by intervention of the master of an American merchant ship, then in port. When news of the incident reached England a squadron of the British Pacific fleet was sent to San Jose, which then had no rail communication and could be reached overland only over very poor roads. However, the British compelled the Guatemalan government to send a battery of artillery from the capital and to fire gun salutes to the British flag continuously from dawn to dusk. On the same day a regiment of Guatemalan soldiers had to march in public over their national flag, trampling it in the dust in expiation. Magee received 100,000 dollars, compensation and remained in Guatemalan to become a wealthy merchant and a Briton held in considerable awe.

The *Champion* returned to England before 1896 and went into reserve. Her type had become obsolete and was replaced on foreign stations by the smaller cruisers of the Naval Defence Act programme. She was still rated as a third class cruiser in 1902 but by 1905 had become a moored tender to HMS *Pembroke,* the training school at Chatham, and was afterwards broken up.

Calliope

BRITISH THIRD CLASS PROTECTED CRUISER 1884 *Plate 65*

Built	Royal Naval dockyard, Portsmouth
Launched	June 1884
Completed	1884
Dimensions	*Length* 235ft
	Breadth 44ft 6in
	Draught 20ft
Displacement	2,770 tons
Machinery	Single screw
	Compound engines by Rennie
	IHP = 4,020 = 14.6 knots
Bunkers	Coal. 300 tons normal. 550 tons maximum
Endurance under steam	4,000 miles at 10 knots
Armament	Four 6-inch breech-loading guns. Single mounts in side sponsons
	Twelve 5-inch breech-loading guns. On broadside
	Nine machine-guns
	Two 18-inch torpedo carriages
Armour	*Protective deck* 1¾-inch
Complement	290
Hull	Wood sheathed and coppered

The *Calliope* was a steel-hulled screw corvette, later re-rated as a third class cruiser. She was an improvement on the sister ship *Comus,* name ship of a series of which each one was slightly different. The *Calliope*'s propeller was of feathering type to reduce resistance, replacing the lifting propeller fitted in earlier ships of the class. These had had to be raised from the shaft up lifting guides when under sail, which was the way these cruisers made long passages.

The *Calliope* commissioned in January 1887 for service on the China station under Captain R.C.Kane, but during December was diverted to the Australian station. During 1888 she was the first ship to enter the Calliope dock at Auckland, New Zealand, offically opening it in company with the wooden warship *Diamond.*

In July 1889 an international political situation developed at the Pacific island of Samoa, where German and American interests were in conflict. German and American warships were confronting each other in the harbour of Apia and a war seemed likely. In those days before wireless communication, captains of British warships on foreign stations had to use their discretion in tense situations and the *Calliope* anchored among the other warships to remind them of the British Navy's interests in the Pacific. Kane was warmly regarded by the Americans and seemed to have a steadying effect on the situation. However, on March 16th a typhoon swept Apia and all ships were in difficulties. The *Calliope* was ready, she slipped her cable and managed to steam out in the teeth of wind and wave to the open sea and safety. The American warships *Trenton, Vandalia* and *Nipsic* were driven ashore and severely damaged. The German warships *Olger, Adler* and *Eber* followed and there was heavy loss of life. The *Calliope*'s escape from the harbour received considerable attention and her engineer-officer was immediately promoted. She paid off in 1890, having steamed and sailed 76,814 sea miles in 633 days during this commission.

In 1897 the *Calliope* commissioned as a training ship and this photograph shows her in this role about 1901. Appearance was unchanged since her completion but the forward and after 6-inch gun sponsons were plated-in. The 5-inch broadside guns were still mounted between the sponsons. Her full rig and association with naval adventure made her a good choice for training.

In 1907 she was unrigged and was towed to the Tyne to become a static training ship for the local Royal Naval Reserve. In 1914 she was renamed *Helicon* to release her name for a light cruiser then completing. She continued to serve by providing training for men of the Royal Naval Volunteer Reserve and the Royal Naval Division – the "sailors dressed as soldiers" of the Western Front.

After 1918 the old ship carried on as a RNR drill vessel and depot, resuming the name *Calliope* in 1931 when the newer cruiser was scrapped, and served until she was discarded in 1951 to be scrapped.

65   CALLIOPE, BRITISH THIRD CLASS PROTECTED CRUISER 1884

66   PRINZESS WILHELM, GERMAN PROTECTED CRUISER 1888

Prinzess Wilhelm

GERMAN PROTECTED CRUISER 1888 *Plate 66*

Built	Germaniawerft, Kiel
Laid down	1886
Launched	September 1887
Completed	1888
Dimensions	*Length overall* 339ft 6in
	Length between perpendiculars 308ft 6in
	Breadth 46ft
	Draught 21ft 6in mean
Displacement	4,400 tons
Machinery	Twin screw
	Two 4-cylinder horizontal compound engines
	Designed IHP 8,000 = 18.7 knots
	Trials = about 19.5 knots
Bunkers	Coal. 540 tons normal. 750 tons maximum
Armament	Four 5.9-inch. 30 calibre. Single mountings in casemates. Two port and two starboard
	Eight 4.1-inch. 22 calibre. Single mountings
	Six 3-pounders
	Eight machine-guns
	Four 14-inch diameter torpedo tubes. One bow submerged. Three above water amidships
Armour	*Deck amidships* 2.9-inch
	Conning tower 2-inch
	Base of funnels 4¾-inch
Complement	320
Hull	Wood sheathed and coppered

The *Prinzess Wilhelm* and her sister ship *Irene* were rated as cruiser-corvettes and were primarily intended for colonial service. The design was influenced by that of the Chilean cruiser *Esmeralda*, built by Armstrong at Elswick in 1883.

The hulls were of iron and these were the first twin-screw ships in the German Navy. They were also the first German cruisers not rigged for sailing and the mainmast being stepped exceptionally far forward gave a distinctive appearance.

The *Prinzess Wilhelm* served in the North Sea and Baltic until 1895, when she was stationed abroad until 1899. Her funnels were heightened during 1894 and she was reboilered in 1901 during a refit lasting from 1899 until 1902. During this her amidship bulwarks were altered. The armament of both ships was redisposed several times.

By February 1914 the *Prinzess Wilhelm* was a mine hulk at Danzig, later being moved to Kiel and then Wilhelmshaven. She was removed from naval service in November 1921 and was broken up at Wilhelmshaven during 1922.

This photograph, taken about 1902, shows the sponson mountings for 4.1-inch guns and her elegant, pointed stern. A German training ship lies to starboard with a cutter-rigged smack beating under her stern. A sightseeing steam yacht views the gathering of yachts and visiting warships in Cowes Roads.

Stromboli

ITALIAN PROTECTED CRUISER 1888 *Plate 67*

Built	R. Arsenale di Venezia (Royal Naval yard, Venice)
Laid down	1884
Launched	1886
Completed	1888
Dimensions	*Length overall* 300ft
	Length waterline 283ft 6in
	Breadth 43ft 1in
	Draught 18ft 8in mean. 20ft maximum
Displacement	approximately 3,600 tons
Machinery	Twin screw
	Two 2-cylinder compound engines by Ansaldo
	Ten cylindrical boilers
	IHP natural draught = 6,169 = 17 knots
	IHP forced draught = 7,480 = 17.8 knots
	IHP later sustained speed = 14.5 knots
Bunkers	Coal. 630 tons
Endurance	3,500 miles at 10 knots
Armament	Two 10-inch. 30 calibre. One forward and one aft
	Six 6-inch. 32 calibre. Three on each side. Single mounts
	Five 6-pounders. 40 calibre
	Two machine-guns
	Four 14-inch diameter torpedo tubes. One submerged bow. Three above water
Armour	*Protective deck* 2-inch – 1-inch
	Conning tower 1-inch
Complement	308

The *Stromboli* was one of the "Etna" class protected cruisers laid down during 1883-4 and including the *Etna*, *Stromboli*, and *Vesuvio*, with a fourth similar ship, the *Ettore Fieramosca*, which was commenced in 1885. These ships were designed under the direction of Engineer Carlo Vigna and were built in Italy. They followed and were copies of Italy's first modern protected cruiser, the *Giovanni Bausan*, designed and built at

148   *67 STROMBOLI, ITALIAN PROTECTED CRUISER 1888*

68   AUSTRALIA, BRITISH FIRST CLASS CRUISER (BELTED) 1889

Elswick by Armstrong and commenced during 1882.

The mounting of two 10-inch guns made the *Stromboli* a formidable cruiser by contemporary standards, backed by six 6-inch. She was a fair sea boat with little top hamper but rather large funnels.

The *Stromboli* was not in action throughout her existence which was spent almost entirely in the Mediterranean, except for occasional ocean-going cruises. This photograph was taken during a visit to England about 1905. She still carried a storm staysail on the forestay and trysails were brailed to each mast. The ventilating cowls were few in number and of moderate size for a ship principally intended for warm climate use.

The *Stromboli* was discarded during 1907 and broken up.

Australia

BRITISH FIRST CLASS CRUISER (BELTED) 1889 *Plate 68*

Built	Napier, Glasgow
Laid down	1885
Launched	1886
Completed	1889
Dimensions	*Length* 300ft
	Breadth 56ft
	Draught 22ft 6in maximum
Displacement	5,600 tons
Machinery	Twin screw
	Two horizontal, triple expansion engines by Napier
	Four double-ended boilers
	IHP natural draught = 5,500 = 16 knots
	Forced draught = 8,500 = 18 knots
Bunkers	Coal. 750 tons normal. 900 tons maximum
Endurance	5,000 miles at 10 knots
Armament	Two 9.2-inch 22-ton guns. 25 calibre, replaced by 30 calibre in 1898. One forward and one aft.
	Ten 6-inch 5-ton guns. Converted to quick-firers in 1898. Single mounts at sides
	Six 6-pounders quick-firers
	Ten 3-pounder quick-firers
	Six Nordenfelt machine-guns
	Four 18-inch diameter torpedo tubes (Removed by 1903)
Armour	*Side belt* 10-inch compound type. 200ft x 5ft 6in
	Transverse bulkheads 16-inch compound
	Deck 3-inch – 2-inch
	Gun positions 4½-inch
	Conning tower 12-inch compound

Complement 497

The *Australia* was one of the "Orlando" class of "belted" or armoured cruisers which included the *Undaunted (Plate 69)*, *Immortalité*, *Narcissus*, *Galatea*, *Aurora* and *Orlando*. These followed the 8,500-ton armoured cruisers *Warspite* and *Impérieuse* of 1885 and were enlargements of the "Mersey" class. The "Orlandos" set the basic pattern of arrangement and appearance for British cruisers for years to follow.

They were designed to have the speed and coal endurance to protect British shipping on ocean trade routes against attack by fast commerce destroyers likely to be sent out by France and Russia, and were armed to be capable of fighting a contemporary second class battleship, which would be the largest antagonist likely to be encountered in distant seas.

The ships fulfilled some expectations but lacked protection for the guns, the 9.2- and 6-inch weapons being in shields and the total armament being too large for the length of ship. However, they aquitted themselves well at manoeuvres, maintaining good speed in bad weather and displaying ability to work the guns at a steady rate of fire. All exceeded designed speed on trials and the *Orlando* steamed the 170 miles from Lyttleton to Wellington, New Zealand, in under ten hours, without forced draft.

Most of the class displaced almost 6,000 tons in fighting trim.

The *Australia* cost £259,390 to build and first commissioned under Captain H.H.Boys for the 1889 naval review and manoeuvres. Many of the class were still completing and were fitted with wooden dummy guns for the occasion.

By 1896 the *Australia* was in the reserve squadron, rated as a tender for training, and during 1898 her 9.2-inch guns were removed and replaced by new weapons of 30 calibres. The 6-inch guns were modified to quick-firers at the same refit. She remained in reserve as the class was obsolete and was sold to be broken up about 1904.

This photograph, taken about 1899, shows the disposition of the armament and the many traditional features retained in a new ship type; yards and fidded topmasts, bow and stern decoration and a "Nelson" style entry port amidships.

Undaunted

BRITISH FIRST CLASS CRUISER (BELTED) 1889 *Plate 69*

Built	Palmers Shipbuilding Co, Jarrow on Tyne
Laid down	April 1885
Launched	November 1886
Completed	1889
Dimensions	*Length* 300ft

151   *69   UNDAUNTED, BRITISH FIRST CLASS CRUISER (BELTED) 1889*

Breadth 56ft
Draught 22ft 6in maximum
Displacement 5,600 tons
Machinery Twin screw
Two horizontal, triple expansion engines by builders
Four double-ended boilers
IHP natural draught = 5,500 = 16 knots
IHP forced draught = 8,500 = 18 knots
IHP forced draught, trials = 19.5 knots for 4 hours
Bunkers Coal. 750 normal. 900 tons maximum
Endurance 5,000 miles at 10 knots
Armament Two 9.2-inch 22-ton guns. One forward and one aft
Ten 6-inch quick-firers. Single mounts on sides
Six 6-pounder quick-firers
Ten 3-pounder quick-firers
Six Nordenfelt machine-guns
Four 18-inch diameter torpedo tubes (Removed by 1903)
Armour *Side belt* 10-inch compound. 200ft x 5ft 6in
Transverse bulkheads 16-inch compound
Deck 3-inch – 2-inch
Gun positions 4½-inch
Conning tower 12-inch compound
Complement 497

The *Undaunted* was another "belted" or armoured cruiser of the "Orlando" class, a sister ship to the *Australia (Plate 68)*. She cost £256,005 to build and first commissioned under Captain M.J.Dunlop to participate in the naval manoeuvres of 1889 which followed a review at Spithead by the German emperor, who held the honorary rank of admiral in the British fleet.

The *Undaunted* commissioned in February 1890 under Sir Charles Beresford for service with the Mediterranean fleet. While lying at Alexandria, preparing for a ball to be held on board, a telegram brought news that the French warship *Siegnelay*, 1,900 tons, was stranded and likely to become a total loss 270 miles away. The *Undaunted* sailed at once and found that the *Siegnelay* had parted her cable and driven ashore in a gale to lie well up a beach. Her commander had notified the French naval command that she was a total loss and French warships had been sent to take off her crew, guns and stores before she was abandoned.

Beresford thought she could be salved, which would be a minor triumph for the Royal Navy, and as such opportunities of action in those peaceful times were rare, prepared to make the most of the circumstances. The *Undaunted*'s first lieutenant and a hundred and thirty men were sent on board the *Siegnelay* to lighten her by removal of stores, ammunition, coal and fittings. 450 tons were removed and the *Undaunted* lay within 850 yards, on the edge of shallow water, while Beresford hired local lighters and small craft with which his crew laid out the *Undaunted's*

cables and hawsers to the stranded ship. By now the British sloop *Melita* and a small Turkish warship had arrived to assist. After working for three days and nights as fast as possible to forestall the weather and the arrival of the other French warships, Beresford ordered the strain to be taken on the tow ropes by all three ships and the *Siegnelay* was towed off.

The *Undaunted* returned to England in May 1893 and paid off. By 1896 she was serving on the China station with her sisters *Immortalité* and *Narsissus*, returning to England to become a seagoing gunnery tender to HMS *Cambridge*, the gunnery school at Devonport. The *Narcissus* served similarly at Portsmouth and the *Immortalité* at Sheerness. This 1899 photograph shows her shorter funnels than her sisters'.

By 1905 the *Undaunted* had been sold to be broken up.

Blonde

BRITISH THIRD CLASS PROTECTED CRUISER 1890 *Plates 70 and 71*

Built Royal Naval dockyard, Pembroke
Launched October 1889
Completed 1890
Dimension *Length overall* 233ft
Length between perpendiculars 220ft
Breadth 35ft
Draught 14ft mean. 16ft maximum
Displacement 1,580 tons
Machinery Twin screw
Two vertical triple expansion engines by Earles Shipbuilding and Engineering Co
Laird type boilers
IHP natural draught = 1,750 = 15 knots
IHP forced draught = 3,000 = 16.5 knots
Bunkers Coal. 160 tons
Endurance 3,400 miles at 10 knots
Armament Six 4.7-inch quick-firers. Two forward. Two aft. Two amidships on sponsons. All in shields
Four 3-pounder quick-firers
Two Nordenfelt machine-guns
Two 14-inch diameter torpedo tubes. Above water. Eight torpedoes carried
Armour *Deck* 2-inch
Gun positions 4½-inch
Complement 159
Hull Wood sheathed and coppered for foreign service

The *Blonde* and her sister ships *Blanche*, *Barrosa* and *Barracouta*, were

153   *70   BLONDE, BRITISH THIRD CLASS PROTECTED CRUISER 1890*

71   BLONDE, BRITISH THIRD CLASS PROTECTED CRUISER 1890

small, third class cruisers. She cost £90,059 to build.

These ships spent most of their life in the Channel and Atlantic fleets.

These photographs were taken in 1898 and show the *Blonde* to be a curious mixture of old and new: a steel-hulled ship with 4.7-inch quick-firing guns yet having the navigating bridge aft, with chartroom under and a conning tower forward. The engine-casings support more boats than such a small ship should have carried or needed. The light masting, stocked bower anchor and the port forward 3-pounder gun in its port are also noteworthy features.

The *Blonde* had some basic similarity in form and appearance with the contemporary torpedo gunboats *(see Plates 119-21)* and during naval manoeuvres of the 1890's a small cruiser of the "Blonde" type often worked with three or four torpedo gunboats, possibly acting as a leader or command ship, though those terms were then unknown.

The *Blonde* was reboilered with water tube boilers in 1902 but by 1905 these ships were relegated to subsidiary duties and were not considered fighting craft, though they remained armed. Soon after they were sold to be scrapped.

Maha Chakrkri

SIAMESE PROTECTED CRUISER 1892 *Plate 72*

Built	Ramage and Ferguson, Leith, Scotland
Launched	June 1892
Completed	1892
Dimensions	*Length overall* 283ft
	Breadth 39ft 4in
	Draught 19ft 6in mean
Displacement	2,500 tons
Machinery	Twin screw
	Two triple-expansion engines
	Five cylindrical boilers
	IHP = 3,000 = 15 knots
Bunkers	Coal. 280 tons normal
Armament	Four 4.7-inch quick-firers. Single mounts
	Ten 6-pounder quick-firers. Single mounts
	Six machine-guns
Armour	*Protective deck* 2-inch
Complement	318

The *Maha Chakrkri* was designed and built by Ramage and Ferguson of Leith, Scotland, noted as builders of many of the finest steam yachts. Her design was based on that of a small, lightly-armed protected cruiser but with generous accommodation added.

The four 4.7-inch quick-firers were mounted on sponsons, two on each side, other light guns being mounted about the upper deck. The square-rigged foremast and trysails on each mast provided useful auxiliary area before the wind on ocean passages, or as steadying canvas in bad weather.

The *Maha Chakrkri* joined the small Siamese fleet which at the time comprised eight small gunboats and a torpedo boat, though three 27-knot destroyers were later built in Japan.

She saw no action throughout her existence and served principally as the royal yacht of the king of Siam, who delighted in cruising on board her. He had previously owned a 128ft steam yacht built on the Clyde. The *Maha Chakrkri* visited England during 1897 to attend the naval review for Queen Victoria's jubilee, where this photograph was taken. She is proudly wearing the Siamese naval ensign with its white elephant on a red ground.

During 1917 the hull of the *Maha Chakrkri* was sold to the Kawasaki Company of Kobe, Japan, to be broken up. Her machinery and fittings were removed to be used in a 298ft steel steam yacht designed and built by the company in 1918 as the new Siamese royal yacht, which bore the same name.

Apollo

BRITISH SECOND CLASS PROTECTED CRUISER 1892 *Plate 73*

Built	Royal Naval dockyard, Chatham
Laid down	1890
Launched	February 1892
Completed	1892
Dimensions	*Length overall* 314ft 6in
	Length between perpendiculars 300ft
	Breadth 43ft 8in
	Draught 13ft 6in mean. 18ft maximum
Displacement	3,400 tons
Machinery	Twin screw
	Two triple expansion engines by Earles Shipbuilding and Engineering Co
	Three double-ended and two single-ended, cylindrical boilers
	IHP = 9,000 = 19.75 knots
Bunkers	Coal. 400 tons normal. 535 tons maximum
Endurance	8,000 miles at 10 knots
Armament	Two 6-inch quick-firers. One forward and one aft
	Six 4.7-inch quick-firers
	Eight 6-pounder quick-firers

72   MAHA CHAKRKRI, SIAMESE PROTECTED CRUISER 1892

157   *73   APOLLO, BRITISH SECOND CLASS PROTECTED CRUISER 1892*

One 3-pounder quick-firer
Four Nordenfelt machine-guns
Four 14-inch diameter torpedo tubes. Carried 12 torpedoes.

Armour   *Deck* 2-inch – 1-inch
            Gun shields 4½-inch
            Engine hatches 5-inch
            Conning tower 3-inch
Complement 273

The *Apollo* was name ship of a class of twenty-one second class protected cruisers laid down under the Naval Defence Act of 1889. She cost £186,361 to build.

Cruisers were then the eyes of a fleet and a brief examination of their part in some of the naval manoeuvres of 1902 is interesting, as only some of the ships involved were fitted with wireless, and flag signalling and cruiser scouting remained the principal means of communication.

The object of the exercises was for the "X" fleet to gain control of the English Channel and its approaches, and of the St George's Channel, to stop vital trade to Britain. They were opposed by the "B" fleet, commanded by Rear-Admiral Sir Gerard Noel, superintendent of reserves, with his flag in the battleship *Revenge*. He had twelve battleships, five first class cruisers, nine second class cruisers, including the *Apollo*, and eight destroyers. There was also a "C" squadron of two cruisers and two torpedo gunboats based on Plymouth, and a flotilla of nine destroyers based on Devonport. A "D" squadron based on Portland and Portsmouth comprised five cruisers and two torpedo gunboats, with a further fifteen destroyers and other torpedo gunboats and torpedo boats for local defence at Plymouth and at Portsmouth, his main fleet base.

The "X" fleet, commanded by Vice-Admiral Arthur Wilson, senior officer in command of the Channel squadron, with his flag in the battleship *Majestic,* had eight battleships, five first class cruisers, eight other cruisers and eight destroyers. His "Y" squadron, based on the Scilly Isles, comprised two second class cruisers and three torpedo gunboats, with eight destroyers and four torpedo boats. A "Z" squadron was based on the Channel Islands and had four cruisers and two torpedo gunboats, with twelve destroyers and six torpedo boats. At Queenstown he had three small ships.

These were the first manoeuvres in which large flotillas of destroyers were used with fleets.

The "X" fleet had the advantage that its bases were to be considered impregnable, while the bases of the "B" fleet at Portsmouth, Portland and Plymouth were considered vulnerable.

Cruisers of the main body of each fleet could be detached as thought necessary before hostilities opened, but the "B" fleet was then to be cruising in the North Sea and fleet "X" off the north of Ireland. The whole of England below the 56th parallel was in the hands of force "B",

and all Ireland, the Channel Isles and the Scillies were force "X" territory. Orders from the Admiralty to commence hostilities might arrive independently to each fleet. Admiral Noel detached three first class cruisers and four second class from his main fleet, led by the *Edgar*. The *Apollo* joined them from Sheerness and two second class cruisers from Plymouth. All had orders to rendezvous ten miles south of the Wolf Rock. Early on the 29th July, before hostilities started, the *Apollo* and the cruiser *Fox* were sent to reconnoitre the enemy at the Scillies and then report to Sennen Cove at Land's End, where force "B" had a signal station.

The cruiser *Latona* was waiting at Sennen for a telegram from the Admiralty to commence the "war". On receipt she steamed at 9.30 am for the rendezvous, where she found only the *Apollo*, which the *Fox* had not accompanied to Sennen. The main force of "B" cruisers were invisible due to haze but had been rejoined by the *Fox*. By chance the "X" force rendezvous for its Channel cruisers was nearby, 35 miles south of the Lizard, and not long afterwards the *Apollo* and *Latona* sighted smoke coming up from the south-east, so they steamed towards what was thought to be the rest of the "B" cruisers, only to run into the enemy. When ten cruisers appeared they put on full power and attempted to run for Plymouth but were overhauled and brought to action by the faster "X" ships until they were declared "captured", being ordered out of action by the umpires.

Meanwhile "B" cruiser force was steaming east, stationed in line three miles apart for good signalling. The gunfire of the chase of the *Apollo* and *Latona* reached them and the squadron steamed to action with the "X" ships but were surprised at their numbers and, as it was too late to run, a spirited "engagement" took place, resulting in four of the "B" cruisers being "disabled" or "sunk" and three of the "X" ships being "put out of action". That engagement was probably typical of what fleet warfare would have been like at the time.

Soon after, the role of the cruiser was to change and ships of the "Apollo" type, suitable for scouting and skirmishing, would become obsolete. By 1903 many of the class were laid up. In 1908 the *Apollo* was converted at Chatham dockyard to a minelayer. Her armament was reduced to four 4.7-inch guns and she carried a hundred mines. The *Andromache, Thetis, Iphigenia, Intrepid, Latona* and *Naiad* were similarly converted and served as a squadron. However, when war commenced they worked from Dover and Sheerness until 1915, then were reduced to subsidiary service when destroyers took over minelaying work. Between them they laid almost 8,000 mines in twenty-two operations and completed war service as depot ships.

The *Apollo* was sold in August 1920 to be broken up at Plymouth. This photograph of her was taken in 1902.

Scylla

BRITISH SECOND CLASS PROTECTED CRUISER 1892 *Plate 74*

Built	Samunda Brothers, Poplar, London
Laid down	1890
Launched	October 1891
Completed	1892
Dimensions	*Length* 300ft
	Breadth 43ft 8in
	Draught 16ft 6in. 18ft maximum
Displacement	3,400 tons
Machinery	Twin screw
	Two vertical triple-expansion engines by Penn
	Three double-ended, one single-ended cylindrical-type boilers
	IHP natural draught, trials = 7,614 = 19 knots
	IHP forced draught, trials = 9,280 = 20 knots
Bunkers	Coal. 400 tons normal. 535 tons maximum
Endurance	9,000 miles at 10 knots
Armament	Two 6-inch quick-firers. One forward and one aft
	Six 4.7-inch quick-firers. In shields on upper deck broadside
	Eight 6-pounder quick-firers
	One 3-pounder
	Four machine-guns
	Four 14-inch diameter torpedo tubes. Above water
Armour	*Deck* 2-inch – 1-inch
	Gun shields 4½-inch
	Engine hatch coamings 6-inch
	Conning tower 3-inch
Complement	273

The 1890's were the heyday of the protected cruiser. In 1894 Britain possessed fifty-four effective second and third class protected cruisers to a combined twenty-four French and Russian ships, besides having twenty-seven older cruisers of this general type and size. The *Scylla* was one of the twenty-one "Apollo" class cruisers built under the 1889 Naval Defence Act. These included the *Apollo, Andromanche, Latona, Melampus, Naiad, Sappho, Scylla, Terpsichore, Thetis,* and *Tribune,* all with unsheathed hulls; and the *Aeolus, Brilliant, Indefatigable* (renamed *Melpomene* in 1911), *Intrepid, Iphigenia, Pique, Rainbow, Retribution, Sirius, Spartan* and *Sybille,* with sheathed hulls for tropical service.

These were of almost yacht-like appearance when in Victorian colours and all were good steamers when new, but many deteriorated quickly However, the *Terpsichore* achieved 20.1 knots in 1908 and the *Aeolus* about

19 in 1909.

The class had some notable captains: Prince George (later King George V) commanded the *Melampus* for one commission, and Captain Percy Scott, later a naval gunnery expert, had the *Scylla* for a time during 1898 when she won the Mediterranean fleet gunnery prize.

This photograph of the *Scylla* was taken in 1902 and shows a compass platform above the wheelhouse, with searchlight and semaphore. Another semaphore is fitted at the after masthead which also carries a long upper gaff for early wireless aerials.

The *Sybille* was wrecked in 1901 and after 1904 several ships of the class were laid up. The *Latona, Thetis, Apollo, Andromache, Iphigenia, Intrepid* and *Thetis* were later converted to minelayers *(Plates 73 and 75)*.

By 1906 the *Seylla's* best speed had dropped to about 17 knots, and that only for short periods. Having little fighting value the class were gradually removed from the effective fleet and the *Scylla* was sold for scrapping after 1910. *Aeolus, Melampus, Melpomene, Pique, Retribution, Terpsichore* and *Tribune* were also sold to be broken up between 1910-14.

Brilliant

BRITISH PROTECTED CRUISER 1893 *Plate 75*

Built	Royal Naval dockyard, Sheerness
Laid down	1890
Launched	June 1891
Completed	1893
Dimensions	*Length overall* 314ft 6in
	Length between perpendiculars 300ft
	Breadth 43ft 8in
	Draught 18ft 6in mean
Displacement	3,600 tons
Machinery	Twin screw
	Two 3-cylinder triple-expansion engines
	Three double-ended, two single-ended cylindrical type boilers
	IHP natural draught, 8 hours trials = 7,552 = 19.2 knots
	IHP forced draught, 4 hours trials = 9,180
Bunkers	Coal. 400 tons normal. 535 tons maximum
Endurance	8,500 miles at 10 knots
Armament	Two 6-inch quick-firers
	Six 4.7-inch quick-firers
	Eight 6-pounder quick-firers
	One 3-pounder
	Four machine-guns
	Four 14-inch diameter torpedo tubes. Above water

74   SCYLLA, BRITISH SECOND CLASS PROTECTED CRUISER 1892

75 BRILLIANT BRITISH PROTECTED CRUISER 1893

Armour	Deck 2-inch
	Gun shields 4½-inch
	Engine hatches 5-inch
	Conning tower 3-inch
Complement	273
Hull	Wood sheathed and coppered

The *Brilliant* was another of the "Apollo" class of protected cruisers, ordered under the Naval Defence Act of 1889.

Beken's camera caught the *Brilliant's* crew at work in the misty light of early morning. A working party pauses on the poop, signalmen man the after bridge and a boat's crew prepares to leave the side, while a painting party works forward.

These ships had limited fighting value and by 1906 were being removed from the effective fleet. By then they could steam at only 17 knots, except for short spurts.

At the outbreak of World War I in 1914 the *Brilliant* served as a depot ship in the river Tyne until 1915. Later she was based at Lerwick, Shetland Isles, until 1918.

By the end of 1917 the German-occupied Belgian ports of Ostend and Zeebrugge were vital bases for German submarines, which voyaged through the Dover Strait, attempting to pass the British barrage and the Dover patrol, to prey on shipping in the English Channel and Atlantic. German destroyers and tropedo boats also used the bases for raids in the Channel and early in 1918 it was planned to close these harbours by sinking ballasted blockships in their entrances. Blockships were selected from obsolete cruiser classes; the *Brilliant* and *Sirius* were to be sunk at Ostend and simultaneously the *Iphigenia*, *Intrepid* and *Thetis* at Zeebrugge. Supporting and distracting operations were to be carried out.

After postponements, the blocking forces sailed on April 22nd 1918. The attempt on Ostend was commanded by Commodore H. Lynes whose attack was confused by the Germans having moved a navigation buoy one mile eastward on the eve of the operation, and after the protective smoke screen was laid a breeze dispersed it and surprise was gone, so the *Brilliant* and *Sirius* had to be sunk about ¼ mile from the east of the entrance, which remained unobstructed.

On May 9th-10th 1918 the attempt on Ostend was repeated, using as blockship the old cruiser *Vindictive*, which had so distinguished herself during the blocking of Zeebrugge. Although she was sunk in the channel, under heavy fire, it was only partially obstructed.

Besides the natural hazards of the Belgian coast, the blockships faced extensive German minefields and heavy coastal batteries, yet the operations were carried through with great gallantry and heavy British losses of officers and men.

Charybdis

BRITISH SECOND CLASS PROTECTED CRUISER 1894 *Plate 76*

Built	Royal Naval dockyard, Sheerness
Laid down	1891
Launched	June 1893
Completed	October 1894
Dimensions	Length 320ft
	Breadth 49ft 6in
	Draught 19ft mean. 21ft maximum
Displacement	4,360 tons
Machinery	Twin screw
	Vertical triple-expansion engines
	Eight single-ended boilers
	IHP natural draught, 8 hours trials = 7,125 = 19.3 knots
	IHP forced draught, 4 hours trials = 9,136 = 20.5 knots
Bunkers	Coal. 400 tons normal. 1,000 tons maximum
Endurance	7,000 miles at 10 knots
Armament	Two 6-inch quick-firers. One forward and one aft
	Eight 4.7-inch quick-firers. Four on each side
	Eight 6-pounders
	One 3-pounder
	Four 18-inch torpedo tubes. Above water
Armour	Deck 2-inch
	Gun shields 4½-inch
	Conning tower 3-inch
	Engine hatches 5-inch
Complement	318

The *Charybdis* was one of the large fleet of cruisers constructed under the Naval Defence Act and was the last sizeable warship built at Sheerness dockyard. She was one of eight sisters of the "Astraea" class which included the *Hermione*, *Astraea*, *Cambrian*, *Flora*, *Forte*. *Fox* and *Bonaventure*.

The displacement was increased by about 1,000 tons over their less successful predecessors, the "Apollo" class, and they were improved in every way, being better sea boats, with more comfortable quarters, and increased steaming radius and armament, carrying the secondary battery one deck higher. They cost about £250,000 each.

Completed for sea in October 1894, the *Charybdis* was commissioned and immediately paid off into reserve due to the shortage of crews caused by the growing size of the British fleet. On January 1st 1896 she commissioned for service with the "flying squadron", to reinforce Britain's views on the German-South African incident. Subsequently she was in the Channel fleet as a scout but after two years' commission was paid off and laid up at Devonport for two years. In the spring of 1900 she recommis-

76   CHARYBDIS, BRITISH SECOND CLASS PROTECTED CRUISER 1894

sioned with the crew of the cruiser *Comus* for service in the North America and West Indies squadron under Captain G.A. Gifford. During the banks fishing season she flew a broad pendant as commodore of the fishery protection squadron, afterwards reverting to station as a private ship.

The *Charybdis* recommissioned at Halifax, Nova Scotia, in 1902 for similar service under command of Commodore R. Montgomorie, who later led a combined squadron of British, German and Italian warships in a blockade of the Venezuela coast, to obtain satisfaction for debts incurred by the republican government, which had repudiated responsibility for them. A mob seized a British merchant ship at Puerto Cabello but the *Charybdis* steamed there at full speed and released the ship, afterwards bombarding the forts of the harbour in retribution.

In 1905 the *Charybdis* returned to refit at Chatham and was placed in the first line of the Nore division of the Home fleet in 1907. During the following year she was principally used for troop carrying, and continued this duty after transfer to the 3rd division, Home fleet. By 1910 she was reduced to a nucleus crew and was transferred to Devonport, apparently to be sold.

In 1914 the *Charybdis* was hurriedly prepaired for sea, principally manned by reservists. She was commanded by Rear-Admiral R. Wemyss as flagship of the 12th cruiser squadron patrolling the western entrance to the English Channel, supported by five French armoured cruisers, to cover the passage of the British expeditionary force troops to France. In October 1914 the *Charybdis* led the escort for the first Canadian troops sent to France.

When Wemyss was transferred to the Dardanelles campaign the *Charybdis* was paid off at Halifax. Her engines were wearing out and she lay there until the end of 1917 when the Bermuda authorities pleaded hardship and requested a replacement ship for vessels taken by the Navy, which had left them without proper trade or passenger communication with America. The *Charybdis* was made available to them and was converted into a merchant ship of sorts. From spring 1918 she maintained a service for passengers and foodstuff between New York and Bermuda, using only the port side engine, under which she made 10 knots but consumed 60 tons of coal a day. In October 1918 she was further converted when the forward boiler-room became an additional hold, allowing her to carry 1,500 tons of cargo. She sheered badly and was uneconomical but served the Bermudans until December 1919 when ordinary shipping again became available.

The *Charybdis* was laid up at Bermuda in 1922 when she was purchased by local owners intending to operate her again as a merchant ship. When freights slumped this did not proceed and in 1923 she was resold to Danish scrappers. The Dutch tug *Willem Barentz* towed her to Rotterdam where she was again sold and broken up.

Endymion

BRITISH FIRST CLASS PROTECTED CRUISER 1894 *Plate 77*

Built	Earle's Shipbuilding and Engineering Co, Hull
Laid down	November 1889
Launched	July 1891
Completed	May 1894
Dimensions	*Length overall* 387ft 6in
	Length between perpendiculars 360ft
	Breadth 60ft
	Draught 23ft 9in normal. About 26ft maximum
Displacement	7,350 tons
Machinery	Twin screw
	Two 3-cylinder triple-expansion engines by builders
	Four double-ended, one single-ended cylindrical boilers
	IHP natural draught = 10,000 = 18.5 knots
	IHP forced draught = 12,000 = 19.5 knots
Bunkers	Coal. 850 tons normal. 1,250 tons maximum
Armament	Two 9.2-inch. 30 calibre. In shields. One forward and one aft
	Ten 6-inch quick-firers. 40 calibre. In shields on upper deck. Four sponsoned, four others in casemates, two port and starboard on main deck
	Twelve 6-pounder quick-firers
	Five 3-pounder quick-firers
	Two maxims
	Four 18-inch torpedo tubes, submerged
Armour	*Deck* 5-inch
	Gun shields and casemates 6-inch
	Hoists to 9.2-inch guns 7-inch
	Hoists to casemates 2-inch
	Conning tower 12-inch
Complement	544

The *Endymion* was one of the six "Edgar" class protected cruisers ordered under the Naval Defence Act of 1889. These included the *Edgar, Hawke, Endymion, Theseus, Grafton, Gibraltar* and *St George*. They cost about £430,000 each and steamed well, achieving 19 knots at sea in moderate conditions, besides being generally free from the usual machinery troubles then common. The rakish funnels and clean hull shape made them handsome ships and they were sheathed and coppered for foreign service.

The *Endymion* joined the Channel squadron in 1894 and served the then customary working-up period in home waters. She paid off in December 1895 and commissioned for particular service in July 1896

77   *ENDYMION, BRITISH FIRST CLASS PROTECTED CRUISER 1894*

until June, then again in August until January 1897, when she laid up at Chatham until 1899.

In June 1899 she commissioned for the China station and served there during the Boxer rising of 1900, returning to pay off in September 1902 and refit at Harland and Wolff's shipyard until 1903. In April 1904 the *Endymion* joined the Channel fleet and served until December 1904.

During January 1905 she commissioned as a gunnery tender to HMS *Wildfire* at Sheerness and remained there until 1912, when she joined the 3rd fleet at Portsmouth. In March 1913 she commissioned as flagship of the vice-admiral commanding the training squadron based on Queenstown. During 1914-15 she served with the 10th cruiser squadron and she was then selected for fitting with side bulges on the hull at the waterline as protection against mine or torpedo explosion. The *Grafton*, *Edgar* and *Theseus* were similarly fitted and the resulting appearance was in contrast to the smart ship in this photograph. Net sweeping gallows were also rigged over the bows for the Dardanelles operations, where the *Endymion* arrived in 1915. She served in the Aegean during 1918 and in March 1920 was sold to T. E. Evans of Cardiff for £24,000. She left the Nore to be broken up in May 1920.

This photograph was taken in 1897.

St George

BRITISH FIRST CLASS PROTECTED CRUISER 1894 *Plate 78*

Built	Earle's Shipbuilding and Engineering Co, Hull
Laid down	April 1890
Launched	June 1892
Completed	October 1894
Dimensions	*Length between perpendiculars* 360ft
	Breadth 60ft 8in
	Draught 23ft 9in normal. About 26ft maximum
Displacement	7,350 tons
Machinery	Twin screw
	Two 3-cylinder inverted triple-expansion engines by Maudslay, Son and Field
	Four double-ended, one single-ended cylindrical boilers
	IHP natural draught 4 hour trials = 10,585 = 20.25 knots
	IHP forced draught = about 12,000
Bunkers	Coal. 850 tons normal. 1,250 tons maximum
Armament	Two 9.2-inch. 30 calibre. In shields. One forward and one aft
	Ten 6-inch quick-firers. 40 calibre. In shields and casemates
	Twelve 6-pounder quick-firers
	Five 3-pounder quick-firers
	Two maxims
	Four 18-inch diameter torpedo tubes. Two submerged
Armour	Deck 5-inch
	Gun shields and casemates 6-inch
	Hoists to 9.2-inch guns 7-inch
	Hoists to casemates 2-inch
	Engine hatches 6-inch
	Conning tower 12-inch
Complement	544
Hull	Wood sheathed and coppered

The *St George* was another of the "Edgar" class cruisers, a sister to the *Endymion (Plate 77)*. She cost £377,204 to build and commissioned during 1894 as flagship of Rear-Admiral Sir Harry Rawson on the Cape and West Africa station. This photograph is believed to have been taken during service there and shows the shape of the 9.2-inch gun-shields and the sponsons of the forward and after broadside upper-deck 6-inch guns.

The cruiser was then the embodiment of defiant British sea power, carrying the country's policies into every ocean. Wherever trouble occurred these instruments of empire appeared and usually subdued it quickly. During 1895-6 the *St George* was Rawson's flagship for operations by a naval brigade sent to the final Ashanti war, eliminating a threat to the Gold Coast.

In 1896 she steamed to Zanzibar, the island off the East African coast where a revolution had occurred in this British protectorate. Britain had transferred considerable areas of land on the African mainland to Germany, who was busy expanding her colonies, and when the sultan of Zanzibar died, Prince Seyyid Khalid ben Baggalah declared himself ruler and seized power with the aid of native troops. British authorities ashore were unable to contain the disturbance and the cruiser *Philomel* and the gunboat *Thrush*, which were in harbour, landed parties of seamen while the *Thrush* trained her guns on the sultan's palace which was being used as the prince's headquarters.

Next day the *St George* and the small cruiser *Racoon* arrived within hours of each other, and on August 23rd the rebels were given an ultimatum to surrender. When this was ignored all warships cleared for action and shipping left the harbour with the exception of the sultan's armed yacht *Glasgow* which remained, manned by rebels and surrounded by armed dhows. On expiration of the ultimatum the British ships opened fire for over thirty minutes, destroying the palace, severely damaging the *Glasgow*, and sinking many dhows. The prince surrendered in favour of a new sultan, who was proclaimed that day.

The *St George* also led the naval punitive expedition to Benin, on the West African coast, where an aggressive ruler was committing atrocities and threatening the stability of the neighbouring Niger Coast Protectorate. The *St George* was accompanied by the cruisers *Philomel*, *Phoebe* and

78 St. GEORGE, BRITISH FIRST CLASS PROTECTED CRUISER 1894

Barossa, with the *Forte* and *Theseus* detached from the Mediterranean and supported by the gunboats *Widgeon*, *Magpie* and *Alecto*. Rawson led a march of 1,200 seamen and marines through the jungle to Benin, where they achieved their object and withdrew, though losing many men from fever.

The *St George* returned to pay off at Portsmouth in July 1898, remaining there until commissioned in October 1899 with the training squadron. In 1900 she transferred to an active cruiser squadron and formed part of the escort of the SS *Ophir*, taking the royal party on their empire tour from March until November 1901.

She paid off in November 1902 and recommissioned in March 1904 as senior officer's ship, South Atlantic, participating in the search for the Russian Volunteer fleet steamers *Smolensk* and *Petersburg* during August and September.

From December 1904 until May 1906 she served as a boy seamen's training ship with the 4th cruiser squadron on the North America and West Indies station, then went into reserve at Devonport from 1906-9.

During 1909-10 the *St George* was converted to a depot ship for destroyers, then termed a "torpedo depot ship", and served the 3rd flotilla at the Nore. She was mother ship to the 6th flotilla during 1912-13, and to the 9th at the Firth of Forth in 1913-14. That October she was based on the Humber with the 7th flotilla and by 1915 was transferred as a depot ship in the Mediterranean, serving there until 1918 when she was again converted to a submarine depot ship and served the 2nd flotilla in the Aegean Sea during 1918-19.

The *St George* paid off in 1920 and was sold in July to be broken up by Castle's of Plymouth.

Royal Arthur

BRITISH FIRST CLASS PROTECTED CRUISER 1893 *Plate 79*

Built	Royal Naval dockyard, Portsmouth
Laid down	August 1889
Launched	February 1891
Completed	1893
Dimensions	*Length overall* 387ft 6in
	Length between perpendiculars 360ft
	Breadth 60ft 8in
	Draught 23ft 9in mean. 24ft 6in loaded
Displacement	7,700 tons
Machinery	Twin screw
	Two 3-cylinder vertical inverted triple-expansion engines by Maudslay, Son and Field
	Six cylindrical type double-ended boilers

	IHP natural draught = 10,000 = 18.5 knots
	IHP forced draught = 12,000 = 19.5 knots
Bunkers	Coal. 850 tons normal. 1,260 tons maximum
Endurance	10,000 miles at 10 knots. 3,000 miles at 18 knots
Armament	One 9.2-inch 22-ton. 30 calibre. Aft
	Twelve 6-inch quick-firers. 40 calibre. Two in shields on foredeck. Six in shields on upper deck broadside. Four in casemates on main deck broadside
	Twelve 6-pounder quick-firers
	Five 3-pounder quick-firers
	Seven machine-guns
	Two 18-inch diameter torpedo tubes, submerged
	A 56ft steam launch equipped with torpedo dropping gear was also carried
Armour	*Deck* 5-inch – 2½-inch
	Gun shields 4½-inch
	Casemates 6-inch – 2-inch
	Ammunition hoists 7-inch
	Coamings 6-inch
	Conning tower 12-inch
Complement	520 – 550
Hull	Wood sheathed and coppered

The *Royal Arthur* was a sister ship of the *Crescent (Plate 80)* and both were first class cruisers developed from the design of the "Edgar" class. They differed in having a raised forecastle on which two 6-inch guns were mounted. Both were intended as flagships for major colonial stations of the Empire and were successful ships of good appearance and speed. The *Royal Arthur* was to have been named *Centaur*, but was christened by Queen Victoria after one of her sons. She sustained 18 knots for forty-eight hours on trials, and cost about £402,400 to build.

In 1893 the *Royal Arthur* became Sir H. Stephenson's flagship on the Pacific station, supported by the third class cruisers *Comus* and *Satellite*, returning to refit at Portsmouth in 1896. In February 1897 she commissioned for particular service until July and again commissioned in November as rear-admiral's flagship for the Australian station. She recommissioned at Sydney in April 1901 and returned to England in June 1904 to pay off for repair; which lasted until 1905.

During July 1905 the *Royal Arthur* became vice-admiral's flagship of the 4th cruiser squadron, North America and West Indies station, returning to pay off in May 1906 and go into reserve at Portsmouth until 1909, when she joined the 4th cruiser squadron, Home fleet, until 1912.

During August 1913 the *Royal Arthur* commissioned for the training squadron at Queenstown, transferring to the 10th cruiser squadron during 1914-15. She became guard ship at Scapa Flow in February 1915 and later was reduced to a depot ship for submarines, attending the 12th flotilla during 1918 and the 1st in 1919.

79 ROYAL ARTHUR, BRITISH FIRST CLASS PROTECTED CRUISER 1893

The *Royal Arthur* paid off in December 1920 and was sold in September 1921 to Cohen's to be towed to Germany for scrapping.

This photograph was taken in 1897.

Crescent

BRITISH FIRST CLASS PROTECTED CRUISER 1894 *Plates 80 and 81*

Built	Royal Naval dockyard, Portsmouth
Laid down	1890
Launched	March 1892
Completed	1894
Dimensions	*Length overall* 387ft 6in
	Length between perpendiculars 360ft
	Breadth 60ft 8in
	Draught 23ft 9in mean. 24ft 6in loaded
Displacement	7,700 tons
Machinery	Twin screw
	Two 3-cylinder vertical inverted triple-expansion engines by Penn
	Six cylindrical double-ended boilers
	IHP natural draught = 10,378 = 18.6 knots
	IHP forced draught = 12,000 = 19.7 knots
Bunkers	Coal. 850 tons normal. 1,260 tons maximum
Endurance	10,000 miles at 10 knots. 3,000 miles at 18 knots
Armament	One 9.2-inch 22-ton gun. 30 calibre. Aft
	Twelve 6-inch quick-firers. 40 calibre. Two in shields on foredeck. Six in shields on upper deck broadside. Four in casemates on main deck broadside
	Twelve 6-pounder quick-firers
	Five 3-pounder quick-firers
	Seven machine-guns
	Two 18-inch diameter submerged torpedo tubes
	A 56ft steam launch equipped with torpedo dropping gear was also carried
Armour	*Deck* 5-inch – 2½-inch
	Gun shields 4½-inch
	Casemates 6-inch – 2-inch
	Ammunition hoists 7-inch
	Coamings 6-inch
	Conning tower 12-inch
Complement	520 – 550
Hull	Wood sheathed and coppered

The *Crescent* and her sister ship *Royal Arthur (Plate 79)* were developments of the similar cruisers of the "Edgar" class, differing in having a raised forecastle on which two 6-inch guns were mounted instead of the single 9.2-inch of the "Edgars". This feature improved their seakeeping and they were always good steamers.

The *Crescent* cost about £383,000 ready for sea during 1894. Her first commission was for special service and relief duties to the China station, during which she steamed over 100,000 miles without trouble.

In March 1895 she commissioned for the North America and West Indies station as flagship of Vice-Admiral Erskine, remaining there with one second class and six third class cruisers until paid off at Portsmouth in October 1897.

In June 1898 the *Crescent* was commissioned by Captain the Duke of York (later King George V) who was then a serving naval officer who had risen from midshipman's rank to command a first class torpedo boat, then the gunboat *Thrush*, the second class cruiser *Melampus* and, after an interval, the *Crescent*.

These photographs, taken during 1898, show the nineteenth-century first class cruiser at a peak of development; well-armed, long-ranging, imposing in appearance (which was then important), and capable of acting as an admiral's flagship on a foreign station. Masts, yards and rigging are still prominent, complemented by graceful buff funnels, but fighting tops are not fitted to the masts. The hull bristles with guns, though the main-deck casemate-mounted 6-inch would have been of little fighting value.

The port bow close-up shows bow scrollwork and the embrasured bow 6-pounders. She is trimmed by the stern, probably being light on fresh and feed water.

The *Crescent* commissioned again in May 1899 as flagship of the North America and West Indies station, returning to England in October 1902 to be refitted by the Thames Ironworks.

During February 1904 the *Crescent* became flagship of the rear-admiral, Cape and West Africa station, and in September participated in the Royal Navy's search for the steamers *Petersburg* and *Smolensk* of the Russian Volunteer fleet during August and September 1904. She returned to pay off in 1907 and in June became part of the Portsmouth division of the Home fleet, serving with the 4th cruiser squadron from 1909 until 1913. In February 1913 the *Crescent* joined the training squadron based on Queenstown, Ireland, until August 1914, when she transferred to the 10th cruiser squadron until she became guardship at Hoy in February 1915. She served for a time as guardship at Portsmouth dockyard, with armament reduced to four 6-inch guns. By 1917 she was reduced to a depot ship for submarines at Scapa Flow and later at Rosyth. She was paid off during 1920 to be purchased by Cohen and in October 1921 she was towed from Rosyth to be broken up in Germany.

80   CRESCENT, BRITISH FIRST CLASS PROTECTED CRUISER 1894

81 CRESCENT,
BRITISH FIRST CLASS PROTECTED CRUISER
1894

82   GEFION, GERMAN PROTECTED CRUISER 1894

Gefion

GERMAN PROTECTED CRUISER 1894 *Plate 82*

Built	Schichau, Danzig
Laid down	1892
Launched	May 1893
Completed	1894
Dimensions	*Length overall* 334ft
	Length waterline 325ft
	Breadth 42ft 7in
	Draught 20ft 3in mean. 21ft 6in maximum
Displacement	3,765 tons
Machinery	Twin screw
	Two vertical triple-expansion engines by Schichau
	Six cylindrical double-ended boilers
	IHP forced draught, 4 hours trials = 9,828 = 20.5 knots
	Normal high speed = 19 knots
Bunkers	Coal. 780 tons normal
Endurance	6,500 miles at 10 knots
Armament	Ten 4.1-inch quick-firers. 35 calibre. Single mounts
	Six 4-pounder quick-firers. 40 calibre
	Eight machine-guns
	Two 17.7-inch torpedo tubes. Deck mounted
Armour	*Protective deck* 3-inch – 1¼-inch – ½-inch
Complement	302

The *Gefion* was well armed with ten 4.1-inch guns disposed in single mountings along her sides. The turtle-back forecastle and well-deck aft of amidships were both features which should have been unnecessary with her generous freeboard. Her appearance was distinctive with three widely-spaced funnels and bridge abaft the foremast. As designed, she could set a storm staysail forward of each mast and a boomless trysail abaft them – one of the last cruisers so equipped.

After completion in 1894, the *Gefion* served with the German fleet in the North Sea and Baltic at a time when German cruiser development had not crystallised to a distinct type, nor were cruiser squadrons regularly attached to the German fleet, which was still primarily a coast defence navy. However, the *Gefion* was interesting as the prototype of many subsequent German cruisers of similar size, principally intended as commerce raiders. These were fast and well-armed ships with designed speeds often surpassed on trials. Most were armed with the 4.1-inch gun, a powerful weapon which could outrange the 6-inch guns of British cruisers in the 1890's.

This photograph was taken in 1897 and later that year the *Gefion* sailed for service abroad, returning in 1901 to refit at Wilhelmshaven. She was

again refitted during 1905 for further fleet service but by 1914 was obsolete and about to be relegated when war commenced. Like many other older German ships she was disarmed in 1916 and became an accommodation ship at Danzig until the end of World War I.

The *Gefion* was discarded by the German Navy in November 1919 and was converted into an uneconomical merchant ship in that time of tonnage shortage and high freight rates. During 1923 she was scrapped at Danzig.

Buenos Aires

ARGENTINIAN PROTECTED CRUISER 1895 *Plate 83*

Built	Armstrong and Co, Elswick
Launched	May 1895
Completed	1895
Dimensions	*Length overall* 424ft
	Length waterline 408ft
	Breadth 47ft 2in
	Draught 18ft mean. 22ft maximum
Displacement	4,780 tons
Machinery	Twin screw
	Two 4-cylinder triple-expansion engines by Humphry and Tennant
	Four double-ended, four single-ended boilers
	IHP natural draught, 6 hours trial = 13,000 = 23.2 knots
	IHP forced draught = 18,000 = 24 knots
Bunkers	Coal. 350 tons normal. 1,000 tons maximum
Endurance	3,500/10,000 miles at economical speed
Armament	Two 8-inch quick-firers. 45 calibre. One forward and one aft
	Four 6-inch quick-firers. 45 calibre. Two forward and two aft
	Six 4.7-inch quick-firers. Three each side
	Four 6-pounders
	Sixteen 3-pounders
	Six maxim guns
	Five torpedo tubes. One bow. Two forward and two aft, submerged
Armour	*Protective deck* Steel. 3-inch – 1.5-inch
	Gun shields 4.5-inch
	Gun hoists 3-inch
	Conning tower 6-inch
Complement	429
Hull	Wood sheathed and coppered

83   BUENOS AIRES, ARGENTINIAN PROTECTED CRUISER 1895

The *Buenos Aires* was another Armstrong "Elswick" cruiser – the type of ship which brought fame to the firm. She followed the smaller Argentine cruisers *Nueve De Juilio* of 1892 and the *Vinte cinco-De-Maio* of 1892 from the same builders. These, with three armoured coast defence ships and two new armoured cruisers, formed the main force of the Argentine fleet.

The *Buenos Aires* was a clean-lined ship for the period, and with an 8-inch gun forward and aft, a 6-inch at each quarter of the superstructure and three 4.7-inch on each beam, was well armed and had excellent speed when built.

She was very similar to the Chilean cruiser *Blanco Encalada,* completed at Elswick in 1894, and Brazil's *Barrozo* of 1897 was from the same yard and perhaps represented a reply to maintain the naval balance on the east coast of South America.

This photograph was taken in 1911, when the *Buenos Aires* attended the Coronation naval review at Spithead. Her bridge was placed abaft the foremast and the large deckhouse and signal platform, to suit the mounting of the forward pair of 6-inch guns. She was an efficient-looking ship and gave good service, but passed a peaceful existence in the Argentine Navy, where smartness and discipline was maintained by frequent exercises and drills.

The *Buenos Aires* was discarded in 1931 to be broken up.

Pothuau

FRENCH ARMOURED CRUISER 1896 *Plate 84*

Built	Granville
Laid down	1893
Launched	1895
Completed	1896
Dimensions	*Length overall* 370ft 8in
	Length waterline 360ft
	Breadth 50ft 2in
	Draught 22ft 6in. 21ft 4in mean
Displacement	5,365 tons
Machinery	Twin screw
	Two horizontal triple-expansion engines
	Sixteen Belleville type boilers
	IHP natural draught, trials = 6,845 = 17.79 knots
	IHP forced draught, trials = 10,200 = 19.2 knots
Bunkers	Coal. 538 tons normal. 638 tons maximum
Armament	Two 7.6-inch. In turrets, one forward and one aft
	Ten 5.5-inch quick-firers
	Ten 3-pounder quick-firers
	Eight 1-pounders
	Four torpedo tubes. Above water
Armour	*Belt* 3.9-inch – 2-inch
	Turrets 9.5-inch
	Protective deck 3.5-inch – 1.6-inch
	Casemates 2.5-inch
	Conning tower 9.4-inch
Complement	461

In 1891 France built the extraordinary-shaped armoured cruiser *Dupuy de Lôme,* the forerunner of a succession of powerfully armed ships, Four of the "Charner" type followed and then the individual ship *Pothuau,* sometimes referred to as the *Amiral Pothuau.* These ships and the subsequent classes of larger French armoured cruisers resulted from a campaign by Admiral Aube and the "young school" of naval thought who considered that battleships and fleet actions were outdated by the torpedo and the torpedo boat and that future war at sea against England, still France's traditional enemy, would best be carried out by commerce raiding by armoured cruisers, to cut off supplies of food and materials.

Aube's ideal commerce raider was an armoured cruiser of considerable range, medium gun power and with sufficient armour to withstand action with a ship of similar characteristics. However, successive French naval ministries continued to build battleships, but also encouraged development of the armoured cruiser in the fleet.

Britain had built armoured cruisers and similar vessels during the 1880's and 1890's and Russia had developed the type during the 1870's. However, Britain continued to favour the protected cruiser for policing the world trade routes until the "Cressy" class of armoured cruisers were commenced in 1899-1901, when the potential threat of commerce raiding by French ships became seriously apparent.

The *Pothuau* perpetuated the long ram bow of contemporary French warships and proved a good sea boat, able to maintain her speed for several years. She cost the equivalent of £384,000. This photograph was taken in 1898 and shows the long superstructure typical of many French ships. The armament of 5.5-inch guns was disposed in this; eight in casemates and two with shields and on side sponsons. The two large gun-turrets were mounted close to the ends and the light bridge structures were typical of the time.

By 1914 the *Pothuau* was serving as a gunnery school ship but from the outbreak of war until 1915 cruised in Mediterranean patrols. She was then ordered to the Cameroons where her landing party took posession of Krivi. At the end of 1915 she commenced a lengthy refit at Lorient and afterwards was stationed at Port Said for the defence of the Suez Canal during 1916-17. Afterwards the *Pothuau* sailed for Saigon in Indo-China, where some refitting took place.

During 1917-18 she was at Toulon, where the mainmast was cut down and she was equipped for operating a kite balloon, later reverting to a gunnery training ship.

84 POTHUAU, FRENCH ARMOURED CRUISER 1896

85   BROOKLYN, UNITED STATES ARMOURED CRUISER 1896

During 1919 the turrets were replaced by anti-aircraft-gun prototype mountings and she continued as a gunnery school ship until November 1927, when she was discarded. The *Pothuau* was scrapped in 1929.

Brooklyn

UNITED STATES ARMOURED CRUISER 1896 *Plate 85*

Official number	CA3
Built	Cramp, Philadelphia, Pennsylvania
Laid down	August 1893
Launched	October 1895
Completed	1896
Dimensions	*Length overall* 402ft 6in
	Length waterline 400ft 6in
	Breadth 64ft 8in
	Draught 24ft mean, normal. 26ft 2in full load
Displacement	9,215 tons normal. 10,068 tons full load
Machinery	Twin screw
	Four reciprocating triple-expansion engines
	Five two-ended and two single-ended boilers
	IHP trials = 18,769 = 21.91 knots mean
Bunkers	Coal. 900 tons normal. 1,650 tons maximum (1903)
Endurance	5,110 miles at 10 knots
Armament	*Original*
	Eight 8-inch. 35 calibre. Two forward and two aft. Two port and starboard
	Twelve 5-inch. 40 calibre. In casemates
	Twelve 6-pounders
	Four 1-pounders
	Four Gatling machine-guns
	Five 18-inch torpedo tubes. Above water. One in stem, others in sides. Howell type
	Armament in 1913 after reconstruction commenced in 1909
	Eight 8-inch (as above)
	Twelve 5-inch (as above)
	Four 6-pounders
	Torpedo tubes removed
	During 1918 secondary armament was amended to:
	Eight 5-inch
	Two 3-inch anti-aircraft
	Four 6-pounders
Armour	Harvey
	Main belt 8-inch amidships to 3-inch. 267ft long by 8ft wide

No armoured bulkheads to ends of belt
Deck 6-inch amidships to 3-inch at ends
Barbettes 8-inch to 6½-inch
Hoods to barbettes 5½-inch
Shields to 5-inch guns 4-inch
Hoists 6-inch
Conning tower 7½-inch
Complement 718

Construction of the *Brooklyn* was authorised during 1892 and she embodied improvements from the similar ship *New York*, completed in 1893. The arrangement of 8-inch guns, considerable freeboard, pronounced tumble home and stern shape indicated French influence in the design, which also had some contemporary German characteristics. She was of striking appearance, with funnels of unusual height.

The *Brooklyn* was generally a successful ship. At the commencement of the Spanish-American war, in May 1898, she was flagship of Commodore Schley of the flying squadron, nominally stationed at Hampton Roads, with orders to protect the United States' coast.

She carried Schley's flag at the battle of Santiago, Cuba, where on July 3rd 1898 the small and inferior Spanish squadron broke out and attempted to escape from the blockading American ships.

The Spanish flagship *Infanta Maria Teresa*, an armoured cruiser, led her sister ships *Vizcaya* and *Colon* to sea, with smaller warships. Although outgunned and suffering serious damage, the Spanish flagship steered boldly for the *Brooklyn*, intending to ram her. As she approached, Schley ordered the *Brroklyn* to turn away from the enemy towards the battleship *Texas*, resulting in temporary confusion in the American line between these ships and the battleship *Iowa*. This and other actions by Commodore Schley before and after the battle caused a subsequent court of inquiry to be held. It exonerated but censured him.

The *Vizcaya* followed the *Teresa* and also attempted to ram the Brooklyn, which avoided the attack by superior speed. Before joining the engagement of this Spanish cruiser, the *Brooklyn* also fired on the emerging *Colon* and joined the battleship *Oregon* in her pursuit, until she was beached. During part of this action the *Brooklyn* steamed at 16 knots without the forward engines.

Reconstruction of the *Brooklyn* was commenced during 1909, when fire controls were added. Her torpedo tubes were removed, her secondary armament was reduced, and two-stage hoists were fitted in the barbettes. She maintained her steaming ability into World War I and in 1919 was flagship to the destroyer force, Asiatic fleet, with her original appearance little changed.

She represented the US Navy at Vladivostok during the allied intervention in Siberia.

The *Brooklyn* was sold out of the US Navy in December 1921 to be broken up.

86   EMPERADOR CARLOS V, SPANISH FIRST CLASS PROTECTED CRUISER 1897

Emperador Carlos V

SPANISH FIRST CLASS PROTECTED CRUISER 1897 *Plate 86*

Built	Naval dockyard, Cadiz
Laid down	1892
Launched	1895
Completed	1897
Dimensions	*Length between perpendiculars* 404ft 8in
	Breadth 67ft
	Draught 25ft mean. 28ft 6in maximum
Displacement	9,903 tons
Machinery	Twin screw
	Two 4-cylinder triple-expansion engines
	Twelve cylindrical boilers
	IHP natural draught = 15,000 = 19 knots
	IHP forced draught = 18,500 = 20 knots
Bunkers	Coal. 1,200 tons normal. 2,040 tons maximum
Armament	Two 11-inch. 35 calibre. One forward and one aft
	Eight 5.5-inch. In side casemates
	Four 4.1-inch. In sides
	Two 12-pounders
	Ten 6-pounders
	Eight 1-pounders
	Two machine-guns
	Two 14-inch torpedo tubes
Armour	*Belt* 2-inch
	Barbettes 10-inch
	Hoods 4-inch
	Deck 2½-inch
	Hoists 8-inch
	Over battery 2-inch
	Conning tower 12-inch
Complement	583

The *Emperador Carlos V* had many similarities to contemporary British cruisers. She was powerfully armed for her size and type, with something of the battle-cruiser concept in mounting two 11-inch guns in a cruiser hull. She was completed before the Spanish-American war of 1898 which cost Spain the best ships of her modest fleet in battles at Santiago, Cuba, and Manila in the Philippines – all then Spanish possessions.

The *Emperador Carlos V* saw no action throughout her career. She formed part of the Spanish war reserve squadron under Admiral Camara, which during May 1898 was ordered to proceed to the Canary Islands, then Spanish, to coal and prepare for a long voyage. On leaving the Canary Islands they were to split into three divisions when out of sight of land. Admiral Camara would lead the first with his flag in the *Emperador Carlos V*, accompanied by the armed liners *Rapido*, *Patriota*, and *Meteor*, and the armed yacht *Giralda*, intending to steam to Bermuda and then carry out operations against the American coast, bombarding and harrassing shipping. After steaming north the squadron was to make for the West Indies and attempt to reach Havana, Santiago or San Juan. The two other divisions were to operate in the eastern Atlantic.

On June 15th the reserve squadron was still preparing for sea at Cadiz when the Spanish government decided to send all available effective ships to the Philippines. Camara was ordered to steam to Port Said with the *Carlos V* and the battleship *Pelayo*, accompanied by the *Rapido* and *Patriota* and convoying two troop transports and five colliers. They would there receive further orders for the Pacific. However, they were refused permission to coal at Port Said so proceeded through the canal to Suez, where the squadron was recalled to Carthagena to reinforce Spanish defence against threat of punitive action by the American battleships *Oregon* and *Iowa*, supported by auxiliary cruisers, which were reported to be preparing to cross the Atlantic under Commodore Watson.

The *Emperador Carlos V*'s subsequent career was uneventful. Spain was neutral during World War I and by 1920 she was renamed *Carlos Quinto* and was classed as a first class cruiser, with duties as flagship of the training squadron. Eight of the 6-pounder guns had been removed but the armament was otherwise unchanged.

By 1927 she was listed as a depot ship at El Ferrol and was no longer seagoing, remaining in this service until 1931 and being broken up in 1932.

This photograph, taken in 1902, shows the high barbettes and cupola-shaped hoods of her two "Honorita" type 11-inch guns.

Eclipse

BRITISH SECOND CLASS PROTECTED CRUISER 1897 *Plate 87*

Built	Royal Naval dockyard, Portsmouth
Laid down	December 1893
Launched	July 1894
Completed	March 1897
Dimensions	*Length overall* 370ft 4in
	Length waterline 364ft
	Breadth 54ft
	Draught 20ft 6in mean. 22ft loaded
Displacement	5,600
Machinery	Twin screw

182   *87   ECLIPSE, BRITISH SECOND CLASS PROTECTED CRUISER 1897*

Two 3-cylinder inverted vertical triple-expansion engines by builders
Eight single-ended boilers
IHP natural draught, trials = 8,220 = 19.2 knots
IHP forced draught, trials = 9,853 = 20.1 knots

Bunkers	Coal. 550 tons normal. 1,000 tons maximum
Endurance	7,000 miles at 10 knots. 5,600 miles at 12 knots. 2,800 miles at 17 knots
Armament	Five 6-inch quick-firers. 45 calibre
	Six 4.7-inch quick-firers
	Nine 12-pounders
	Six 3-pounders
	Two maxims
	Three 18-inch diameter torpedo tubes. One above water aft. Two submerged broadside. Ten torpedoes carried
Armour	*Deck* 3-inch – 1½-inch
	Gun shields 4½-inch
	Engine hatches 6-inch
	Conning tower 6-inch
Complement	420
Hull	Wood sheathed and coppered

The *Eclipse* was the name ship of a class which included the *Diana*, *Dido*, *Doris*, *Isis*, *Juno*, *Minerva*, *Talbot*, and *Venus*. These followed the "Astraea" class but had 1,140 tons greater displacement and improved protection.

The *Eclipse* cost £279,345 to build. On completion she commissioned as flagship of the rear-admiral commanding the East Indies station, paying off in September 1900 for refit at Chatham. She served on the China station from May 1901 to September 1904 and went into reserve at Devonport during 1904-5. In September 1905 she became a cadets' training ship in the 4th cruiser squadron on the North America and West Indies station, paying off in July 1906 to remain in reserve at Portsmouth until commissioned to be attached to the Royal Naval College, Osborne, Isle of Wight. She served there from 1907 until 1912 and this photograph shows her lying off Cowes during this time.

The *Eclipse* joined the 3rd fleet at Portsmouth during 1912-13 and was at Devonport during 1913-14. Early in 1914 she escorted the submarines *AE 1* and *AE 2* to Singapore, returning to join cruiser force "G" in the Channel in August 1914. She captured the German small sailing ship *Johanna* in August and the *Orlanda* a month later. In February 1915 she transferred to the 12th cruiser squadron, Channel fleet, and in 1916 was reduced to a submarine depot ship. In 1918-19 the *Eclipse* was at Devonport and was sold in September 1921 to be broken up in Germany.

Talbot

BRITISH SECOND CLASS PROTECTED CRUISER 1896 *Plate 88*

Built	Royal Naval dockyard, Devonport
Laid down	March 1894
Launched	April 1895
Completed	September 1896
Dimensions	*Length overall* 370ft 4in
	Length waterline 364ft
	Breadth 54ft
	Draught 20ft 6in mean. 22ft loaded
Displacement	5,600 tons
Machinery	Twin screw
	Two 3-cylinder inverted triple-expansion engines by builders
	Eight single-ended boilers
	IHP natural draught, trials = 8,462 = 19.2 knots
	IHP forced draught, trials = 9,766 = 20 knots
Bunkers	Coal. 550 tons normal. 1,000 tons maximum
Endurance	7,000 miles at 10 knots. 5,600 miles at 12 knots. 2,800 miles at 17 knots
Armament	*Original*
	Five 6-inch quick-firers. 45 calibre
	Six 4.7-inch quick-firers
	Nine 12-pounders
	Six 3-pounders
	Two maxims
	Three 18-inch diameter torpedo tubes. One above water aft. One on each broadside submerged. Ten torpedoes carried
	Armament modified 1902
	Eleven 6-inch Mark VII quick-firers. 45 calibre
	Eight 12-pounder quick-firers
	One 3-pounder
	Remainder as above
Armour	*Deck* 3-inch – 1½-inch
	Gun shields 4½-inch
	Engine hatches 6-inch
	Conning tower 6-inch
Complement	420
Hull	Wood sheathed and coppered

The *Talbot* was another of the "Eclipse" class protected cruisers. She cost £273,856 to build and commissioned for the North America and West Indies station during 1896, returning to refit at Devonport during 1899.

88   TALBOT, BRITISH SECOND CLASS PROTECTED CRUISER 1896

In 1901 she sailed for the China station and served there until 1904. She paid off at Chatham in August 1904 for refitting and was in reserve at the Nore during 1905-6, then at Devonport during 1906-7. In 1907 she commissioned with the Channel fleet for two years and was attached to the 2nd battle squadron during 1909-10.

The *Talbot* was stationed at Hawlbowline from 1911-12 and joined the 3rd fleet during 1912, grounding in the Suez Canal that September. During 1913 she was attached to the 7th destroyer flotilla before rejoining the 3rd fleet at Devonport during 1913-14. In August 1914 the *Talbot* was serving with cruiser force "G" in the English Channel and captured the German ship *Goldbek*, 2,630 tons, off the Lizard in September. By February 1915 she was with the 12th cruiser squadron until April, when she arrived at the Dardanelles. From May 1916 to 1917 the *Talbot* patrolled the East African coast and was on the Cape of Good Hope station in 1918 with the *Charybdis* as flagship, eight French cruisers and one light cruiser, on trade-route patrol work.

The *Talbot* returned to the Mediterranean in 1919 and then to Devonport in November to be paid off. She was sold to Messrs Castle of Plymouth in July 1920 to be broken up, and was towed to Queenstown and was resold in December 1921 to Multilocular Shipbreaking Co of Stranraer, but was finally scrapped at Copenhagen in 1924.

Minerva

BRITISH SECOND CLASS PROTECTED CRUISER 1897 *Plate 89*

Built	Royal Naval dockyard, Chatham
Laid down	December 1893
Launched	September 1895
Completed	February 1897
Dimensions	Length overall 370ft 4in
	Length waterline 364ft
	Breadth 54ft
	Draught 20ft 6in mean. 23ft maximum
Displacement	5,600 tons
Machinery	Twin screw
	Two inverted 3-cylinder triple-expansion engines by builders
	Eight single-ended type boilers
	IHP natural draught, trials = 8,221 = 19.6 knots
	IHP forced draught, trials = 9,891 = 20.3 knots
Bunkers	Coal. 550 tons normal. 1,076 tons maximum
Armament	*Original*
	Five 6-inch quick-firers. 45 calibre
	Six 4.7-inch quick-firers
	Nine 12-pounders
	Six 3-pounders
	Two Maxims
	Three 18-inch diameter torpedo tubes. One above water aft. One on each broadside, submerged
	Armament modified 1902
	Eleven 6-inch Mark VII quick-firers. 45 calibre
	Eight 12-pounders
	Remainder as above
Armour	Deck 3-inch – 1½-inch
	Gun shields 4½-inch
	Engine hatches 6-inch
	Conning tower 6-inch
Complement	437
Bottom	Wood sheathed and coppered

The *Minerva* was completed in 1897 as another of the "Eclipse" class of second class protected cruisers. This included the *Eclipse, Talbot, Minerva, Venus, Juno, Diana, Dido, Doris,* and *Isis*. They each cost an average of £237,000.

The *Minerva* was commissioned for particular service in January 1897 and was at Chatham during 1897-9. She formed part of the training squadron during 1899-1900 and transferred to a cruiser squadron for 1900-3, paying off in November 1903 for a refit at Devonport dockyard. In June 1904 she sailed for the Mediterranean, where she served until 1912.

During 1912-13 she was attached to the 3rd fleet at Devonport and assisted in the salvage of the submarine *B 2* in October 1912. During 1913 the *Minerva* was attached to the 6th destroyer flotilla and was based at Portsmouth in 1913-14. In August 1914 she was one of the 11th cruiser squadron, which included the *Doris, Isis, Juno* and *Venus*, based on Ireland. Later she was transferred to the 5th cruiser squadron with the *Diana* and *Talbot* and on the 3rd September the *Minerva* sank the Austrian steamer *Bathori*, 2,200 tons, off Cape Finisterre.

By November 1914 she was at Suez, attached to the force of British and French warships defending Egypt and particularly the Suez Canal against Turkish invasion. She and the French *d'Entrecasteaux* were the only cruisers supporting the old British battleships *Swiftsure* at Port Said and *Ocean* at Suez, with the French coast defence battleship *Réquin* in Lake Timsah, the sloop *Clio* and the Indian marine armed transport *Hardinge*, six old torpedo boats and the armed ship *Himalaya*. Turkish army units did cross the canal but were repulsed.

In April 1915 the *Minerva* sank the Turkish destroyers *Demir-Hissar* off Chios. During 1916 she was on the China station and the following January was patrolling the Indian Ocean and the Red Sea. From March 1917 until 1919 the *Minerva* served off the East African coast with the *Talbot*.

89   MINERVA, BRITISH SECOND CLASS PROTECTED CRUISER 1897

90   FURIOUS, BRITISH SECOND CLASS CRUISER 1897

In May 1920 she was offered for sale at Queenstown, Ireland, and that November was sold to H. Austen Ltd for £20,000. Her hull was towed away to be scrapped abroad in January 1921.

Furious

BRITISH SECOND CLASS CRUISER 1897 *Plate 90*

Built	Royal Naval dockyard, Devonport
Laid down	June 1895
Launched	December 1896
Completed	1897
Dimensions	*Length between perpendiculars* 320ft
	Breadth 57ft 6in
	Draught 22ft normal. 24ft maximum
Displacement	5,750 tons
Machinery	Twin screw
	Two vertical triple-expansion engines by Earles Shipbuilding and Engineering Co
	Eighteen Belleville type boilers
	IHP natural draught, trials = 7,155 = 18.7 knots
	IHP forced draught = 10,272 = 20.1 knots
Bunkers	Coal. 500 tons normal = 3,800 miles at 10 knots. 1,175 maximum = 9,000 miles at 10 knots
Armament	*Original*
	Four 6-inch quick-firers
	Six 4.7-inch quick-firers
	Eight 12-pounder quick-firers
	Three 3-pounders
	Five machine-guns
	Two 18-inch diameter torpedo tubes. Submerged broadside
	Alterations 1903-4
	4.7-inch guns removed and 6-inch guns substituted, making ten 6-inch quick-firers
Armour	*Bow belt* 2-inch at forefoot, extended 40ft aft
	Decks 3-inch
	Gun positions 3-inch
	Engine hatches 4-inch
	Conning tower 8¾-inch
Complement	450

The *Furious* was one of a class of four protected cruisers which also included the *Arrogant*, *Gladiator* and *Vindictive*.

They were comparatively short ships for their displacement and were designed to act as rams, having an armoured stem and double rudders, the forward one being between the propellors, enabling them to turn in their own length. The principle of ramming an enemy is an old one in naval warfare and with the use of steam for propulsion a small number of special ram ships were built for various navies, though they were little favoured in the British Navy. However, most armoured and many other warships built between about 1865 and the outbreak of World War I were built with a ram bow, sometimes reinforced and occasionally unfortunately proving itself an efficient means of sinking ships of the same fleet in peacetime accidents. By the end of the 19th century it was rare for specially-built rams to be constructed, which makes the ordering of this class of cruiser more remarkable.

The *Furious* cost £280,772 and was sheathed and coppered for tropical service. Her main armament was changed during a refit in 1903-4, when the 4.7-inch guns were removed and replaced by 6-inch. By then her speed had dropped to 19.7 knots and coal consumption was heavy. This photograph was taken in 1902.

During 1912 the *Furious* was converted to a depot hulk. She was laid up when World War I commenced but in 1915 was brought into use as a training ship and renamed *Forte* to release her name for a new large cruiser, then building. She was sold in May 1923 to be broken up.

The *Arrogant*'s engines were worn out by 1911 and she was converted to a submarine depot ship. The *Gladiator* was sunk in collision during 1908. Only the *Vindictive* remained active during World War I, and she was to become famous for her exploit at Zeebrugge and later as an Ostend blockship in 1918.

Carlo Alberto

ITALIAN ARMOURED CRUISER 1898 *Plate 91*

Built	Royal Naval yard, Spezia
Laid down	February 1892
Launched	September 1896
Completed	May 1898
Dimensions	*Length between perpendiculars* 324ft 9in
	Breadth 59ft
	Draught 24ft 3in maximum
Displacement	6,500 tons
Machinery	Twin screw
	Two 3-cylinder triple-expansion engines by Ansaldo
	Eight cylindrical boilers
	IHP natural draught, trials = 8,221 = 17.7 knots
	IHP forced draught = 13,116 = 19.11 knots
Bunkers	Coal. 600 tons normal. 1,000 tons maximum. Plus some oil

91 CARLO ALBERTO, ITALIAN ARMOURED CRUISER 1898

fuel

Armament	Twelve 6-inch. 40 calibre
	Six 4.7-inch. 40 calibre
	Fourteen 6-pounders
	Ten 1-pounders
	Six machine-guns
	Torpedo tubes. Four 17.7-inch submerged (Modified to four above water in 1904)
Armour	Harvey
	Belt 6-inch amidships to 4½-inch at ends
	Deck 1½-inch
	Lower deck 6-inch
	Battery 6-inch
	Deck above main deck battery 2-inch
	Screen in battery 2-inch
	Gun shields 4½-inch
	Conning tower 6-inch
Complement	500

Completed during 1898, the *Carlo Alberto* and her almost identical sister ship *Vettor Pisani*, completed in 1899, were comparatively lightly armed for contemporary armoured cruisers.

Both ships led an uneventful life for several years. The *Carlo Alberto* was refitted during 1904 when her torpedo tubes were removed to above-water positions and the 1-pounder guns were reduced to six.

On September 29th 1911 Italy declared war on Turkey after her refusal to allow Italian occupation of Tripoli, then a Turkish posession. Italy then had a fleet far superior to the Turks' and there was little doubt she would dominate the Mediterranean. The *Carlo Alberto* at the time formed part of the training squadron under Rear-Admiral Ricci, which included the sister battleships *Sardegna*, *Re Umberto* and *Sicilia*. She sailed from Spezia on September 24th, attached to the 4th and 2nd divisions under Rear-Admiral P. Thaon di Revel, which were reinforced by the cruiser *Filiberto*, to blockade the coast of Tripoli.

During the bombardment of Tripoli on October 3rd 1911, the *Carlo Alberto* engaged the lighthouse battery and the mole fort in company with the battleship *Brin* and the *Filiberto;* an action continued the following day until the works were wrecked. The *Carlo Alberto* remained part of the blockading force and on April 10th she was part of a squadron to convoy troopships with a force of 12,000 troops to be landed on the Tripoli coast. The squadron included the battleships *Sardegna*, *Re Umberto* and *Sicilia*, with the cruiser *Marco Polo* and the scouts *Agordat* and *Coatit*, plus two auxiliary cruisers and six torpedo boats. After bombarding Turkish positions at Zuara, the army was successfully landed at Macbez, near the Tunisian frontier, and thereafter the active role of the Italian fleet shifted to the Aegean. The *Carlo Alberto* remained part of the fleet covering the central Mediterranean, still a useful cruiser capable of 18 knots.

Italy entered World War I on the side of Britain and France in May 1915 and the Italian fleet's principal task was to confine the powerful Austro-Hungarian fleet within the Adriatic. This was done with the help of the British, French and other allied warships.

After early Austrian action against shore positions and towns in the north Adriatic, the sea war settled down mainly to raids by the Austrians and occasional actions involving small craft, though there were also attacks and disasters involving capital ships on both sides.

The Italian army fighting on the Isonzo front at the head of the Adriatic was supported on the seaward flank by small destroyers which were covered by the *Carlo Alberto* and the old battleship *Sardegna*.

During 1917 the *Carlo Alberto* commenced conversion to a troop transport at the Royal Naval dockyard, Venice. Her armour was removed, a further deck constructed, and accommodation modified. She was completed during 1917-18 at the naval dockyard, Taranto, being renamed *Zenson*, and recommissioned in April 1918. She was discarded in June 1920 and was broken up.

Takasago

JAPANESE PROTECTED CRUISER 1898 *Plate 92*

Built	Armstrong Whitworth, Elswick
Laid down	April 1896
Launched	May 1897
Completed	May 1898
Dimensions	Length overall 387ft 6in
	Length between perpendiculars 360ft
	Breadth 46ft 6in
	Draught 17ft normal. 20ft 6in full load
Displacement	4,160 tons normal. 5,260 tons full load
Machinery	Twin screw
	Two triple-expansion engines by Humphrys and Tennant
	Four double-ended cylindrical type, and four single-ended cylindrical type boilers
	IHP natural draught = 10,850
	IHP forced draught = 12,990 = 22.9 knots
	Sea speed = 21 knots
Bunkers	Coal. 350 tons normal. 1,000 tons maximum
Armament	Two 8-inch quick-firers. 40 calibre. One forward and one aft
	Ten 4.7-inch quick-firers. 40 calibre. Single mounts
	Twelve 12-pounders. Single mounts
	Six 2½-pounders. Single mounts

92 *TAKASAGO, JAPANESE PROTECTED CRUISER 1898*

Five 18-inch diameter torpedo tubes above water

Armour   Harvey nickel steel
Deck 4½-inch – 2½-inch
8-inch gun shield fronts 4½-inch
8-inch gun shield sides 2½-inch
4.7-inch gun shields 2½-inch
Conning tower and hoists protected

Complement   425

The *Takasago* was a typical protected cruiser of contemporary British type, built by Armstrong to the design of Sir Philip Watts; she was one of the many "Elswick" cruisers built for foreign navies at the time. The hull was arranged with a forecastle and poop and had considerable freeboard. This, coupled with the weight of the two 8-inch guns (15 tons each) and the 4.7-inch guns (2 tons each) made her roll considerably and she was lively at sea. The armour was designed to resist 8-inch armour-piercing shells – a considerable protection. The fighting tops were fitted low on the masts to aid stability, and a pair of 2½-pounder guns were fitted in each.

The *Takasago* was slightly smaller but similar to the American-built protected cruisers *Kasagi* and *Chitose* of 1898. At the commencement of the war between Japan and Russia (1904-5) the *Takasago*, together with the *Kasagi*, *Yoshino* and *Takasago*, formed the third cruiser division of four ships under Rear-Admiral Deva whose flagship was the *Chitose*. This "greyhoud squadron" of fast cruisers saw much action.

The *Takasago*, with the *Chitose* and *Kasagi* and reinforced by *Tokiwa* and *Asama,* were in action with the Russian armoured cruiser *Bayan* off Port Arthur during the morning of April 13th 1904, and later that day the *Takasago* and others decoyed the Russian battleships *Petropavlovsk* and *Poltava* and the *Bayan* fifteen miles seaward of Port Arthur, allowing the Japanese battleships to attack.

The *Takasago* struck a Russian mine off Port Arthur on 12th December 1904 and sank next day with the loss of two hundred and seventy-four officers and men.

Rossia

RUSSIAN ARMOURED CRUISER 1898 *Plates 93 and 94*

Built   Baltic Works, St Petersburg
Laid down   1893
Launched   May 1896
Completed   1898
Dimensions   *Length overall* 480ft
               Length waterline 472ft

Breadth 68ft 6in
Draught 26ft 6in mean

Displacement 12,130 tons
Machinery   Triple screw
                Three vertical triple-expansion engines by builders
                Thirty-two Belleville type boilers
                IHP natural draught = 14,500 = 19 knots
                IHP forced draught, trials = 18,446 = 20.25 knots
Bunkers   Coal. 1,000 tons normal. 2,500 tons maximum. Plus oil fuel
                by 1902
Endurance   19,000 miles at 10 knots. 3,000 miles at 19 knots
Armament   *Original*
                Four 8-inch. Two forward and two aft. Single mounts
                Sixteen 6-inch quick-firers. Single mounts
                Six 4.7-inch quick-firers. Single mounts
                Twelve 12-pounder quick-firers
                Twenty 3-pounder quick-firers
                Sixteen 1-pounder quick-firers
                Six torpedo tubes. Above water. Bow, stern and broadside
                Four small torpedo boats carried
                Alterations after refit 1907
                Four 8-inch. 45 calibre. Two forward and two aft. Single
                mounts
                Fourteen 6-inch. Single mounts
                Two 3-pounders
                Two machine-guns
                All torpedo tubes removed 1907
Armour   Harvey steel
                Belt 354ft long, 7ft wide. 8-inch – 5-inch – 4-inch
                Bulkheads 6-inch
                Casemates 8-inch – 2-inch
                Deck 2½-inch
                Lower deck 6-inch
                Battery bulkheads 2-inch
Complement   735 – 833
Hull   Wood sheathed and coppered

The *Rossia* was built as an improvement on the armoured cruiser *Rurik* – a 10,950-ton ship completed in 1896 of similar characteristics. As she was probably intended for ocean commerce destruction the *Rurik* attracted great interest in major navies, and Britain constructed the large protected cruisers *Powerful* and *Terrible* (Plates 95 and 96) in reply. However, the *Rurik* suffered from mixed armament and from being heavily rigged as a barque for long passages, – a mistake in a ship capable of steaming at 18 knots and having good coal endurance.

The *Rossia* cost the equivalent of £900,000 to build. She did not attain her designed speed but could sustain about 18-19 knots for long periods.

93 ROSSIA, RUSSIAN ARMOURED CRUISER 1898

194   *94   ROSSIA, RUSSIAN ARMOURED CRUISER 1898*

She also suffered from mixed armament, which complicated ammunition-handling and magazines. The four 8-inch guns were powerful weapons with high muzzle-velocity and were the first 45-calibre guns of this type. When built, the *Rossia* had three masts, with fidded topmasts, capable of setting trysails and staysails. *Plate 93* shows her with this rig in 1902, painted in contemporary Russian naval colours. The *Gromboi*, an almost identical armoured cruiser, was launched in 1899.

At the commencement of the Russo-Japanese war in 1904, the *Rossia* was flagship of the Vladivostock squadron which included the *Gromboi* and *Rurik*, with the protected cruiser *Bogatyr* and destroyers. Captain Reitzenstein commanded the force and was succeeded by Rear-Admiral Yessen. Orders were to attack the Japanese coast and their sea communications with the mainland in attempts to detach Japanese warships from the main fleet. Occasional Japanese sorties were made off Vladivostok to tempt the Russian ships to battle, when they were under orders to remain within a day's steaming of the port.

On April 24th 1904 the *Rossia*, *Gromboi* and *Bogatyr*, with two torpedo boats, under Rear-Admiral Yessen, sank some small Japanese steamers. On June 12th the *Rossia*, *Gromboi* and *Rurik*, under Vice-Admiral Bezobrazoff, sailed to attack Japanese communications in the Gulf of Korea. On the 15th they were sighted off Shimonoseki by the Japanese cruiser *Tsushima* which sent wireless messages of alarm, despite Russian jamming. The Russian ships sank three Japanese transports, one carrying heavy artillery, and despite attempted interception by four armoured cruisers, returned safely to Vladivostok, seizing a British collier carrying coal for Japanese forces on the way.

These cruisers continued to raid Japanese shipping during June and July. On 14th August 1904 the *Rossia*, *Gromboi* and *Rurik* were in the Straits of Korea to assist in the attempted break-out of the major Russian fleet blockaded in Port Arthur. However, the attempt failed and Rear-Admiral Yessen was confronted by the Japanese armoured cruisers *Idzumo*, *Adzuma*, *Tokiwa* and *Iwate*, under Admiral Kamimura. The Japanese manoeuvred to cut off escape to Vladivostok and the Russian ships were out-gunned. The *Rossia* was engaged by the *Adzuma* and fires were started on all the Russian ships, which fought bravely. The *Rurik* began to lose speed and eventually was disabled. The others turned to her aid but the *Rossia* was seriously on fire and most of her guns were silenced. The *Gromboi* was considerably damaged and as the *Rurik* was sinking under heavy fire the *Rossia* and *Gromboi* escaped when Japanese manoeuvring gave the opportunity. They continued to fire at the pursuing Japanese ships, and the *Iwate* suffered a great explosion and fire. The Russian ships steamed slightly faster than the Japanese and as they drew away firing slackened. The Japanese ships returned to pound the sinking *Rurik* which went down gallantly.

This engagement, which became known as the battle of the Japan Sea, cost the *Rossia* forty-seven killed and a hundred and fifty-three wounded. She sustained thirty-one shell hits but although hull damage looked serious it was soon repaired. However, all but four of her 8- and 6-inch guns were irreparable. She was afterwards refitted and reboilered during 1907, and *Plate 94* shows her attending the 1911 Coronation naval review at Spithead. The mainmast was removed and the photo shows the forward starboard 8-inch gun cleared away and trained outboard and the after one on the sponsons which supported them. The multiplicity of guns, tumble home in the sides, and bow armament were interesting features.

Russia and Germany were at war on 1st August 1914 and the Russian Baltic fleet was active to defend the eastern Baltic against the larger German fleet. There were raids and mining forays, some brisk actions between major ships and constant submarine and patrol activity. Both fleets were busy supporting land forces and covering movement by sea of men and supplies.

The *Rossia* served with the Baltic fleet with five other armoured cruisers which were among the most active ships. On September 1st-2nd the *Rossia* was with the cruisers *Bogatyr*, *Oleg* and *Rurik* (built in 1910), under Admiral von Essen. They swept westward and contacted German patrolling cruisers, pushing the German scouts back to the level of Windau.

Later, many cruisers, including the *Rossia*, were fitted for minelaying. On July 12th 1915 the minelayers *Rossia*, *Oleg*, *Bogatyr* and *Rurik*, supported by the armoured cruisers *Bayan* and *Admiral Makaroff*, made a minelaying sortie. The *Rossia* laid ninety-eight of her hundred mines north of Arcona, and when returning she encountered the small German cruiser *Undine* but managed to remain unobserved to preserve the secrecy of her mission and returned to base at Uto. On 25th July the German patrol cruiser *Gazelle* was severely damaged by striking one of her mines.

Thereafter the *Rossia* seems to have been inactive and may have been laid up due to age and the need of crews for the many smaller craft coming into service. On December 5th 1917 an armistice was agreed between Germany and Russia. The Russian warships had acquitted themselves well against a technically superior enemy.

The *Rossia* was scrapped at a Russian port during 1922.

Powerful

BRITISH FIRST CLASS PROTECTED CRUISER 1898 *Plate 95*

Built	Naval Construction and Armaments Company, Barrow in Furness
Laid down	1894
Launched	May 1895
Completed	1898

95   POWERFUL, BRITISH FIRST CLASS PROTECTED CRUISER 1898

Dimensions	Length overall 538ft
	Length between perpendiculars 500ft
	Breadth 71ft
	Draught 27ft normal. 30ft maximum
Displacement	14,440 tons
Machinery	Twin screw
	Two vertical three-stage compound engines by builders
	Forty-eight Belleville type water-tube boilers
	IHP full power trials = 25,000 = 22.81 knots
Bunkers	Coal. 1,500 tons normal. 3,000 tons maximum. 400 tons oil fuel added 1903
Endurance	3,000 miles at 22 knots. 4,500 miles at 17½ knots. 7,000 miles at 14 knots
Armament	Original
	Two 9.2-inch. 40 calibre. One forward and one aft
	Twelve 6-inch quick-firers. 40 calibre. Eight on main deck.
	Four on upper deck
	Sixteen 12-pounder quick-firers
	Twelve 3-pounder quick-firers
	Two maxims
	Four 18-inch diameter torpedo tubes. Submerged
	Increased 1902-3
	Four 6-inch quick-firers added in casemates on upper deck
Armour	Deck 6-inch – 34 inch Harvey steel
	9.2-inch gun mounts 6-inch
	Casemates for 6-inch guns 6-inch – 2-inch
	9.2-inch gun shields 6-inch
	Conning tower 12-inch
Complement	894
Hull	Wood sheathed and coppered

The design of the *Powerful* and her sister ship *Terrible (Plate 96)* resulted from the British Admiralty's exaggerated impression of the potential of the Russian cruiser *Rurik*, which was intended primarily as a commerce destroyer, should the need arise.

These huge protected cruisers were Britain's extreme long-range trade-route protectors. A third ship of the class was projected but never built, though the fleet gave her the tentative name of *Horrible*. When new, these were the longest warships in any fleet and probably the most expensive to maintain, as their fighting potential was small. Machinery spaces occupied 240ft of the 538ft overall length and the turning circle was 1,100 yards.

In spite of their faults they were striking ships which, with four funnels and high freeboard, had considerable "flag showing" value and public appeal; qualities which were useful in contemporary naval policy.

The *Powerful* cost £674,879 to build and sailed for the China station under Captain the Hon. H. Lambton in 1898. She was the largest ship in

the area and augmented a current show of British force there. She suffered many machinery defects on the passage out and coal consumption was high – about 25 tons per day at full power. As a result of naval and parliamentary agitation she later ran experimental steaming trials and eventually consumption was reduced to 18 tons per day.

The *Powerful* returned to England for refitting during 1902-3, when additional 6-inch guns were mounted. However, these ships were by then obsolete and subsequently spent much time in reserve.

By 1913 the *Powerful* was on the subsidiary list and during 1914 became a training hulk at Devonport, serving throughout World War I. In November 1919 she was renamed *Impregnable* and was not sold to be broken up until 1929.

This photograph was taken in 1902.

Terrible

BRITISH FIRST CLASS PROTECTED CRUISER 1898 *Plate 96*

Built	J. and G. Thompson Ltd, Clydebank
Laid down	1894
Launched	1895
Completed	1898
Dimensions	Length overall 538ft
	Length waterline 520ft
	Breadth 71ft
	Draught 27ft mean. 31ft maximum
Displacement	14,200 tons normal. Approximately 19,000 tons full load
Machinery	Twin screw
	Two reciprocating 4-cylinder triple-expansion engines by Thompson
	Forty-eight Belleville type water-tube boilers
	IHP natural draught, 30 hours trials = 18,493 = 20.96 knots
	IHP forced draught, 4 hours trials = 25,572 = 22.4 knots
Bunkers	Coal. 3,000 tons. Originally burned 21 tons per hour at full speed
Armament	Original
	Two 9.2-inch. 40 calibre. One forward and one aft
	Twelve 6-inch quick-firers. 40 calibre
	Eighteen 12-pounders
	Twelve 3-pounders
	Two maxim machine-guns
	Four 18-inch torpedo tubes. Submerged
	Alterations 1903
	A further four 6-inch guns were added and two 12-

96 *TERRIBLE, BRITISH FIRST CLASS PROTECTED CRUISER 1898*

Armour   pounders removed
        Deck 6-inch – 3-inch
        Casemates and barbettes 6-inch
        Conning tower 6-inch
Complement   894

The *Terrible* exceeded her designed displacement and draught. Her coal consumption was high at full power and caused concern for bunker supplies when cruising. Her propellers were both arranged to turn inwards for convenience in engine-room layout, which made her unhandy at low speed. She carried her way for five miles from full speed to stop, without putting engines astern. The water tube boilers, of an early type unfamiliar to naval personnel, gave much trouble.

The *Terrible* was first commissioned for the 1897 manoeuvres but immediately afterwards paid off into reserve, probably because of the need for alterations to ensure full effectiveness and also because of scarcity of men to man the large numbers of warships coming into service.

In 1898 she was commissioned for special service under Captain G. Robinson, but developed machinery and other defects, so was not included in the 1899 summer manoeuvres. During 1899 Captain Percy Scott, a noted gunnery expert, took command with orders to relieve the *Powerful* on the China station. The Boer war broke out during her passage and in November 1899 she landed a naval brigade from amongst her crew to operate with the Natal field force in the relief of Ladysmith. Some of her guns were mounted on improvised field carriages and under Captain Scott's direction were used effectively against the Boers.

During March 1900 the *Terrible* proceeded to China where in June she again landed a naval brigade to assist in the northern Chinese operations against the Boxer rebellion. The *Terrible* returned to pay off at Portsmouth in October 1902 after a distinguished commission and proceeded to John Brown's shipyard at Clydebank for a refit lasting eighteen months, during which a further four 6-inch guns were added in casemates on the upper deck amidships. A major refit was then unusual in a private yard.

A special service commission followed, from June to December 1904. Then she went into reserve until August 1905 when she recommissioned to escort the battleship *Renown*, conveying the Prince and Princess of Wales, later King George V and Queen Mary, on a visit to India. Next year, because of her unusual amount of 'tween deck space, she was used to carry troops to China, returning with others and with government officials. Five hundred miles out from Hong Kong one tail shaft broke and the propeller was lost. She came home on the other propeller. .

The *Terrible* then went into the reserve division of the Home fleet at Portsmouth and although she could still steam at 20 knots, was regarded as of little fighting value compared with her maintenance costs. During 1911 she replaced the cruiser *Argonaut* as parent ship of the 1st division of the Home fleet, where her extensive below-deck space again provided useful accommodation. After short service at the Nore station she went into reserve at Pembroke and in June 1914 was ordered to be paid off and prepared for sale. However, outbreak of war intervened and she was retained. During 1915 she was recommissioned for the Dardanelles campaign as a troopship under Captain C. Hughes-Onslow, but her neglected machinery caused frequent breakdown.

The *Terrible* returned to become part of the artificer training establishment HMS *Fisgard*. In September 1919 she was paid off but later replaced a wooden ship as *Fisgard III*. With the upper deck housed in, one mast removed and one funnel remaining, she served until 1931 when the *Fisgard* became a shore establishment. The *Terrible* was then considered as a replacement for the training ship *Arethusa*, but she was too large, so was broken up at Newport during autumn 1932.

Niobe

BRITISH FIRST CLASS PROTECTED CRUISER 1898 *Plate 97*

Built	Vickers, Barrow-in-Furness
Laid down	December 1895
Launched	February 1897
Completed	1898
Dimensions	*Length overall* 462ft 6in
	Length between perpendiculars 435ft
	Breadth 69ft
	Draught 25ft 3in mean. 27ft 6in maximum
Displacement	11,000 tons
Machinery	Twin screw
	Two 4-cylinder inverted triple-expansion engines by builders
	Thirty Belleville boilers
	IHP 30 hours trial = 12,961 = 19.3 knots
	IHP 8 hours full power trial = 16,834 = 20.5 knots
Bunkers	Coal. 1,000 tons normal. About 2,000 maximum
Endurance	About 4,000 miles at 17 knots. 2,200 miles at full speed
Armament	Sixteen 6-inch quick-firers. Two in shields on foredeck. Two in shields on poop. Twelve in side casemates
	Fourteen 12-pounder quick-firers
	Twelve 3-pounders
	Two Maxims
	Three 18-inch diameter torpedo tubes. Two submerged
Armour	*Deck* 4-inch – 2½-inch
	Casemates for 6-inch guns 4½-inch – 2-inch
	Gun shields 4½-inch – 2-inch
	Ammunition hoists 2-inch

97   NIOBE, BRITISH FIRST CLASS PROTECTED CRUISER 1898

Conning tower 12-inch
Complement 677
Hull bottom Wood sheathed and coppered

The *Niobe* was one of four large protected cruisers ordered by the 1895-6 naval estimates to be ships of a size between the "Powerful" type and the earlier *Blenheim* and *Blake*, 9,000-tonners built in 1890. Known as the "Diadem" class they were designed under the supervision of Sir William White to be fit to engage the Russian commerce-raiding type cruisers *Rurik* or *Rossia* and their predecessors. However, there was criticism of their armament of 6-inch guns when many foreign cruisers were mounting 8- and 10-inch. The *Niobe*, *Andromeda*, *Diadem* and *Europa* cost about £600,000 each. Their four funnels and pole masts without fighting tops made them rather bare-looking ships but they steamed well and were good sea boats, though the turning circle was about 1,000 yards.

The *Niobe* commissioned with the Channel fleet during 1898 and served temporarily at the Cape in March 1900, returning to the Channel fleet and then escorting the SS *Ophir* from England to India in 1901, when she was acting as a royal yacht. The *Niobe* refitted at Barrow in 1903-4 and went into reserve at Devonport during 1905, becoming flagship of the rear-admiral, reserve squadron, and refitting in reserve in 1908.

She commissioned in April 1909 with the 4th division of the Home fleet at Devonport, paying off in September 1910 when she was sold to the Canadian government for £215,000 and arrived at Halifax the following month to become flagship of the Royal Canadian naval forces. She stranded off Cape Sable in July 1911 and was towed off by HMS *Cornwall* to be repaired at Halifax.

The *Niobe* was at New York in October 1914 and received an unexpected addition to her crew of British naval reservists from the crew of the racing yacht *Shamrock IV*, challenger for the Americas Cup, which arrived at New York after declaration of war. She remained with the Royal Canadian Navy until February 1915 but then transferred to the 4th cruiser squadron which included the *Suffolk*, *Berwick*, *Bristol*, *Essex*, *Lancaster*, one armed merchant cruiser and the old battleship *Glory*, engaged on Atlantic patrols and escort duties. However, the *Niobe*'s machinery was wearing out and in October 1915 she was paid off at Halifax and was disarmed to become a depot ship. She was damaged by the explosion at Halifax in December 1917 of the munition ship *Mont Blanc*. The *Niobe* was sold out of the service in 1920 and was broken up at Philadelphia, USA in 1922.

Ariadne

BRITISH FIRST CLASS PROTECTED CRUISER 1900 *Plate 98*

Built	J. and G. Thomson, Clydebank, Scotland
Laid down	October 1896
Launched	April 1898
Completed	1900
Dimensions	*Length overall* 462ft 6in
	Length between perpendiculars 435ft
	Breadth 69ft
	Draught 25ft 3in mean. 26ft maximum
Displacement	11,000 tons
Machinery	Twin screw
	Two 4-cylinder inverted triple-expansion engines by builders
	Thirty Belleville type boilers
	IHP natural draught = 18,000 = 20.75 knots
	IHP 8 hours trials = 19,156 = 21.5 knots
	IHP 30 hours trials = 14,046 = 20.1 knots
Bunkers	Coal. 1,000 tons normal. About 2,000 tons maximum
Endurance	About 4,000 miles at 17 knots
Armament	Sixteen 6-inch quick-firers. 45 calibre. Two on foredeck. Two aft. Twelve in side casemates
	Twelve 12-pounder quick-firers
	Four 3-pounder quick-firers
	Two Maxims
	Three 18-inch diameter torpedo tubes. One aft above water. Two submerged broadside
Armour	*Deck* 4-inch – 2½-inch
	6-inch gun casemates 6-inch
	Gun shields 4½-inch
	Conning tower 12-inch
Complement	677
Hull bottom	Wood sheathed and coppered

Despite the defects of the "Diadem" type the Admiralty ordered four slightly improved sister ships with half a knot more speed. These were the *Ariadne*, *Spartiate*, *Amphitrite* and *Argonaut*, laid down under the 1896-7 naval estimates as the last first class protected cruisers to be built for the Royal Navy. They were vulnerable ships of 11,000 tons displacement as designed, but approaching 12,000 tons in fighting trim.

The *Ariadne* first commissioned with the North American and West Indies squadron from 1902-5, serving as flagship of the vice-admiral off Venezuela during 1902-3 and joining the 4th cruiser squadron as flagship in 1904. In August 1905 she went into reserve at Plymouth, as

98   ARIADNE, BRITISH FIRST CLASS PROTECTED CRUISER 1900

99   HAI CHI, CHINESE PROTECTED CRUISER 1899

the type were becoming obsolete, and remained laid up until 1912-13 when she transferred to the 3rd fleet. She became a stokers' training ship at Portsmouth until 1914 when she was moved to Devonport.

During 1916 she was converted to a minelayer with accommodation for four hundred mines and armament reduced to four 6-inch and one 4-inch guns. During 1917 she laid seven hundred and eight mines in the Heligoland Bight. On 26th July 1917 the *Ariadne* was torpedoed off Beachy Head by the *UC 65* and sank with loss of thirty-eight lives. The survivors were rescued by the paddle minesweeper *Lorna Doone*.

This photograph of the *Ariadne* was taken in 1900 and shows the large number of boats carried by ships at the time. Although steaming easily here, the *Ariadne* and her sisters burned about 16 tons of coal per hour at full power.

Hai Chi

CHINESE PROTECTED CRUISER 1899 *Plate 99*

Built	Armstrong, Elswick
Launched	January 1898
Completed	1899
Dimensions	*Length overall* 396ft
	Breadth 46ft 10in
	Draught 16ft 9in mean. 19ft maximum
Displacement	4,300 tons
Machinery	Twin screw
	Two 4-cylinder triple-expansion engines
	Four single-ended and four double-ended Hawthorn, Leslie type boilers
	Natural draught, trials = 22.5 knots
	IHP forced draught, trials = 17,000 = 24 knots
Bunkers	Coal. 400 tons normal. 990 tons maximum
Endurance	8,000 miles at economical speed
Armament	Two 8-inch Elswick type, quick-firers. 45 calibre. One forward and one aft
	Ten 4.7-inch Elswick type, quick-firers. 45 calibre. Single mounts at sides
	Twelve 3-pounder quick-firers
	Four 1-pounders
	Six Maxims
	Five 18-inch diameter torpedo tubes. Above water
Armour	Harvey nickel steel
	Protective deck 5-inch amidships to 1½-inch at ends
	8-inch gun shields 4½-inch
	8-inch gun hoists 4-inch

Conning tower 6-inch
Complement 374

The *Hai Chi* and her sister ship *Hai Tien* may be compared to the similar Argentine cruiser *Buenos Aires*, also built by Armstrong's at Elswick, in 1895 *(Plate 83)*. Like dozens of Elswick warships they were designed and built under the direction of Philip Watts.

Watts had spent his early life in British Admiralty service, rising to become a naval constructor. In May 1885, at the age of thirty-nine, he resigned in order to succeed William White as naval architect and general manager at Armstrong's. White himself had been appointed Director of Naval Construction at the Admiralty, and Watts was later to succeed him here also.

When built, the *Hai Chi* was painted black, white and buff but is seen here in grey at 1911 Coronation naval review, showing China's dragon ensign at Spithead. When new these cruisers were the major force of the Chinese fleet which also included three new, German-built cruisers, five torpedo gunboats, a destroyer and some smaller craft. Unfortunately, the ships were then generally poorly officered, but the fleet's fighting potential was good. The Japanese fleet had decisively defeated the Chinese in a war of 1894-5 and remained their likeliest antagonists.

By 1913 a Chinese republican regime reorganised the ministry of marine and was generally supported by the Navy. Chinese warships were often involved in the then turbulent internal politics of their country. During 1919-20 the *Hai Chi* was at Canton in a force including the cruisers *Chao Ho* and *Hai Chen*, two destroyers, four gunboats, a despatch vessel and a transport, whose crews were loyal to the secessionist local government which had declared independence. This represented about half the effective Chinese fleet, but during 1920 the ships returned to the Peking government flag.

The *Hai Chi* fought against the Japanese during the war of the 1930's, and was sunk in action during 1937.

Szigetvar

AUSTRO-HUNGARIAN PROTECTED CRUISER 1901 *Plate 100*

Built	Stabilimento Tecnico, Pola
Laid down	June 1899
Launched	October 1900
Completed	1901
Dimensions	*Length* 313ft 6in
	Breadth 39ft 4in
	Draught 14ft 6in mean. 17ft maximum
Displacement	2,437 tons

100 SZIGETVAR, AUSTRO-HUNGARIAN PROTECTED CRUISER 1901

Machinery	Twin screw
	Two triple-expansion engines by builders
	Eight Yarrow type boilers
	Designed IHP natural draught = 5,000 = 17.5 knots
	Designed IHP forced draught = 7,200 = 20 knots
Bunkers	Coal. 300 tons normal. 475 tons maximum
Endurance	2,000 miles at 10 knots
Armament	Eight 4.7-inch quick-firers. 40 calibre. One forward and one aft. Two port and two starboard, single mountings on sponsons. One port and starboard amidships
	Ten 3-pounders
	Four machine-guns
	Two 17.7-inch diameter torpedo tubes. Above water
Armour	Deck amidships 2-inch
	Deck ends 1.2-inch
Complement	305
Hull	Wood sheathed and coppered

The *Szigetvar* and her sister ships *Zenta* and *Aspern* each cost about £155,000 in contemporary values. They were sometimes referred to as "torpedo cruisers" and were primarily designed for Adriatic and Mediterranean service with the then rapidly expanding Austro-Hungarian fleet – a force with efficient ships and personnel.

In the author's opinion this is one of the best photographs ever taken of a warship, evoking the smartness of a trim little ship on her mettle during a visit to a foreign country, seen in the jobble of tide in Cowes Roads during 1902.

During 1913 it was proposed to replace the reciprocating engines of the *Szigetvar* and *Aspern* by turbines and to give them new boilers, but this does not seem to have been done. A crow's nest was added to the fore mast when Austro-Hungary entered World War I in 1914. By 1917 both ships were equipped for minelaying.

The *Zenta* was sunk by French warships off the Dalmatian coast on August 16th 1914. One hundred and thirty of the crew were killed and one hundred and eighty-three captured.

The *Szigetvar* saw little action other than patrols and sorties. In 1920 she was assigned to Britain as an ex-enemy warship, to be broken up.

Hyacinth

BRITISH CRUISER 1901 *Plate 101*

Built	The London and Glasgow Shipbuilding Co, Glasgow
Laid down	January 1897
Launched	October 1898
Completed	1901
Dimensions	Length overall 373ft
	Length between perpendiculars 350ft
	Breadth 54ft
	Draught 20ft 6in mean. 22ft maximum
Displacement	5,650 tons
Machinery	Twin screw
	Two 4-cylinder vertical triple-expansion engines by builders
	Eighteen Belleville type boilers
	IHP 30 hours trials = 7,718 = 17.34 knots
	IHP 8 hours trials = 10,536 = 19.4 knots (foul bottom)
	Later made 21 knots
Bunkers	Coal. 600 tons normal. 1,100 tons maximum
Endurance	5,500 miles at 10 knots. 3,000 miles at 17 knots
Armament	Eleven 6-inch quick-firers. One forward, two aft. Four on upper deck each broadside
	Nine 12-pounders
	Six 3-pounders
	Two Maxims
	Two 18-inch diameter torpedo tubes, submerged. Seven torpedoes carried
Armour	Deck 3-inch – 1½-inch
	Gun shields 3-inch
	Engine hatches 5-inch
	Conning tower 6-inch
Complement	437
Hull	Wood sheathed and coppered for foreign services

The *Hyacinth* and her sisters *Hermes* and *Highflyer* were ordered under the 1896-7 naval estimates, the *Hyacinth* costing £282,741.

This photograph was taken in 1902, her last year in Victorian colours. The fidded topmasts and yards contrast with her quick-firing armament and the semaphores.

She was one of an active class and in 1914 the *Hyacinth* formed part of the Cape of Good Hope squadron, with the old cruisers *Astraea* and *Pegasus*. She could then steam at 19.7 knots and was a useful ship. About August 1st the squadron encountered the German light cruiser *Köningsberg* off Dar-es-Salaam but as war was undeclared could do nothing. The German cruiser increased speed to 22 knots and soon left the shadowing British ships astern. During her subsequent cruise along the East African coast, the *Köningsberg*, pursued by the old battleship *Goliath* and the cruisers *Hyacinth*, *Dartmouth*, *Weymouth*, *Pyramus*, *Pioneer*, *Fox* and *Astraea*, took one prize and sank the old British cruiser *Pegasus* at Zanzibar. She finally took refuge up the Rufiji River where she was shelled and blockaded until she was destroyed by the monitors *Mersey* and *Severn* in 1915.

101 HYACINTH, BRITISH CRUISER *1901*

102   SUTLEJ, BRITISH ARMOURED CRUISER 1902

The *Hyacinth* remained on the Cape and East African station throughout the war. In 1920 she was placed on the disposal list and was under consideration for sale to India. However, during 1923 she was sold to be scrapped at Swansea.

Sutlej

BRITISH ARMOURED CRUISER 1902 *Plate 102*

Built	John Brown and Co Ltd, Clydebank
Laid down	August 1898
Launched	November 1899
Completed	1902
Dimensions	*Length overall* 472ft
	Length waterline 454ft
	Breadth 69ft 6in
	Draught 25ft 9in mean. 28ft maximum
Displacement	11,700 tons
Machinery	Twin screw
	Two 4-cylinder triple-expansion engines by builders
	Thirty Belleville type boilers
	IHP forced draught, trials = 21,261 = 21.77 knots
Bunkers	Coal. 800 tons normal. 1,600 tons maximum
Armament	*Original*
	Two 9.2-inch. One forward and one aft
	Twelve 6-inch quick-firers. In side casemates
	Fourteen 12-pounder quick-firers
	Three 3-pounders
	Eight machine-guns
	Two 18-inch diameter torpedo tubes. Submerged
	Alterations
	Four 6-inch quick-firers added in casemates during 1903
	Four 6-inch guns removed during 1916
Armour	Krupp
	Belt 6-inch. 230ft long by 11ft 6in wide
	Forward side 2-inch
	Bulkheads 5-inch
	Deck 3-inch – 1½-inch
	Barbettes 6-inch
	Turrets 6-inch
	Casemates 5-inch
	Conning tower 12-inch
Complement	700. 745 as flagship

The *Sutlej* and her sisters *Cressy*, who gave her name to the class, *Aboukir*,

Bacchante, *Euryalus* and *Hogue* (*Plate 104*) were ordered under the 1897-8 supplementary naval estimates as the first British armoured cruisers since the "Orlando" type of 1886. The design initiated several subsequent classes of similar and improved ships which formed the major force of British cruiser squadrons for fifteen years. This class were the first British warships in which the wooden fittings were impregnated with a fire-preventitive.

This photograph was taken in 1902 and shows the new *Sutlej* as of purposeful but stark appearance. Windsails are rigged in place of ventilating cowls – a rather impractical method of ventilating at sea. The twin-funnelled picket boat is under the after derrick and the after mast semaphore and signalling gaff were still the longest-range method of communication.

The *Sutlej* joined the Channel fleet in May 1902 and on 18th September 1903 ran down and sank the barque *Charles Chalmers* in the North Sea. She refitted at Chatham during 1904 and sailed for the China station in November, serving there until May 1906. Later that year she commissioned as a training ship for boy seamen with the 4th cruiser squadron on the North America and West Indies station, returning to reserve at Chatham for a short period during 1907, before rejoining the station until 1909, when she returned to become flagship of the 3rd fleet at Devonport, 1909-10. A boiler explosion killed two men during manoeuvres in July 1910.

The *Sutlej* laid in reserve at Devonport during 1911-12, then commissioned with the 6th cruiser squadron until 1914, going into reserve in June but joining the 9th cruiser squadron in August and transferring to the 11th cruiser squadron, based on Ireland, in February 1915. She was at Santa Cruz in February 1916 and rejoined the 9th cruiser squadron in September 1916, on the West Coast of Africa station.

The *Sutlej* was reduced to an accommodation ship at Rosyth in January 1918, being renamed *Crescent*, changing to *Hogue* in 1919.

She was sold in May 1921 to Thomas Ward and was towed to Belfast from Rosyth in March 1924 and from there to Preston, where she was scrapped.

The 1902 Coronation Naval Review

Plate 103

A four-funnelled British cruiser steams slowly to her review station between lines of battleships and cruisers attending the Coronation naval review of King Edward VII in 1902. Steam pinnaces, yachts, passenger steamers and tugs view and attend the fleet which was gathering for the last time in Victorian colours and with ships unaffected by wireless and submarines.

103 *THE 1902 CORONATION NAVAL REVIEW*

Hogue

BRITISH ARMOURED CRUISER 1902 *Plate 104*

Built	Vickers Ltd, Barrow-in-Furness
Laid down	July 1898
Launched	August 1900
Completed	1902
Dimensions	*Length overall* 472ft
	Length waterline 454ft
	Breadth 69ft 6in
	Draught 25ft 9in mean. 28ft maximum
Displacement	11,700 tons
Machinery	Twin screw
	Two 4-cylinder triple-expansion engines by builders
	Thirty Belleville type boilers
	IHP forced draught, trials = 21,065 = 22.1 knots
Bunkers	Coal. 800 tons normal. 1,600 tons maximum
Armament	*Original*
	Two 9.2-inch. One forward and one aft
	Twelve 6-inch quick-firers. In side casemates
	Fourteen 12-pounder quick-firers
	Three 3-pounders
	Eight machine-guns
	Two 18-inch diameter torpedo tubes. Submerged
	Alterations 1903
	Four 6-inch quick-firers added in casemates
Armour	Krupp
	Belt 6-inch. 230ft long by 11ft 6in wide
	Forward side 2-inch
	Bulkheads 5-inch
	Deck 3-inch – 1½-inch
	Barbettes 6-inch
	Turrets 6-inch
	Casemates 5-inch
	Conning tower 12-inch
Complement	700. 745 as flagship

The *Hogue* was another armoured cruiser of the Cressy class, a sister of the *Sutlej (Plate 102)*.

She cost about £790,000 to build and when new steamed at 17 knots for four days during manoeuvres, afterwards running a full power trial and achieving 22.4 knots. This was her best speed and it consumed 17 tons of coal per hour.

The *Hogue* commissioned with the Channel fleet in November 1902. On 11th March 1904 she collided with the steamship *Meurthe* off Europa

Point and returned home to pay off in May and refit at Devonport. She served on the China station from the end of 1904 until May 1906, then commissioned as a training ship for boy seamen with the 4th cruiser squadron on the North America and West Indies station. Returning in May 1908, she paid off into reserve at Devonport until 1909.

She joined the 3rd division of the Home fleet at the Nore during 1909 and a bunker explosion killed two men in October. During 1912 she paid off for refitting at Chatham until 1913, when she recommissioned during September with the Home fleet at the Nore.

This photograph was taken in 1912 and clearly shows the side casemates and anchoring arrangements.

At the outbreak of World War I the *Hogue* was a unit of the 7th cruiser squadron, under the command of Rear-Admiral A. H. Christian. This included the sister ships *Aboukir*, *Euryalus* and *Cressy*, with the *Bacchante* and the light cruiser *Amethyst*. On 28th August 1914 this squadron formed part of a force led by the battlecruisers *Lion*, *Queen Mary*, *Princess Royal*, *Indomitable* and *New Zealand*, supported by six light cruisers, submarines and destroyers, which carried out a North Sea sweep against German warships, attempting to draw the German fleet out for a major battle. This culminated in the battle of the Heligoland Bight. At the close of this indecisive action in which the Germans lost three light cruisers and one destroyer, the British light cruiser *Arethusa* was severely damaged and was taken in tow by the *Hogue*, which brought her safe to port.

On September 22nd 1914 the *Hogue*, *Aboukir* and *Cressy* were patrolling between the German minefields in the southern North Sea and the Dutch coast, steaming at 10 knots, two miles apart. The destroyer screen had to return to port due to bad weather and the ships were not zig-zagging against submarine attack. The First Lord of the Admiralty, Winston Churchill, had a few days earlier ordered that these ships should not be risked on patrol without destroyer protection, but the decision was not passed on by naval staff. The cruisers' movements were repetitive and the German staff were well aware of their position.

At 6.30 am they were about 30 miles west of Ymuiden when an explosion shattered the side of the *Aboukir,* which began to sink. It was assumed she had struck a mine as no submarine had been sighted. Orders had not then been given for British warships not to approach a sinking ship and the *Hogue* immediately steamed to the aid of the *Aboukir* but was hit by two torpedoes, sinking ten minutes later. The *Aboukir* sank twenty-five minutes after being torpedoed. The *Cressy* came up and remained stopped to pick up survivors. As she began to move away a torpedo struck, quickly followed by a second. She capsized and quickly sank.

The three ships were sunk by German submarine *U 9*, commanded by Lieutenant-Commander Weddigen; a 500-ton boat with a crew of twenty-eight, she had four torpedo tubes and carried six torpedoes. Weddigen reported that the cruisers were easy targets, and the action stimulated German determination to develop submarine warfare.

104   HOGUE, BRITISH ARMOURED CRUISER 1902

It demonstrated that the older warships were vulnerable to torpedo attack as all three had their watertight doors closed. Later, similar old ships were fitted with bulges at the waterline for anti-torpedo and mine protection.

This disaster was not published in the British press as its effect on national morale would have been severe. Sixty-two officers and one thousand three hundred and ninety-seven men were lost; sixty officers and seven hundred and seventy-seven men were saved, largely by the efforts of the Dutch steamers *Flora* and *Titan*.

Asama

JAPANESE ARMOURED CRUISER 1899 *Plate 105*

Built	Armstrong, Elswick
Laid down	November 1896
Launched	March 1898
Completed	March 1899
Dimensions	*Length overall* 442ft
	Length between perpendiculars 408ft
	Breadth 67ft 3in
	Draught 24ft 6in mean
Displacement	9,750 tons normal. 10,519 tons full load
Machinery	Twin screw
	Two 4-cylinder triple-expansion engines by Humphrys and Tennant
	Cylindrical type boilers
	IHP natural draught, trials = 14,718 = 20.87 knots
	IHP forced draught, trials = 20,550 = 23 knots
Bunkers	Coal. 600 tons normal. 1,406 tons maximum
Endurance	4,600 miles at 11.6 knots
Armament	Four 8-inch quick-firers. 40 calibre. Two forward and two aft
	Fourteen 6-inch quick-firers. 40 calibre. Single mounts
	Twelve 12-pounder quick-firers. 40 calibre. Single mounts
	Eight 2½-pounder quick-firers. Single mounts
	Five 18-inch diameter torpedo tubes. One bow, above water. Four submerged
Armour	Harvey nickel steel
	Belt 7-inch – 3½-inch. 280ft long by 7ft wide
	Bulkheads 3½-inch
	Barbette bases 6-inch
	Casemates and turrets 6-inch
	Deck 2-inch
	Citadel to maindeck 5-inch
	Ammunition hoists 3-inch
	Conning tower 14-inch
Complement	500

The *Asama* and her sister ship *Tokiwa* was ordered under the second Japanese naval expansion programme of March 1897, which authorised construction of six armoured cruisers as a compromise between a further squadron of battleships, which would have been ideal, and the need for more cruisers.

The intention was for one of these ships to be built in Japan, but eventually all were ordered in Europe, and the *Asama* and *Tokiwa* were to be built by Armstrong's at Elswick under the design direction of Sir Philip Watts. They were based on the Chilean cruiser *O'Higgins*, launched in 1897, but with additional armour and improved armament.

The ships were fast and both exceeded design speed on three-hour, full-power trials. They were economical when built but declined until by 1903 the *Asama* could only steam at 19 knots.

This photograph was taken in 1902, and although the negative is damaged it shows the principal features of the *Asama*, which saw more action than most armoured cruisers.

At the outbreak of the Russo-Japanese war in February 1904 the *Asama* was one of six armoured cruisers forming the 2nd division of the 2nd squadron of the fleet, which was a formidable force manned by good seamen and commanded by skilled and dedicated officers, many of whom had experienced naval warfare in the conflict with China ten years previously.

When hostilities commenced the *Asama*, under Rear-Admiral Uriu, with protected cruisers and destroyers, was detailed to convoy transports landing Japanese troops in Korea and to deal with Russian warships at Chemulpo. When the Russian protected cruiser *Variag* and the old cruiser *Korietz* came out, the *Asama*'s fierce gunfire drove them back. the *Variag* severely damaged. Both were subsequently scuttled.

In April the *Asama* was in action off Port Arthur, the Russian naval base, supporting the *Tokiwa* and several protected cruisers which intercepted the Russian cruisers *Bayan*, *Diana*, *Askold* and *Novik*. These were driven back to Port Arthur, which the Japanese were attempting to block with scuttled ships.

The *Asama* was detached from patrol duty in March to demonstrate off Vladivostok, with other ships.

After the fall of Port Arthur in January 1905, the *Asama*, *Adzuma* and other craft were sent to blockade Russian warships at Vladivostok, to prevent them breaking out to join the Russian 2nd Pacific squadron (popularly known as the Baltic fleet) which were steaming to the east from the Baltic on an unprecedented voyage half-way round the world, to attempt to defeat the Japanese in their home waters. The two fleets met at the battle of Tsushima on May 27th-28th 1905, when the Japanese triumphed over the stubbornly fighting Russian fleet, whose

105   ASAMA, JAPANESE ARMOURED CRUISER 1899

task had been hopeless from the start.

The *Asama* joined the main fleet on the day before the battle. She and the armoured cruiser *Iwate* engaged the Russian *Sissoi Veliki* and set her on fire, but soon after the *Asama* received concentrated fire from the rear Russian ships and a 12-inch shell smashed the steering-gear and caused serious leaks. Other hits followed and she retired to make repairs, afterwards rejoining Admiral Kamimura's squadron of five armoured cruisers. She was steering badly, drew 5ft more than normal and could only steam slowly. The eleven hits killed three and wounded thirteen. It was her last action in that war.

By 1912 the *Asama* needed reboiling and could only steam at about 16 knots.

In December 1914 she grounded on the Pacific coast of Central America and was badly damaged, but was refloated and repaired. She remained rated as a first class cruiser into the early 1920's and was later rated as a coast defence ship and sometimes acted as a training ship.

Like many Japanese warships, the *Asama* was long lived, being broken up by the Hitachi Shipbuilding Co in 1946.

Chacabuco

CHILEAN PROTECTED CRUISER 1902 *Plate 106*

Built	Armstrong, Elswick
Laid down	1897
Launched	1898
Completed	1902
Dimensions	*Length between perpendiculars* 360ft
	Breadth 46ft 6in
	Draught 17ft normal. 20ft maximum
Displacement	4,300 tons
Machinery	Twin screw
	Two triple-expansion engines
	Cylindrical double-ended boilers
	IHP forced draught = 15,500 = 24 knots
Bunkers	Coal. 300 tons normal. 1,028 tons maximum
Armament	*Original*
	Two 8-inch Elswick guns. 40 calibre. One forward and one aft
	Ten 4.7 quick-firers. 40 calibre. Single mounts in side sponsons
	Twelve 12-pounder quick-firers
	Six 3-pounder quick-firers. In tops
	Five 18-inch torpedo tubes. One above water in bow. Four submerged
	Rearmed 1941
	Six 6-inch
	Ten 20-mm
	Twlve machine-guns
	Two depth-charge throwers
Armour	Harvey nickel steel
	Deck 4½-inch – 1¾-inch
	8-inch gun shields 4½-inch fronts. 2½-inch sides
	4.7-inch gun shields 2½-inch
	Conning tower 5-inch
Complement	400

The *Chacabuco* was laid down at Elswick as a speculation, designed as an ideal general-purpose protected cruiser. The firm were at the height of their cruiser-building fame, producing ships for many foreign countries from Chile to China.

The *Chacabuco* was a sister to the Japanese cruiser *Takasago* (Plate 92) and was purchased by Chile in February 1902 when nearly complete, being first named *Fourth of July*. This photograph was taken when she was fresh from the shipyard. With raked funnels and well-proportioned masts and hull-profile she was a smart and efficient-looking ship. The length of the 8-inch guns was great in comparison to the size of the gunhouses.

She joined a fleet comprising the old battleship *Captain Prat* and the coast defence ship *Huascar*, the Elswick-built armoured cruisers *O'Higgins* and *Esmeralda*, the protected cruisers *Ministro Zenteno* and *Blanco Encalada*, and the small cruisers *Presidente Errazuriz* and *Presidente Pinto*, backed by torpedo gunboats, destroyers, torpedo boats and smaller ships to form a balanced and efficient force.

During 1903 it was persistently rumoured that the *Chacabuco* and the armoured cruiser *Esmeralda* were to be sold to a private American buyer. Nothing came of this but it almost caused international complications as the Russian-Japanese war was in progress and the ships would probably have been re-sold to the Russians.

The *Chacabuco* pursued a peaceful existence in the smartly-manned and maintained Chilean fleet which, despite the vagaries of politicians, has always enjoyed close ties with the British Navy since the service in Chile of Admiral Lord Cochrane during 1818-22.

The *Chacabuco* retained her speed for many years and could make 23 knots in 1920. She was thoroughly refitted in 1941 when the old guns were removed and replaced by six 6-inch and others, and the bridge was rebuilt. She had the distinction of being the last Elswick cruiser to exist and was not discarded by the Chilean Navy until 1952 when she was broken up.

106   CHACABUCO, CHILEAN PROTECTED CRUISER 1902

107   MONTCALM, FRENCH ARMOURED CRUISER 1902

Montcalm

FRENCH ARMOURED CRUISER 1902 *Plate 107*

Built	La Seyne
Laid down	January 1898
Launched	March 1900
Completed	1902
Dimensions	*Length overall* 459ft
	Length waterline 452ft 8in
	Breadth 63ft 8in
	Draught 24ft 6in. 25ft maximum
Displacement	9,516 tons
Machinery	Triple screw
	Three vertical triple-expansion engines by builders
	Twenty Normand type boilers
	IHP forced draught, trials = 18,200 = 20.85 knots
Bunkers	Coal. 1,020 tons normal. 1,650 tons maximum. Plus some oil fuel
Endurance	6,500 miles and 10,000 miles at 10 knots. 1,200 miles and 1,920 miles at full speed
Armament	Two 7.6-inch. In single turrets, forward and aft
	Eight 6.4-inch quick-firers. In side casemates
	Four 3.9-inch quick-firers. In shields
	Sixteen 3-pounder quick-firers
	Six 1-pounder quick-firers
	Two 18-inch diameter torpedo tubes. Submerged
Armour	Harvey nickle steel
	Belt 7ft 6in wide. 6¾-inch – 4-inch
	Upper belt 3.7-inch – 2.4-inch
	Bulkhead aft 3.4-inch
	Protective deck 2-inch plus splinterdeck
	Turrets 8-inch
	Turret bases 5-inch
	Casemates 4-inch
	Conning tower 6-inch
Complement	612

By 1900 many armoured cruisers were built for the French Navy, four classes being constructed at once in continuing development from the *Dupuy de Lôme* of 1891 and her successors such as the *Pothuau (Plate 84)*. The *Montcalm* was a sister ship of the *Dupetit-Thouars* and *Amiral de Gueydon*. She cost the equivalent of £902,809. Like many French warships, she had triple screws; an arrangement unusual in most navies.

Plate 107 was taken in 1902 and shows the single turrets of the two 7.6-inch guns and the four-port casemates of the 6.4-inch. The widely-spaced boiler-rooms and peculiarly shaped funnels were features of many contemporary French cruisers and battleships. She was fitted with mechanical ventilation, evident by lack of cowls and the trunking fitted amidships and close to the funnels. The tall topmasts and long fore gaff were for signalling.

The *Montcalm* could be compared with the British armoured cruisers *Aboukir*, *Cressy*, *Hogue* and *Sutlej*, and the Russian *Rossia (Plates 93, 102, 104)*.

After service in home waters the *Montcalm* was stationed in the Pacific, where there were French island colonies. At the outbreak of World War I she formed part of a force under Rear-Admiral Sir G. E. Patey, commanding the Australian station with his flag in the battlecruiser *Australia* and accompanied by the *Montcalm* and the small cruisers *Melbourne*, *Psyche*, *Pyramus* and *Philomel*. On August 30th 1914 these ships escorted transports with New Zealand troops to the German base at Apia on the island of Samoa. The wireless station was captured and a small garrison established.

At this time a powerful squadron of German cruisers under Admiral von Spee was cruising the Pacific to destroy British and allied commerce, and Patey's force was able to concentrate only because Japanese warships were patrolling allied trade routes in the Pacific. Von Spee learned of the attack on Samoa and steamed there to attack the squadron, but they had sailed, so he steamed east to Tahiti and subsequently into the east Pacific, where he took part in the battle of Coronel and subsequently met his end in the battle of the Falklands.

During 1915 the *Montcalm* joined other units in the Suez Canal for defensive operations and from January to September 1916 was refitting. She sailed for the 4th cruiser squadron, West Indies, and spent from July to November 1918 as an escort for troopship convoys across the Atlantic from America to France. Later she participated in the Baltic and Murmansk operations of 1918-19.

She again refitted during 1920, though the armoured cruiser was an obsolete type. Appearance remained unchanged but she was re-rated as a second class cruiser – one of fifteen armoured cruisers still forming the principal French cruiser strength. In October 1928 the *Montcalm* was removed from the effective list but was maintained as a floating barracks until 1931, when she became a school tender. In October 1937 she was renamed *Tremintin* and was dismantled during World War II.

Donegal

BRITISH ARMOURED CRUISER 1903 *Plate 108*

Built	Fairfield Shipbuilding and Engineering Co, Glasgow
Laid down	February 1901

108   DONEGAL, BRITISH ARMOURED CRUISER *1903*

Launched	September 1902
Completed	1903
Dimensions	*Length overall* 463ft 6in
	Length waterline 440ft
	Breadth 66ft
	Mean draught 24ft 6in
Displacement	9,800 tons
Machinery	Twin screw
	Two 4-cylinder inverted vertical triple-expansion engines by builders
	Thirty-one Niclausse type boilers
	IHP = 22,154 = 23.7 knots
Bunkers	Coal. 800 tons normal. 1,600 tons maximum. Plus 400 tons oil fuel
Armament	Fourteen 6-inch Mark VII quick-firers. 45 calibres. Two in twin turrets forward and aft, the remainder in side casemates
	Ten 12-pounder quick-firers
	Three 3-pounders
	Eight pompoms
	Eight machine-guns
	Two 18-inch diameter torpedo tubes. Submerged. Nine torpedoes carried
Armour	Krupp steel
	Belt 4-inch. 330ft long by 11ft 6in wide
	Forward side 2-inch
	Deck 2-inch – ¾-inch
	Main deck 1¼-inch
	Aft bulkhead 5-inch
	Barbettes and turrets 5-inch
	Casemates 4-inch
	Conning tower 10-inch
Complement	678

The *Donegal* was one of the "County" class armoured cruisers which comprised the *Bedford, Berwick, Cornwall, Cumberland, Donegal, Essex, Kent, Lancaster, Monmouth,* and *Suffolk*. These were contemporary with the larger "King Alfred" class (*Plate 109*), but were smaller and perhaps more economical ships. The *Essex* and *Kent* were laid down under the 1898 supplementary naval estimates and the remainder by the 1899 and 1900 estimates. Each cost about £775,000 to build.

These ships were an answer to the growing numbers of foreign armoured cruisers and were intended to work either with a battle fleet or for trade-route protection and patrol. All except one exceeded contract speed in service and the *Suffolk* almost achieved 25 knots.

The mounting of two pairs of 6-inch guns in twin turrets forward and aft was an advance on previous practice of having one large gun at each end. The lower casemate guns, seen in this photograph taken in 1911, were of little practical value, being ineffective in a seaway. It also shows the elaborate rigging for early wireless transmitting; useful to a cruiser but very vulnerable in action.

The "County" class were active fleet units and the *Bedford* was wrecked during 1910.

In 1914 the *Donegal* was with the 6th cruiser squadron, Grand fleet. During 1915 she was transferred to the 7th cruiser squadron, still with the Grand fleet. Late in 1916 the *Donegal* was sent to the West Africa station with the *King Alfred* and *Sutlej (Plates 109 and 102)* supporting the cruisers *Astraea, Sirius* and *Highflyer*, with two armed merchant cruisers. During 1917 she sailed for the North America and West Indies station which was then largely made up of armoured cruisers, and remained there until after the war when she transferred to the China station before returning to be paid off.

The *Donegal* was sold in July 1920 to Castle, the shipbreakers, who resold her to the Granton Shipbreaking Co for demolition.

The "County" class saw much war service. The *Monmouth* was sunk at the battle of Coronel in 1914, but was avenged by the *Kent*, perhaps the most famous of the class, which chased and sank the German cruiser *Nüremburg* at the subsequent battle of the Falkland Islands on 8th December 1914.

The "County" class were followed by six very similar ships known as the "Devonshire" class which had two single 7.5-inch guns forward and aft in place of the twin turret 6-inch.

King Alfred

BRITISH ARMOURED CRUISER 1903 *Plate 109*

Built	J. and G. Thomson, Clydebank, Glasgow
Laid down	August 1899
Launched	October 1901
Completed	1903
Dimensions	*Length overall* 529ft 6in
	Length between perpendiculars 500ft
	Breadth 71ft
	Draught 26ft mean. 28ft maximum
Displacement	14,100
Machinery	Twin screw
	Two 4-cylinder triple-expansion inverted engines by builders
	Forty-three Belleville type water tube boilers
	IHP 8 hours full power trial = 30,893 = 23.46 knots
Bunkers	Coal. 1,250 tons normal. 2,500 tons maximum

109 KING ALFRED,
BRITISH ARMOURED
CRUISER 1903

Endurance	2,150-4,300 miles at 19 knots. 1,150-2,300 at full speed
Armament	Two 9.2-inch. 45 calibre. One forward and one aft
	Sixteen 6-inch Mark VII quick-firers. 45 calibre. In side casemates
	Fourteen 12-pounder quick-firers
	Three 3-pounder quick-firers
	Nine machine-guns
	Two 18-inch diameter torpedo tubes. Submerged
Armour	*Belt* 6-inch. 400ft long by 11ft 6in wide
	Forward side 2-inch
	Deck 3-inch – 2-inch
	Main deck 1-inch
	Aft bulkheads 8-inch
	Barbettes 6-inch
	Casemates 5-inch
Complement	900

The *King Alfred* was one of the "Drake" class of armoured cruisers, which also included the *Leviathan* and the *Good Hope*, sunk at the battle of Coronel in 1914. They succeeded the "Cressy" class *(Plate 104)* and proved to be good sea boats, but very lively. All exceeded contract speed but burned about 20 tons of coal per hour. Each cost just over £1,000,000 and when new were hailed as "mighty cruisers" by the First Lord of the Admiralty, though the lower side-mounted 6-inch guns were unable to be used in a seaway and as a result many condemned the ships as failures.

They were succeeded by a new style armoured cruiser in the *Black Prince* and *Duke of Edinburgh* which had six 9.2-inch and ten 6-inch guns, making them almost second class battleships. These were intended for service with a battle fleet and fostered several improved classes. However, the *Black Prince* type did not prove altogether superior to the "Drakes"; during a cruiser "action" in the 1906 naval manoeuvres, in big seas, the *Black Prince* was quickly "disabled" by the *Leviathan*.

This photograph of the *King Alfred* was taken in 1911 when she was wearing the flag of admiral of a cruiser squadron. At the commencement of World War I she was with the 6th cruiser squadron of the Grand fleet. By 1915 she was on the West Coast of Africa station with the armoured cruiser *Essex* and two armed merchant cruisers, patrolling the southwestern Atlantic on commerce protection; part of a thinly spread series of similar cruiser squadrons covering the central Atlantic, the Cape and Indian Ocean. The *King Alfred* remained there until 1917 as part of what became the 9th cruiser squadron, when the importance of the area increased. By January 1918 she was on the North America and West Indies station for convoy work and patrols with twelve other armoured cruisers, serving there until the war's end.

The *King Alfred* was sold during 1920 to be broken up in Holland.

Hamidieh (ex Abdul Hamid)

TURKISH PROTECTED CRUISER 1904 *Plate 110*

Built	Armstrong, Whitworth and Co, Elswick
Laid down	1902
Launched	1903
Completed	1904
Dimensions	*Length overall* 368ft
	Length waterline 345ft
	Breadth 47ft 6in
	Draught 16ft mean
Displacement	3,830 tons
Machinery	Twin screw
	Two 4-cylinder triple-expansion engines by Hawthorn, Leslie and Co
	Cylindrical Niclausse type boilers
	IHP forced draught, trials = 12,500 = 22.2 knots
Bunkers	Coal. 275 tons normal. 750 tons maximum
Endurance	5,550 miles at 10 knots
Armament	Two 5.9-inch. 45 calibre. One forward and one aft
	Eight 4.7-inch. Single mounts on broadsides
	Two 3-pounders
	Two 1-pounders
	Two 18-inch diameter torpedo tubes. Above water
Armour	*Deck* 4-inch – 1½-inch
Complement	302

The *Hamidieh*, completed in 1904, was built as the *Abdul Hamid*, her name being changed about 1907. She was a slightly larger cruiser than the *Medjidieh* which had been built for the Turkish Navy by Cramp of Philadelphia, USA, and completed in 1903. The two ships formed the principal cruiser strength of the fleet for forty years and when new were its only modern major warships.

At the outbreak of war with Italy in September 1911 the *Hamidieh* was at sea with the newly-acquired battleships *Torgut Reis* and *Heireddin Barbarossa (Plates 21 and 23)*, the light cruiser *Medjidieh* and several destroyers. When warning of war was received on the 30th the squadron returned to the Dardanelles, and did not venture out for some time.

By October 1912 Turkey was at war with Greece, Montenegro and Bulgaria. On October 19th the *Hamidieh*, with the *Heireddin Barbarossa*, *Torgut Reis*, the old ironclad *Messudieh* and four torpedo boats, appeared off the Bulgarian port of Varna in the Black Sea and shelled the town and coastal installations.

On November 21st the *Hamidieh* was torpedoed off Varna by one of four Bulgarian torpedo boats making a daylight attack. She was badly

110 HAMIDIEH, TURKISH PROTECTED CRUISER 1904

damaged and just reached Constantinople with the foredeck awash.

On December 3rd Montenegro and Bulgaria signed an armistice with Turkey, but Greece fought on. The *Hamidieh* was repaired and on January 14th 1913 slipped out of the Dardanelles, through the blockading Greek warships, and gained the open sea unobserved. She steamed to the small island of Syra, where the Greeks had large magazines. After shelling these without result, she turned her guns on the Greek armed merchant cruiser *Macedonia*, until she was burnt out. The raid alarmed the Greek government and the approaches to Piraeus were fortified, but the *Hamidieh* was short of coal and steamed for Port Said, arriving on January 19th. However, the British authorities ruled she could only stay for twenty-four hours, so she steamed through the Suez canal into the Red Sea, remaining there until February 9th, when she came back through the canal and steamed via Beirut to Malta, which she entered under stress of weather on February 15th.

Meanwhile the old Greek armoured ship *Psara* and four destroyers had been sent in pursuit of the *Hamidieh*, but the *Psara* was much too slow to catch the cruiser.

On March 11th the *Hamidieh* appeared off Durazzo, in the Adriatic, and shelled an army camp of Greece's Serbian allies. Next day she fired on a Greek transport off San Giovanni di Medua, while Serbian troops were embarking. A few field guns were landed and the Serbs drove her off with shelling. She then sailed for Alexandria to coal, then to Beirut and on to the Suez canal, re-entering the Red Sea on April 9th, where she remained, a constant source of anxiety to Greek communications, until the war ended on April 24th 1913.

When Turkey joined the side of Germany and Austro-Hungary in 1914, the *Hamidieh* was first active in the Black Sea against the Russians. On October 29th 1914 she took part with the *Medjidieh* and the German battlecruiser *Goeben* and cruiser *Breslau*, which had run through the Mediterranean at the Commencement of hostilities to reinforce the Turkish fleet, in a series of actions against shore installations, shelling the port of Theodosia in the Crimea.

On April 3rd 1915 the *Hamidieh* and *Medjidieh* were cruising in the Black Sea off Otchakoff when the *Medjidieh* struck a mine and sank. Thereafter the *Hamidieh* saw no further action in the war. She remained rated as a cruiser in the Turkish fleet into the 1940's, and with the *Goeben*, renamed *Yavuz*, and the raised and restored cruiser *Medjidieh*, she formed the main force, backed by modern destroyers.

The *Hamidieh* was broken up soon after 1945.

Francesco Ferruccio

ITALIAN ARMOURED CRUISER 1905 *Plate 111*

Built	R. Arsenale di Venezia (Royal Naval yard, Venice)
Laid down	September 1899
Launched	April 1902
Completed	September 1905
Dimensions	*Length between perpendiculars* 344ft
	Breadth 59ft 9in
	Draught approximately 24ft maximum
Displacement	7,350 tons
Machinery	Twin screw
	Two triple-expansion engines by Hawthorn Guppy
	Twenty-four Niclausse type boilers
	IHP = 13,635 full power = 19 knots approximately
Bunkers	Coal. 650 tons normal. 1,215 tons maximum
Armament	*Original*
	One 10-inch. 45 calibre. In turret aft
	Two 8-inch. 45 calibre. In turret forward
	Fourteen 6-inch. 40 calibre. Ten in side casemates. Two pairs on upper deck
	Ten 12-pounder quick-firers
	Six 3-pounders
	Two 1-pounders
	Four 18-inch diameter torpedo tubes. Above water in casemates
	Armament 1920
	One 10-inch
	Two 8-inch
	Four 6-inch. 40 calibre
	Six 14-pounders
	Five 14-pounder anti-aircraft
	One machine-gun
	Two 3-pounders
	Four 18-inch diameter torpedo tubes
Armour	Terni
	Belt 6-inch – 3-inch
	Deck 1½-inch
	Lower deck redoubt 6-inch
	Barbettes 6-inch
	Turrets 6-inch
	Battery 6-inch
	Battery bulkheads 5-inch
	Conning tower 6-inch
Complement	517

111   FRANCESO FERRUCCIO, ITALIAN ARMOURED CRUISER 1905

In 1894 the Italian Navy ordered a medium-sized armoured cruiser, designed under the direction of Engineer General Eduardo Masdea, which was the prototype of a very successful class of ship intended to steam at about 19 knots, with good armour protection and to mount one 10-inch and two 8-inch long-range guns, backed by a strong secondary armament. A balanced profile was achieved, the single mast being amidships, funnels equally spaced and armament evenly distributed.

The first ship, to be named *Giuseppe Garibaldi*, was bought on the stocks by Argentina and was completed as the *General Garibaldi* in 1896. The Argentine also purchased her sister ships *Varese I*, which became the *General San Martin*, and the *Varese II*, renamed *General Belgrano*. A fourth ship intended for the Italian fleet and also to have been named *Giuseppe Garibaldi*, was sold to Spain to become the *Cristobal Colon*. Still incomplete, she was sunk in the battle of Santiago de Cuba in 1898.

The fifth ship for Italy, yet another projected "Garibaldi", was also sold to Argentina during construction and became the *General Pueyrredon*.

In a flurry of naval expansion Argentina ordered two more ships of the type in 1902 but both were sold to Japan before completion in 1904; the *Mitra* becoming the *Kasuga* and the *Roca* the *Nisshin*. Both fought with distinction during the war with Russia 1904-5, and proved the ability of the design.

In 1898 the Italian fleet's first ship of the type to be delivered was laid down and completed as the *Varese*. The *Giuseppe Garibaldi* followed; both were completed during 1901. A third ship, the *Francesco Ferruccio*, was commenced at the naval yard. Venice during 1899, but was not completed until 1905. She incorporated amendments including the fitting of distinctive funnels with large cowls similar to those on the two Japanese ships. She cost about £600,000 to build in contemporary values.

During the Italian-Turkish war which commenced in September 1911, the *Francesco Ferruccio* served in the 4th division of the fleet with her two sister ships, the smaller cruiser *Marco Polo*, the torpedo gunboat *Coatit* and the minelayer *Minerva*. The three armoured cruisers participated in the bombardment of Tripoli by the Italian fleet on October 3rd-4th 1911, sustaining no damage.

On February 20th 1912 the *Francesco Ferruccio* and her sisters sailed from Tobruk for Beirut, where they demanded the surrender of the old Turkish corvette *Avni-Illah* and the gunboat *Angora*. Receiving no reply the Italian ships opened fire, sinking the *Avni-Illah* as she returned the fire. The *Angora* retreated up the harbour to shelter behind neutral shipping, but the *Garibaldi* followed her in and sank her with gunfire.

The three cruisers then joined the remainder of the 4th division and the 1st and 2nd divisions of the Italian fleet at the island of Stampalia, which they had seized as a base from which to attack the Dardanelles. On April 18th 1912 the battleships *Vittorio Emmanuele*, *Roma*, *Napoli*, *Regina Margherita*, *St Bon* and the cruisers *Francesco Ferruccio*, *Varese*, *Garibaldi* and *Vettor Pisani*, joined by a decoy squadron of the cruisers *San Marco*, *Pisa* and *Amalfi* appeared off the Dardanelles, where a Turkish squadron was anchored under Nagara. A Turkish destroyer came out to scout, but was chased back to the shelter of the forts, which the Italian ships then bombarded for two hours, firing 342 rounds at Orkanieh and Kum Kaleh, but inflicting little actual damage. The Turks replied but no hits were made on the Italian ships, though the *Francesco Ferruccio* had her ensign shot away.

Afterwards the Turks closed the Dardanelles with mines and the Italian fleet kept a close blockade until the war's end.

During World War I the *Francesco Ferruccio* served mainly in the Adriatic, where the *Garibaldi* was torpedoed during July 1915. In February 1916 the *Francesco Ferruccio* and *Varese*, with four "Roma" class battleships, were sent to Valona, on the opposite shore of the vital Straits of Otranto. The port had been occupied by the Italians in July 1915 and was now being threatened by Bulgarian and Austrian troops. The ships gave supporting fire to the Italian army.

The *Francesco Ferruccio* remained effective after the war and in 1924 became a training ship, relieving her sister ship *Varese*. She served until 1929 and was then laid up until sold in April 1930 to be scrapped.

This photograph was taken in 1911 and shows the *Francesco Ferruccio* at saluting stations. The casemate guns are run in and the shutters closed.

Fylgia

SWEDISH ARMOURED CRUISER 1906 *Plate 112*

Built	Bergsund Co, Finnboda
Laid down	1903
Launched	1905
Completed	1906
Dimensions	*Length waterline* 377ft 8in
	Breadth 48ft 6in
	Draught 20ft 8in maximum
Displacement	4,980 tons
Machinery	Twin screw
	Two triple-expansion engines by builders
	Twelve Yarrow type water-tube boilers
	IHP trials = 12,440 = 22.7 knots
Bunkers	Coal. 350 tons normal. 900 tons maximum
Endurance	5,770 miles at 10 knots
Armament	Eight 5.9-inch. 45 calibre. Twin mounts in four turrets.
	Two amidships, one forward and one aft
	Fourteen 6-pounders
	Two 1-pounders
	Two 18-inch diameter torpedo tubes. Submerged
Armour	*Belt* 4-inch

112 FYLGIA, SWEDISH ARMOURED CRUISER 1906

Deck 2-inch
Turrets 5-inch – 2-inch
Turret hoists 4-inch
Conning tower 4-inch
Complement 321

It is difficult to understand what prompted the construction of this single armoured cruiser of the Swedish fleet, the major force of which then comprised armoured coast defence ships averaging about 3,500 tons.

The *Fylgia* exhibited German influence in design and cost the equivalent of £385,700 to build. She had a progressive arrangement of main armament in four paired turrets mounted one forward and one aft and one on each beam amidships. However, these contrasted with the side sponson-mounting of the 6-pounders which would have been ineffective in a seaway.

This photograph, taken in 1911, shows her well-poroportioned and smart appearance. The large bow badge was then carried by all major Swedish warships; a unique feature. The *Fylgia* retained this colour-scheme until about 1920.

She saw no action throughout her existence, Sweden being neutral during both World Wars.

The *Fylgia* was thoroughly refitted during 1927 when two 3-inch anti-aircraft guns were fitted. She remained rated as a cruiser until 1940, when she commenced reconstruction as a cadet training ship which lasted until 1941. She emerged with only two funnels and a modernised appearance.

By 1950 the *Fylgia* had served her purpose and was converted to a gunnery target. She is believed to have been sunk by practice gunnery in 1955, somewhere off the Swedish coast.

TORPEDO BOATS
TORPEDO GUNBOATS
TORPEDO BOAT DESTROYERS

A self-propelled torpedo was evolved in 1860 by Commander Luppis, an Austrian naval officer who four years later engaged the assistance of Robert Whitehead, the English manager of an engineering works at Fiume, to solve technical problems in its perfection. This fish-shaped weapon was eventually improved and had a motor operated by compressed air which drove a propeller at one end. It had depth setting and stabilising arrangements, and a rudder to keep it running towards a target.

The invention became established as the most practical type of torpedo and was at first launched from carriages on the decks of large warships. Then a tube was used which projected the torpedo, with its propeller revolving, more accurately towards its target.

These torpedoes were intended to be used in action between major warships but during the 1870's the torpedo boat was introduced: as a fast, small, light-draught craft with the torpedo as main armament, whose function was to attack and destroy or disable larger warships in harbour or at sea. Speed was essential, both for approach and escape and to increase operating range in darkness, which was the favoured time of attack; and size was critical – if too large they became unhandy and a target for defensive gunfire; if too small they were unable to keep the sea in moderately rough conditions.

The earliest fast torpedo boat was built in 1873 for the Norwegian Navy by Thornycroft, at Chiswick on Thames: a 53ft long steam launch capable of 15 knots and carrying a spar torpedo, a charge on a long spar which was thrust against an enemy ship's waterline to explode, leading to almost certain loss of boat and crew.

The British Admiralty took little interest in torpedo craft until the Russian Navy acquired many of them during 1877, when Russia was at war with Turkey and Britain seemed likely to become involved. That year the 85ft long torpedo boat *Lightning* was ordered from Thornycroft, designed to fire a self-propelled torpedo from a tube at her bow. She could steam at 19 knots with 460 IHP and attracted such attention that a dozen similar boats were quickly ordered from several yards, the principal builders in England being Thornycroft and Yarrow on the Thames,

and White's at Cowes. One of Yarrow's boats soon achieved 22 knots, but self-propelled torpedoes were still directionally and mechanically unreliable and were not regarded as serious weapons in the British fleet, though France and Russia built large numbers of torpedo boats. By the mid-1880's the principal theory of torpedo boat use was that of attack in force. Multiple attack would confuse an enemy and since the cost of the boats and the size of crew were comparatively small, it was considered acceptable to risk boats in this way.

Need for seakeeping led to the building of a larger British type, such as the 127ft 6in Torpedo boat *No 27 (Plate 113)* and *No 57 (Plate 114)*. This type of craft was also intended to act as a defensive screen against attacks by enemy torpedo boats on a British fleet blockading the French coast, then still regarded as a probable situation in war. For this role the boats were fitted with mountings for light guns, but could be converted to attack craft by the installation of torpedo tubes.

The boats proved efficient during naval manoeuvres but the speed of larger warships rapidly increased to equal or surpass these torpedo boats and many naval harbours constructed new breakwaters with heavily-guarded boomed entrances, making attack almost impossible. However, the existence of torpedo boats nevertheless caused potential enemies considerable expense on defence. Night attacks on roadsteads or on fleets at sea or on exposed anchorages became the torpedo boats' principal hope of success against major ships and for this reason they were usually painted black all over.

During 1880-4 the British Admiralty ordered some second class, 17-knot torpedo boats for coastal defence, carrying a torpedo in dropping gear on each side; a method also used in large steam pinnaces carried on board battleships and large cruisers.

In 1885 Russia owned one hundred and fifteen large torpedo boats, France had fifty and Britain only nineteen. Suddenly the Admiralty ordered sixty more and Yarrow built those with the first turtle-backed foredeck to throw off head seas.

Two years later more boats were ordered, with a length of 134ft 6in, and *No 80* of this type reached 23 knots with 1,540 IHP. British torpedo boat flotillas grew more slowly after that. They were considered very minor warships, so were not named. Life on board was spartan, more so than in the later torpedo boat destroyers, but the young officers and men probably appreciated the less formal discipline and more flexible life compared to that of larger warships.

In some circumstances torpedo boats were to accompany a fleet to sea, attempting to keep up with the bigger ships while their coal lasted. There were even plans for them to be recoaled at immense effort from a larger ship. Their potential might have been considerable in an engagement, but in those peaceful years this did not arise, and if the weather became rough, torpedo boats would be left behind to ride it out to sea anchors, hopefully to return to port under their own steam when it moderated.

In 1896 Britain had forty-three seagoing torpedo boats of from 125-150ft length, compared to France with forty-four and Russia with fifty-five. Surprisingly, Germany owned sixty-four, Italy one hundred and five and Austro-Hungary thirty.

Torpedo boats were also to be used in blockading an enemy port as an "inshore squadron", particularly at night, and for defensively patrolling the approaches to naval anchorages and ports. By then the first class torpedo boats of from 115-27ft were considered best for these duties and Britain owned twenty-six, France sixty-three, Russia six, Germany sixty-one and Italy and Austro-Hungary none. There were smaller boats. Most fleets then owned only four or five second class torpedo boats, except France with eighty-four. The third class or "Vedette" type boats, reckoned to be under 85ft long, were owned in large numbers and many were the largest boats which a battleship or large cruiser could hoist in and carry on board. Most Vedettes were about 52ft long and were not easy to hoist-out or recover in a seaway, as well as being vulnerable to damage when carried on a ship in action.

All these torpedo boat classifications were arbitrary and the larger boats undertook varying duties in exercises or in the few wars in which they were involved.

By 1886 the Admiralty were seriously concerned by the large numbers of French seagoing torpedo boats and particularly at the "Bombe" and "Léger" classes of fast torpedo cruiser or support ships for flotillas: 197ft long, they carried many guns and had a speed of 18 knots.

So the building of British "torpedo catchers", as they were at first called, was commenced. These were well armed with quick-firing guns and also had torpedo tubes. The 550-ton *Rattlesnake* was built at Birkenhead by Laird as a prototype and was completed in 1887, soon followed by two others. Laird's constructed her engines more heavily than the Admiralty specifications and were fined £1,000 for it, but she steamed at 18.5 knots and was mechanically reliable.

After the *Rattlesnake*'s success in the 1888 fleet manoeuvres, which were observed and reported on by a special committee, the use of torpedo boats and the new "torpedo gunboats", as the *Rattlesnake* type became known, was better appreciated. The "Alarm" class which followed

(Plates 119 and 120) had the forward freeboard raised. Three classes of torpedo gunboats were built for Britain during the short vogue for the type and all were failures as torpedo catchers. These were soon relegated to fleet scouting, despatch duties or gunboat service and were displaced by the fast and slightly more seaworthy "torpedo boat destroyers" (the name later shortened to "destroyers"), which first appeared in 1893 with the British *Havock* and *Hornet* which achieved 27 knots.

This further type arose from urgent need to counter the growing speed of French torpedo boats which were steaming at 24 knots, with one builder anticipating reaching 30 in a short time. Failure of the torpedo gunboat type meant that an entirely new concept was necessary to hunt and destroy fast seagoing torpedo boats and in 1893 Yarrow's and the Naval Constructor's department collaborated to produce the design for the *Havock*.

The *Havock* and *Hornet* participated in the manoeuvres of 1894 and were regarded as "seagoing torpedo boats". The following year's manoeuvres were the first in which destroyers operated as a distinct type, which by 1896 was accepted as having replaced the torpedo boat as a serious seagoing torpedo attack craft, though their original function remained for some years as the outrunning and outfighting of torpedo boats by superior gun armament.

More British builders joined in: Thornycroft, Doxford, Fairfield, Palmer, White, Earle and others, and forty-two 27-knot destroyers were designed and built for the British Navy by 1895 *(Plates 122,123,124)*. Fast and sophisticated torpedo craft were also being built for foreign navies by Normand of Le Havre, Schichau at Elbing in Germany, Herreshoff at Newport, Rhode Island, and other specialist yards. Many small navies bought them as they offered good offensive potential for comparatively small outlay.

When the French-built destroyer *Forban* and the British-built Russian *Sokol* reached 31 knots on trials, the British Admiralty decided that all future British destroyers must be capable of 30 knots, though the boats would never reach this in service trim. Rapid development continued, with speeds increasing in succeeding classes but with propulsion still by high-speed steam reciprocating engines and ever-improving boilers. Gradually length increased and the torpedo armament became more important as the destroyers became both hunter and hunted in naval manoeuvres.

In 1899 Hawthorn, Leslie and Co on the Tyne launched the *Viper* as the first destroyer to have steam turbine machinery, developed by the Parsons Co and producing 10,000 HP to achieve 31 knots.

By 1906 one hundred and fifty-one destroyers had been built for the British Navy *(Plate 125)*, including thirty-four of the "River" class, then coming into service. These were 225ft long and steamed at a realistic 26 knots, fully armed and stored. Armament of one 12-pounder and five 6-pounders, backed by two torpedo tubes, made them formidable little ships and the turtle-backed foredeck was replaced in this class by a

230

113   TORPEDO BOAT NO 27, BRITISH FIRST CLASS TORPEDO BOAT 1886

forecastle, making them better sea boats.

For the next fifty years the destroyer was a constantly developing warship type, often associated with high speed, light construction and plenty of action. In 1906, when this review closes, torpedo boats of substantial size were still being built *(Plate 126)* and most of the torpedo craft of the 1890's and afterwards survived to serve in the 1914-18 war.

Torpedo Boat No 27

BRITISH FIRST CLASS TORPEDO BOAT 1886 *Plate 113*

Built	John I. Thornycroft and Co, Chiswick
Laid down	1886
Launched	1886
Completed	1886
Dimensions	*Length* 127ft 6in
	Breadth 12ft 6in
	Draught 6ft 2in
Displacement	60 tons
Machinery	Single screw
	One triple-expansion engine by builders
	IHP = 600 = 21 knots
Bunkers	Coal. About 15 tons
Armament	One 3-pounder quick-firer
	Two 1-inch Nordenfelt machine-guns
	Four 14-inch torpedo tubes. Two forward and two amidships
Complement	15

Torpedo boat *No 27* was a first class boat of a type numbered from 25-9 – all built by Thornycroft.

The design was intended to achieve improved seaworthiness and speed; 21 knots was very fast in 1886, achieved with reciprocating steam engines.

Considerations of attack dictated low freeboard and minimal deck erections, resulting in a poorly-protected bridge, though a shelter was provided for the after wheel immediately forward of a binnacle. The two forward torpedo tubes are visible but the after pair are screened by dodgers. These long, narrow and shallow-draught hulls slid thorough smooth water with little fuss, but were very wet in a seaway.

This boat was later renumbered *027* and served in the Portsmouth local defence flotillas during World War I with her sisters *Nos 026* and *028*. *No 029* went through the war at the Cape of Good Hope station; a long voyage for so small a craft, which must have been towed out.

No 027 was sold in November 1919 to be scrapped.

Torpedo Boat No 57

BRITISH FIRST CLASS TORPEDO BOAT 1886 *Plate 114*

Built	John I. Thornycroft and Co, Chiswick
Laid down	1886
Launched	1886
Completed	1886
Dimensions	*Length* 127ft 6in
	Breadth 12ft 6in
	Draught 6ft 2in
Displacement	60 tons
Machinery	Single screw
	One triple-expansion engine by builders
	IHP = 700 = 21 knots
Bunkers	Coal. About 15 tons
Armament	Two 1-inch Nordenfelt machine-guns
	Four 14-inch diameter torpedo tubes. Two forward and two aft
Armament as guard boat	Two 3-pounder quick-firers. No tubes
Complement	15

No 57 was one of a class of twenty boats built by Thornycroft at Chiswick during 1886. Fifty-one first class torpedo boats were built that year for the British Navy.

Her hull dimensions and form were almost identical to that of *No 27* *(Plate 113)* and propulsion remained single-screw, with steam reciprocating engine, but horsepower had risen to 700 for the same speed of 21 knots, indicating need for reserve power to sustain speed.

Revised boiler arrangements resulted in a single funnel, with deck arrangement generally as for the earlier boats. A topmast was fitted for signalling at sea.

Only two torpedo tubes are visible in this photograph, though four are stated to be carried. The guns appear to be Nordenfelt machine-guns but when serving as guard boats these craft mounted two 3-pounder quick-firers instead of torpedo tubes.

This class were regarded as good boats for their size. *No 57* was renumbered *057* when later torpedo boats came into service during the early 1900's. She served in the Portsmouth local defence flotillas during World War I and was sold to be scrapped in November 1919.

114   TORPEDO BOAT NO 57, BRITISH FIRST CLASS TORPEDO BOAT *1886*

115 TORPEDO BOAT NO 95, BRITISH FIRST CLASS TORPEDO BOAT 1894

116   TORPEDO BOAT NO 95, BRITISH FIRST CLASS TORPEDO BOAT 1894

Torpedo Boat No 95

BRITISH FIRST CLASS TORPEDO BOAT 1894 *Plates 115 and 116*

Built	John Samuel White, East Cowes, Isle of Wight
Laid down	1893
Launched	1894
Completed	1894
Dimensions	*Length* 140ft
	Breadth 15ft 6in
	Draught 6ft
Displacement	130 tons
Machinery	Single screw
	One vertical triple-expansion engine by G.E. Belliss & Co
	IHP = 2,000 = 23.2 knots
Bunkers	Coal. 25 tons
Armament	Three 3-pounder quick-firers. One on top of conning tower
	Three 18-inch diameter torpedo tubes. One in bow. Two on deck
Complement	18

Torpedo boat *No 95* was one of three boats numbered *94-6*, designed and built by John Samuel White in 1894, the year after the first torpedo boat destroyers had appeared. Her size and arrangement may be compared with the early "destroyer" *Conflict*, designed and built by White the same year *(Plate 122)*.

Torpedo boat freeboard had increased with size, and stern shape was altering to improve steering before a sea. Armament had increased to three 3-pounder guns and three 18-inch tubes, one of which was mounted in the stem, with headroom for its crew and space for its machinery provided by the turtle-backed foredeck, which also aided seaworthiness and had the small conning tower at its after end. The dramatic rise in horsepower to 2,000 can be compared with that of Torpedo boats *Nos 27* and *57*, which steamed at 21 knots. *No 95* gained 2.2 knots for a further 1,300 horsepower.

Plate 115 shows *No 95* fitting out in the Medina River at Cowes, with part of White's yard in the background. *Plate 116* shows a stern view and the after steering position and graceful appearance of this class, which resembled some German boats by Schichau. A spritsail barge sails downstream past East Cowes waterfront.

Torpedo boat *No 95* served at Gibraltar throughout World War I as a local patrol and guard vessel. She was sold in November 1919 to be broken up.

Torpedo Boat No 109

BRITISH FIRST CLASS TORPEDO BOAT 1902 *Plate 117*

Built	John I. Thornycroft and Co, Chiswick
Laid down	1901
Launched	July 1902
Completed	1902
Dimensions	*Length between perpendiculars* 166ft
	Breadth 17ft 3in
	Draught 8ft 5in
Displacement	200 tons
Machinery	Single screw
	One triple-expansion engine by builders
	IHP = 2,900 = 25 knots
Bunkers	Coal. 42 tons
Armament	Three 3-pounder quick-firers
	Three 18-inch torpedo tubes. Two forward and one aft
Complement	32

Torpedo boat *No 109* was the first ship of a class of five built by Thornycroft at their yard on the Thames.

By 1902 the development of the torpedo boat destroyer had relegated the role of torpedo boats in major navies to the defence of naval harbours and anchorages, and to coastal patrol work. The larger destroyers early assumed the torpedo boats' original task of attacking enemy ships at sea. However, torpedo boats continued to be built for several years and *No 109* showed development from *No 95 (Plates 115 and 116)*. A bow torpedo tube was not fitted in these later boats due to the difficulty in maintaining its watertightness in a sea. A pair of tubes were mounted abaft the bridge, protected by the turtle-back deck and covered with canvas coats against the spray which constantly swept these small craft at sea. The scalloped awning aft adds a bizarre touch.

No 109 served throughout World War I in the local defence flotillas at the Nore and at Portsmouth. She was sold in March 1920 to be broken up.

Torpedo Boat No 116

BRITISH FIRST CLASS TORPEDO BOAT 1904 *Plate 118*

Built	John Samuel White and Co, East Cowes, Isle of Wight
Laid down	1903
Launched	1903

237   *117   TORPEDO BOAT NO 109, BRITISH FIRST CLASS TORPEDO BOAT 1902*

118 TORPEDO BOAT NO 116, BRITISH FIRST CLASS TORPEDO BOAT 1904

Completed	1904
Dimensions	*Length* 165ft
	Breadth 17ft 7in
	Draught 8ft 9in
Displacement	197 tons
Machinery	Single screw
	One triple-expansion engine
	IHP = 2,900 = 25 knots
Bunkers	Coal. 28 tons
Armament	Three 3-pounder quick-firers
	Three 18-inch diameter torpedo tubes
Complement	32

Torpedo boat *No 116* was one of four boats built by White and numbered *114-17*. She is shown here at sea with a flotilla of similar craft on manoeuvres. The arrangement differed from *No 109 (Plate 117)* in having a larger bridge.

Torpedo boats and destroyers first took part in large scale manoeuvres with the Channel fleet during the summer of 1901. The fleet was divided into two "fleets" for the exercises. Each included many battleships and cruisers and fleet "X" had twenty-eight destroyers and ten first class torpedo boats. Fleet "B" included thirty-two destroyers and ten first class torpedo boats. The object of the manoeuvres was for one fleet to disrupt trade in the Channel and the other to protect it.

The results were disappointing. Umpires judged that fleet "X" torpedo craft had "sunk" one fleet "B" cruiser for the "loss of" six destroyers and the "disablement" of six more. Fleet "B" were judged to have "sunk" a fleet "X" cruiser but to have "lost" six destroyers and five torpedo boats; with ten destroyers and two torpedo boats disabled and Torpedo boat *No 81* actually sunk during the exercise. The destroyer *Viper* was also stranded and lost during the manoeuvres.

The rigorous conditions and results indicated that the potential of torpedo craft in contemporary warfare had been overestimated.

A feature of the design of Torpedo boats *Nos 114-17* was that all the principal parts of the engines were standardised and interchangable and spares, including a set of main cylinders, were carried for them as a class, improving the boats' reliability and speeding repair.

Torpedo boat *No 116* served throughout World War I and in 1920 was amongst the three steam torpedo boats remaining in the Royal Navy. She was sold to be scrapped before 1924.

Circe

BRITISH TORPEDO GUNBOAT 1892 *Plate 119*

Built	Royal Naval dockyard, Sheerness
Launched	June 1892
Completed	1892
Dimensions	*Length* 230ft
	Breadth 27ft
	Draught 8ft 9in mean
Displacement	810 tons
Machinery	Twin screw
	Two vertical triple-expansion engines by builders
	Four marine locomotive type boilers
	IHP natural draught = 2,500 = 17.75 knots
	IHP forced draught = 3,500 = 19.25 knots
	Re-engined and new boilers by Fairfield, 1903
	IHP = 5,700 = 20.8 knots
Bunkers	Coal. 100 tons normal. 160 tons maximum
Endurance	2,500 miles at 10 knots
Armament	Two 4.7-inch quick-firers
	Four 3-pounders
	One machine-gun
	Five 18-inch diameter torpedo tubes. One bow. Two pairs amidships. Carried six torpedoes
Armour	*Gun shields* 4½-inch
Complement	91

The *Circe* was one of the "Alarm" class of torpedo gunboats which included the *Alarm, Hebe, Jason, Leda, Niger, Onyx* and *Renard*. The similar *Speedy* had three funnels and other differences.

These were the second class of torpedo gunboats to be built for the British Navy, following the earlier "Gossamer" class of 1888 to 1890, but suffered from slow speed like their predecessors, which made the type ineffective in their conceived role. A correspondent covering the naval manoeuvres of 1893 wrote of the torpedo gunboats involved: "The majority of these vessels are complete failures. They are a perpetual source of anxiety to the commander of a seagoing fleet . . . They are increasingly breaking down and their speed at sea constantly falls short of their nominal speed on paper by as much as 30-40 per cent." However, they were excellent sea boats; the *Gleaner* crossed the Bay of Biscay in a gale which caused the battleship *Resolution* to return to harbour, and the *Speedwell* performed well with the Channel fleet.

By 1895 torpedo gunboats were being used as scout cruisers in fleet manoeuvres, as it was realised that their potential as catchers of torpedo boats was limited. Their speed continued to fall with age, and the *Circe*

119   CIRCE, BRITISH TORPEDO GUNBOAT 1892

120   JASON, BRITISH TORPEDO GUNBOAT 1892

was one of several which were re-engined and re-boiled about 1903, increasing the speed to over 20 knots.

By 1913 most of the remaining ships of the class were fitted for minesweeping. *Circe*, *Hebe* and *Leda* survived World War I as minesweepers and were sold to be broken up in 1919-20.

Jason

BRITISH TORPEDO GUNBOAT 1892 *Plate 120*

Built	The Naval Construction and Armaments Co, Barrow-in-Furness
Laid down	1891
Launched	May 1892
Completed	1892
Dimensions	*Length* 230ft
	Breadth 27ft
	Draught 8ft 9in mean
Displacement	810 tons
Machinery	Twin screw
	Two vertical triple-expansion engines by builders
	Marine locomotive type boilers
	Original IHP = 3,540 = 19.25 knots
	Re-engined and re-boiled by Fairfield Co, 1903
	IHP natural draught = 2,500 = 17.5 knots
	IHP forced draught = 5,700 = 20.8 knots
Bunkers	Coal. 100 tons
Endurance	2,500 miles at 10 knots
Armament	Two 4.7-inch quick-firers
	Four 3-pounder quick-firers
	One machine-gun
	Three 18-inch diameter torpedo tubes. Six torpedoes carried
Armour	*Gun shields* 4½-inch
Complement	85

The *Jason* was one of the "Alarm" class torpedo gunboats, a sister ship to the *Circe (Plate 119)*. However, she differed from the others by having double rudders for improved manoeuvring. She cost £49,253 to build.

This photograph, taken in 1897, shows the *Jason*'s open bridge with its curious wing lookout shelters, the torpedo tubes amidships and the flying bridge connecting the forecastle with the after deckhouse – necessary in a seaway, as these ships were very lively and had little freeboard aft. The tall buff funnels and narrow beam gave them a remarkably yacht-like appearance and were some of the handsomest warships ever built.

The *Jason* spent her whole life in British waters. She was re-engined and re-boiled by the Fairfield Co in 1903 and, like most of her sisters which survived, became a minesweeper in 1909. She was mined off the west coast of Scotland during 1917 and was lost.

Hazard

BRITISH TORPEDO GUNBOAT 1894 *Plate 121*

Built	Royal Naval dockyard, Pembroke
Launched	February 1894
Completed	1894
Dimensions	*Length* 250ft
	Breadth 30ft 6in
	Draught 9ft mean. 13ft maximum
Displacement	1,070 tons
Machinery	Twin screw
	Two vertical inverted triple-expansion engines by Fairfield S.B. and E. Co,
	Four marine locomotive type boilers
	IHP natural draught = 2,500 = 17 knots
	IHP forced draught = 3,500 = 18.5 knots
Bunkers	Coal. 100 tons normal. 160 tons maximum
Endurance	2,500 miles at 10 knots
Armament	Two 4.7-inch quick-firers
	Four 6-pounders
	One machine-gun
	Five 18-inch diameter torpedo tubes. One bow. All above water. Carried six torpedoes
Armour	*Gun positions* 4½-inch
Complement	115

The *Hazard* was one of the "Dryad" class of first class torpedo gunboats built between 1893-4 and including the *Dryad*, *Halcyon*, *Harrier*, *Hazard* and *Hussar*. These were intended as improvements on the "Alarm" type of 1892-3 and the "Gossamer" type of 1890. Unfortunately their speed was slightly less than the earlier boats and gradually deteriorated. As they were useless for catching torpedo boats they were used as scout cruisers in fleet manoeuvres and were probably regarded as little better than despatch vessels in ordinary fleet duties.

The poop of these craft gave them an unusual appearance, though it made them better sea boats than their predecessors.

The *Hazard* cost £74,070 to build. By 1906 her speed had fallen to about 17 knots and she was acting as an improvised depot ship for a small flotilla of the early British submarines. In 1913, when this photograph was taken, she was relegated to secondary duties and by then most

121 HAZARD, BRITISH TORPEDO GUNBOAT 1894

122   CONFLICT, BRITISH TORPEDO BOAT DESTROYER 1894

of the class were used for minesweeping, having a stern gallows fitted to handle sweep gear.

In 1918 the *Hazard* had again become a depot ship and was sunk in collision off Portland, that year.

The remainder of the class were sold during 1919-20 to be scrapped.

Conflict

BRITISH TORPEDO BOAT DESTROYER 1894 *Plate 122*

Built	John Samuel White, East Cowes
Launched and completed	December 1894
Dimensions	*Length* 205ft 6in
	Breadth 20ft
	Draught 6ft
Displacement	270 tons
Machinery	Two screws
	Vertical triple-expansion engines by Maudslay
	White-Forster type boilers
	IHP = 4,370 = 27.2 knots
Bunkers	Coal. 60 tons
Armament	One 12-pounder quick-firer. On bridge
	Five 6-pounder quick-firers. On deck
	Two single 18-inch diameter torpedo tubes. On deck
Complement	53

The *Conflict* was the prototype of a class which had a contract speed of 27 knots and included the *Teazer* and *Wizard,* also built by White, and the *Zebra* built by the Thames Ironworks Co.

Beken's photograph shows the *Conflict* during builders' trials in 1894, with a trials crew of shipyard employees and the ship in charge of the yard skipper and a pilot. The tattered Union Jack at the masthead was in typical disdain for flag etiquette, but expressed the bravado which the destroyer type engendered amongst shipbuilders and engineers as well as the crews. Shipyards rivalled each other to build and engine the fastest boat, and gains of half a knot on trials were celebrated as major achievements leading to further orders.

A spurting engine-room discharge hints at the power pulsing below in the lightly-built hull and this was a serious design problem in early destroyers where the tremendous vibration of high-speed reciprocating engines was difficult to disperse. Eventually it was relieved by balancing the engines and was further reduced with the introduction of turbine propelling machinery.

The length, fine lines and lightness were emphasised by the unclut-

tered deck of this incomplete destroyer. Hull construction was of riveted steel and the lines of priming paint over the rivet points in way of frames and plate seams emphasised her shape. Soon her armament, equipment and stores would be on board and she would be ready for commissioning.

During 1913 the 27-knot destroyers became reclassified as the "A" type and were fitted with wireless at the time. Colouring remained black until grey became universal in 1916.

The *Conflict* served on patrol duty throughout World War I as a unit of the Portsmouth local defence forces. She was sold in May 1920 to be broken up at Milford Haven by Thomas Ward.

Starfish

BRITISH TORPEDO BOAT DESTROYER 1895 *Plate 123*

Built	The Barrow Shipbuilding Co
Launched	1894
Completed	1895
Dimensions	*Length* 195ft
	Breadth 20ft 6in
	Draught 7ft 3in. 8ft 5in deep-loaded
Displacement	265 tons
Machinery	Two screws
	Vertical triple-expansion engines by the builders
	Blechynden type boilers
	IHP = 4,000 = 27.8 knots
Bunkers	Coal. 60 tons
Armament	One 12-pounder quick-firer. On bridge
	Five 6-pounder quick-firers. On deck
	Two single 18-inch diameter torpedo tubes. On deck
Complement	45

By 1893 there was concern regarding the large numbers and speed of French torpedo boats which were achieving about 24 knots, with one noted builder anticipating reaching 30 knots before long. The failure of the British "torpedo catchers" indicated that an entirely new concept would be required to hunt and destroy torpedo boats and during 1893 the Naval Construction Corps combined with Yarrow and Co of Poplar, on the Thames, to design HMS *Havock*, the first "torpedo boat destroyer" – a term later shortened to the now familiar "destroyer".

The *Havock* was 180ft long, 18ft 6in beam and drew 7ft 6in. She displaced 240 tons and had reciprocating steam engines developing 3,000 IHP to achieve a speed of 26.7 knots. Her prime object was to catch and outgun torpedo boats and she mounted one 12-pounder and three

123   STARFISH, BRITISH TORPEDO BOAT DESTROYER 1895

6-pounder guns, besides three torpedo tubes. Almost simultaneously John I. Thornycroft, further up the Thames at Chiswick, built the similar *Hornet* which made 27.3 knots. The *Havock* and *Hornet* participated in the 1894 manoeuvres, where they were regarded as seagoing torpedo boats. Next year " torpedo boat destroyers" took part as a distinct type and by 1896 were accepted as having ousted the torpedo boat as a serious seagoing torpedo carrier, though their primary function was still to hunt torpedo boats.

The success of the *Havock* and *Hornet* caused forty-two destroyers of their general type to be ordered, all designed for a speed of 27 knots. Although this was obtained on trials, usually by running the boats in light condition, it dropped in service where 13 knots was an economical speed.

The *Starfish* was one of a group of eight destroyers built during 1894-5, the last of the "27 knotters" as they became known. Her sisters included the *Opossum, Ranger, Skate, Spitfire, Sturgeon, Sunfish* and *Swordfish*. The builders were Hawthorn, Leslie and Co, Elswick, and Vickers. Though nominally sister ships, each differed in detail.

The *Starfish* served in home waters where destroyers operated singly or in small groups until they were formed into flotillas in 1905. Usually they worked from bases on the Channel coast and occasionally from the east coast. Most of *Starfish*'s life was spent in the Channel and this photograph shows her dashing past Cowes at about 15 knots.

The painting of turtle-back decks white, to contrast with the black hull, was fashionable for a time in early destroyers, where attitudes to many naval traditions were flexible as the ships were so small. Spray dodgers were rigged abaft the bulwarks sheltering the forward 6-pounders, which was where waves broke on board in a seaway.

A second steering position to be used in action was arranged aft behind a splinter screen. The rudders were hung from the stern, projecting beyond the hull, and sponsoned guards were built out to protect them. A gunners' platform was built around the after 6-pounder.

In 1901 the *Starfish* was experimentally equipped with a spar torpedo-boom as an anti-submarine weapon in those days before depth bombs. This was an explosive charge on the end of a spar projecting below water before the bow, where, hopefully, it would strike a submarine being attacked near the surface. During 1905 the *Starfish* was experimentally fitted with torpedo tubes of aluminium construction in an attempt to reduce the weight of tubes for new destroyers. However, the rapid corrosion prevented their adoption and the tubes were removed.

The *Starfish* was sold during 1911 to be scrapped.

Snapper

BRITISH TORPEDO BOAT DESTROYER 1895 *Plate 124*

Built	Earle and Co, Hull
Launched and completed	1895
Dimensions	Length 200ft
	Breadth 19ft 6in
	Draught 5ft 6in
Displacement	270 tons
Machinery	Two shafts
	Vertical triple-expansion engines by the builders
	Yarrow type boilers
	IHP = 4,500 = 27.9 knots
Bunkers	Coal. 60 tons
Armament	One 12-pounder quick-firer. On bridge
	Five 6-pounder quick-firers. On deck
	Two single 18-inch diameter torpedo tubes. On deck
Complement	53

The *Snapper* and her sister ship *Salmon* were the thirty-first and thirty-second torpedo boat destroyers to be built for the British fleet and were completed only two years after the first – HMS *Havock*, built in 1893.

Already length had grown from the 180ft of the *Havock* to the 200ft of the *Snapper* and would continue to increase in the search for speed and the need for greater displacement to carry larger guns and more torpedo tubes, and in the effort to achieve greater endurance and improved seakeeping. They soon surpassed the torpedo boats they were conceived to destroy, and their forerunners, the "torpedo catchers" and in a rapidly developing pattern of battle fleet warfare and submarine attack their role widened to assume that of fleet and later convoy screen, which they shared with cruisers, besides routine patrol duties.

Although photographed at anchor, the impression of speed is inherent in the *Snapper*'s fine bow and narrow hull with almost straight sheer. Somehow in that cramped shell fifty-three men lived in great discomfort, well deserving their "hard lying" money paid to the crews of destroyers and torpedo boats for that reason.

The 12-pounder gun was mounted on the tiny bridge above the conning tower, which was flanked by two 6-pounders behind bulwarks at the after end of the turtle-back deck designed in unsuccessful attempt to deflect seas from sweeping aft. Three other 6-pounders were mounted amidships and aft but her two on-deck torpedo tubes were her most deadly weapons.

The *Snapper*'s four-funnel arrangement was dictated by need for funnel draught and boiler-room arrangements. Too seldom are the demands of the

124   SNAPPER, BRITISH TORPEDO BOAT DESTROYER 1895

machinery on the destroyers' crews mentioned in the many books on their development: tiny stokeholds operating with coal-fired furnaces, and lightweight reciprocating engines working at high revolutions in an engine-room suffocating with a haze of lubricating oil and lagging fumes. The boisterous excitement of a watch on deck at speed was restful by comparison with conditions of the engineers and stokers.

After serving in home waters on the south and east coasts, the *Snapper* was sold during 1911 to be broken up.

Myrmidon

BRITISH TORPEDO BOAT DESTROYER 1901 *Plate 125*

Built	Palmers Co, Jarrow-on-Tyne
Launched	May 1900
Completed	1901
Dimensions	*Length* 215ft
	Breadth 20ft 10in
	Draught 6ft 10in
Displacement	335 tons
Machinery	Two shafts
	Vertical triple-expansion engines by the builders
	Reed type boilers
	IHP = 6,500 = 30.2 knots
Bunkers	Coal. 91 tons
Armament	One 12-pounder. On bridge
	Five 6-pounder quick-firers
	Two single 18-inch diameter torpedo tubes. On deck
Complement	62

The speeds of foreign torpedo boats and destroyers continued to increase and during 1895 it was thought necessary for the British Navy to order numbers of destroyers capable of 30 knots. Although this does not now seem great, it was extreme speed by contemporary standards. However, it was only obtained on trials or during occasional spurts in service; the effects on boilers, engines and crew being considerable. This potential engendered a spirit of zestful dash about destroyer service which clung to it until they became as large as light cruisers and had long lost the old "hard lying" associations.

The *Myrmidon* and her sisters *Kangaroo*, *Peterel*, *Spiteful* and *Syren* were built on the Tyne by Palmers. Most British destroyers were in home waters until 1905, except for a few sent to the Mediterranean and the China station. The *Myrmidon* and *Kangaroo* steamed out to Malta for service with the Mediterranean fleet, returning for many years' service with home flotillas.

In this photograph the *Myrmidon* is probably running at full speed, judging by the spray feathering up her lean bows and the wake roaring astern. Ventilation cowls had increased in area to gulp greater quantities of air into the boiler- and engine-rooms.

Although four funnels were fitted, the amidships pair were combined in one casing and these destroyers had special funnel caps to prevent spray entering the space between the uptake and the outer casing. As they had four funnels this class were given the distinctive letter "B" in the 1913 reclassification of destroyers.

The *Myrmidon* and *Kangaroo* served in the Dover patrol during World War I and the *Myrmidon* was run down and sunk by the merchant ship *Hamborn* during March 1917. All her sisters survived the war and were sold during 1919-20 to be scrapped.

Spider

BRITISH COASTAL DESTROYER 1906 *Plate 126*

Built	John Samuel White, East Cowes, Isle of Wight
Laid down	1906
Launched	December 1906
Completed	1906
Dimensions	*Length overall* 175ft
	Length between perpendiculars 167ft
	Breadth 17ft 6in
	Draught 5ft 10in
Displacement	235 tons
Machinery	Triple screw
	Three turbines
	HP = 3,750 = 26.5 knots
Bunkers	20 tons
Endurance	1,000 miles
Armament	Two 12-pounder quick-firers
	Three 18-inch torpedo tubes
Complement	35

By 1905 the roles of the smaller destroyer and the torpedo boat were becoming indistinguishable and the Admiralty naval programme of 1905-6 included a large class of "coastal destroyers" which had the dimensions and speed of the original destroyers such as the *Conflict* or *Snapper (Plates 122 and 124)*.

The *Spider* was one of the first five of the class built by John Samuel White. Numbers 6-10 were by Thornycroft and 11-12 by Yarrow. All were named. White's later built nos 13-16 and 25-8 of this class.

During 1906 the class were reclassified as torpedo boats and were

125   MYRMIDON, BRITISH TORPEDO BOAT DESTROYER 1901

126   SPIDER, BRITISH COASTAL DESTROYER 1906

given numbers, the *Spider* becoming Torpedo boat *No 5*.

She is seen here on trials and represented the development of the torpedo boat into a patrol vessel. Turbine machinery had become general in destroyers since the ill-fated *Viper* of 1899 and was by 1906 being fitted in the smallest classes. The increase of speed to 26.5 knots was achieved at cost of using triple screws and a shaft horsepower of 3,750.

During World War I Torpedo boat *No 5* served in the North Sea patrol flotillas and in the Nore local defence force. She was sold in 1920 to be scrapped.

MISCELLANEOUS CRAFT

Few specialised types of miscellaneous naval vessels needed to be evolved during the period covered by this book.

Royal and official yachts were among the most imposing and were sometimes conveniently rated as "despatch vessels" to justify the expense. Apart from rare state visits, these yachts were used for reviews and other formal occasions enjoyed by major navies during a long period of general peace.

There were still few depot ships, repair vessels, naval support or logistics ships in the modern tradition of a "fleet train". Coal, the vital necessity of contemporary steam warships, was carried by colliers chartered by naval authorities, with the British Admiralty taking up large numbers to supply bunkering facilities around the world. Coaling at sea was practised occasionally in fine weather towards the end of the period, when oil was beginning to be used as supplementary fuel in many fleets. The grimy task of "coaling ship" was made into a competitive evolution whenever possible, with officers and men of most ranks as well as ratings, taking part and working against the clock to fill the bunkers in large ships.

There were naval storeships, but ammunition and other supplies were also often carried in chartered merchant ships, and governments subsidised the construction of some of the large, fast liners so that they could act as armed merchant cruisers in war – though their value here was overrated. Others were earmarked for use as transports. Britain used specially-built ships for Indian trooping (Plate 1). White and buff troopers such as the 7,300-ton *Dufferin* carried British regiments to and from India on their imperial duty, perhaps meeting a battleship bound for the China station during their traverse of the Suez canal.

There were only small numbers of specialised dockyard craft at that time: tugs, mooring vessels, harbour launches, water carriers, ammunition lighters and other ancillaries. Sailing and stationary training ships were familiar sights at most naval ports, and mining launches and old gunboats used as boom defence vessels were often seen exercising. Defensive-mining of British Naval ports came at different times under the authority of the War Office (army) or the Admiralty; an unsatisfactory arrangement leading to inter-service friction.

Boatwork under oars and sail was an everyday part of naval life, as only the largest ships carried steam launches and these were for use of officers and visitors, for guard patrol, for towing ship's boats on exercises or for bringing off numbers of men or quantities of stores (Plate 132).

Sloops and submarines are the only warlike intruders in this section. In the sail and steam navy, sloops were a type of ship between the steam corvette or third class cruiser and the gun vessel. Sloops were much used on foreign service where a British sloop such as the *Racer (Plate 128)* might have to be prepared to participate in operations ranging from crushing a local rebellion or capturing a slave ship, to assisting in a scientific expedition or oceanographic survey work.

The British Navy's first submarines were *Nos 1-5* of the 63ft 4in American-designed "Holland" type, completed during 1902-3 with a single hull and one compartment, including the conning tower. Submerged displacement was 122 tons and only 9 tons of water ballast was used, so any defect allowing a sudden inrush of water meant disaster. This type were propelled by petrol engines and speed on the surface was 10 knots. Diving time was from 15-20 minutes and armament was one bow torpedo tube. Five torpedoes were carried.

The following Admiralty "A" class submarines had a 100ft long hull, similar to the "Holland" boats, with a displacement of 180/200 tons. Later "A" class boats were 150ft long and achieved 11 knots on the surface and could motor for 1,000 miles, using petrol engines on the surface and electric motors when submerged. These had two torpedo tubes and were still relatively simple craft (Plate 133). Sub-division of British submarines came with the "E" type of 1910, as size continued to increase. The submarine's potential was not fully realised until the 1914-18 war and development continues to make them the most formidable type of warship.

127 *KAISERADLER, GERMAN DESPATCH VESSEL ROYAL YACHT 1876*

Kaiseradler (ex Hohenzollern)

GERMAN DESPATCH VESSEL/ROYAL YACHT 1876 *Plate 127*

Built	North German Shipbuilding Co, Kiel
Laid down	1875
Launched	July 1876
Completed	1876
Dimensions	*Length* 269ft
	Breadth 32ft 9in
	Draught 13ft 9in mean
Displacement	1,707 tons
Machinery	Paddle-wheels. Single-expansion engine
	IHP = 3,000 = 16 knots
Bunkers	Coal
Sail area	3,560 sq ft. Steadying rig
Armament	Two 3.4-inch guns
Complement	145

The *Kaiseradler* was an iron-hulled paddle-steamer built as the despatch vessel *Hohenzollern*, which was probably a cover for her actual use as the royal yacht. In 1880 she was officially rated as royal yacht and served until the new and larger *Hohenzollern* was completed in 1892, when she was renamed *Kaiseradler*.

During 1904 she became the yacht of the German crown prince and is seen here steaming up Spithead, probably to attend a naval review or to visit Cowes week. This graceful craft was broken up at Danzig in 1912.

Racer

BRITISH SLOOP 1884 *Plate 128*

Built	Royal Naval dockyard, Devonport
Laid down	April 1883
Launched	1884
Completed	1884
Dimensions	*Length* 167ft
	Breadth 32ft
	Draught 14ft mean
Displacement	970 tons
Machinery	Single screw
	Compound engine by Hawthorn, Leslie and Co
	Cylindrical boilers
	IHP = 920 = 11.5 knots
Bunkers	Coal. 150 tons
Endurance	2,300 miles under steam at 10 knots
Armament	*Original*
	Eight 5-inch breech-loaders
	Eight smaller guns
	One torpedo launching carriage
	Alterations 1903
	Armament reduced to two 5-inch breech-loading guns on poop for training purposes
Armour	None

Until the 1890's sloops were used for many of the duties on foreign stations which were later carried out by small cruisers. The type grew out of the steam gun vessel and the *Racer* was one of the six sloops of the "Reindeer" class, laid down during 1882-3 as gun vessels but re-rated as sloops in 1884. The *Racer* and three of her sisters were built at the Royal Naval dockyard, Devonport. She was of composite construction and commissioned in April 1885 to join the Channel fleet, preparatory to sailing for the Cape and West Coast of Africa station. During 1886 she participated in a punitive expedition up the river Niger and in 1887 took part in the defence of Suakin against the dervishes. The West Coast of Africa was an unhealthy station and British warships usually spent only half a commission there, the *Racer* proceeding to the Mediterranean to complete service before paying off. She recommissioned for further service at the Cape, afterwards sailing for the South-East Coast of America station.

During 1894 she paid off into reserve at Devonport but commissioned during 1897 as a tender to the *Britannia*, an old wooden first rate line of battleship lying at Dartmouth with the similar hulk *Hindustan* as training establishments for naval cadets. The still fully rigged *Racer* enabled them to experience sail training. In 1903 the *Britannia* hulks were replaced by a new shore college at Dartmouth and the age of entry for cadets was reduced to twelve-thirteen years, with early training taking place at a new naval college at Queen Victoria's old residence of Osborne, Isle of Wight, before they went on to the *Britannia* at Dartmouth.

The *Racer* was attached to Osborne and remained fully rigged and painted in Victorian colours for some years. Eventually she was reduced to the pole-masted rig shown in the photograph, taken in 1903. A spike bowsprit was retained. She continued attached to Osborne until 1914 but was converted to a salvage ship during the war. From 1920-5 she was engaged in recovering the gold from the White Star liner *Laurentic*, sunk by a mine off Ireland on passage to America.

The *Racer* was sold in 1928 to be broken up.

128   RACER, BRITISH SLOOP 1884

129   MARTIN, BRITISH TRAINING BRIG 1890

130   MARTIN BRITISH TRAINING BRIG 1890

131 PRESIDENTE SARMIENTO, ARGENTINIAN TRAINING SHIP, 1898

Martin

BRITISH TRAINING BRIG 1890 *Plates 129 and 130*

Built	Royal Naval dockyard, Pembroke
Launched	January 1890
Completed	1890
Dimensions	*Length* 105ft
	Breadth 33ft 6in
	Draught 13ft 6in mean
Displacement	508 tons
Rig	Brig
Armament	None
Complement	27 permanent crew, plus 100 boys

The *Martin* was one of several training brigs in service with the Royal Navy at the turn of the century. She and the similar brig *Pilot* were built at Pembroke during 1890. The *Martin*, originally named *Mayflower*, was tender to the moored training ship *St Vincent* at Portsmouth. The *Pilot* was tender to the *Impregnable* and the older brig *Seaflower* to the *Boscawen*. These were the last square-rigged sailing vessels in the Royal Navy and cruised the Channel with boys in training, often in company as a squadron, instilling true seamanship in an age already totally committed to the mechanical warfare of steel and steam.

Plate 129 shows the *Martin* under sail in light airs. *Plate 130* was taken at Plymouth where her boys were manning the yards for a birthday of King Edward VII.

Presidente Sarmiento

ARGENTINIAN TRAINING SHIP 1898 *Plate 131*

Built	Cammell, Laird and Co, Birkenhead
Laid down	1896
Launched	August 1897
Completed	July 1898
Dimensions	*Length between perpendiculars* 265ft
	Breadth 43ft 3in
	Draught 18ft 6in mean. 23ft 3in maximum
Displacement	2,750 tons
Machinery	Single screw. Feathering propeller
	3-cylinder compound engine
	One Niclausse type, one Yarrow type, two cylindrical single-ended type boilers

	IHP trials = 2,800 = 13.5 knots
Bunkers	Coal. 330 tons
Rig	Ship
Armament	*Original*
	Five 4.7-inch quick-firers. 50 calibre
	Two 14-pounder Maxim-Nordenfelt quick-firers
	Two 6-pounder Maxim-Nordenfelt quick-firers
	Two 3-pounder Maxim-Nordenfelt quick-firers
	Two 1-inch Maxim machine-guns
	Two 6-pounder Hotchkiss quick-firers
	Two 3-pounder Hotchkiss quick-firers
	Two Maxim machine-guns
	Two 18-inch diameter torpedo tubes. One in bow. One stern
	Amended by 1920
	Two 4.7-inch quick-firers. 50 calibre
	Two 4-inch
	Two 6-pounders
	Two 3-pounders
	Two 18-inch diameter torpedo tubes
Complement	294 (400 maximum)

The *Presidente Sarmiento* was designed and built as a training ship for the efficient and expanding Argentine Navy, which she served until 1961.

The variety of armament was intended to give a wide range of training with weapons.

She is seen here anchored in Spithead during 1902 on one of her visits to English waters. The bulwarks in way of the starboard 4.7-inch guns are lowered, and studding-sail booms are rigged on the yards. The bow torpedo tube appears incongruous in such a hull but the *Presidente Sarmiento* looks everything a training ship should be.

She was discarded by the Navy in January 1961, has since been preserved at Buenos Aires as a national and cultural monument, and is one of the few surviving warships of the nineteenth century.

Boat's crew of the Austro-Hungarian steam corvette DONAU

ABOUT 1900 *Plate 132*

Although steam and some motor launches were in use by large warships in the early twentieth century, smartness in boat-handling under oars or sails remained the pride of all fleets and good oarsmen were prized in ship's companies. Here seamen of the Austro-Hungarian corvette *Donau*

132   BOAT'S CREW OF THE AUSTRO-HUNGARIAN STEAM CORVETTE DONAU, ABOUT 1900

133   'A' CLASS SUBMARINE, PROBABLY 'A 9' BRITISH 1904

134   ST VINCENT, BRITISH STATIONARY TRAINING SHIP FOR BOYS 1815

pull one of her cutters through the anchorage during a visit to Spithead about 1900.

The men who manned Franz Josef's fleet were a mixture of races from his empire. Generally they had the reputation of being smart natural boatmen, which was not true of all naval seamen. Many were from fishing and coasting families of the Istrian and Dalmatian coasts, accustomed to boat-handling from an early age. Competitive rowing between ships in anchorages and on foreign stations was a feature of naval life in the century of peace following the Napoleonic wars. It promoted fitness and introduced interest in the often mundane work of boating personnel and supplies.

"A" Class Submarine

PROBABLY "A 9" BRITISH 1904 *Plate 133*

Built	Vickers, Barrow-in-Furness
Completed	1904
Dimensions	*Length* 150ft
	Breadth 12ft 9in
	Depth 11ft 6in
Displacement	204 tons submerged. 180 tons surface
Machinery	Single screw
	Wolsey 12-cylinder 550 HP petrol motor (Altered from original 16-cylinder)
	Accumulators = 150 HP
	Speeds 7 knots submerged. 11.5 knots surface
Endurance	1,000 miles
	Submerged 3 hours
Armament	Two bow torpedo tubes
Complement	11

Submarine *A 9* was one of the type numbered from *A 5* to *A 13* built at Barrow during 1903-4. Four earlier "A" type boats were smaller and a subsequent boat, *A 14,* was an experimental boat to the builder's design. All had been preceded by submarines *Nos 1-5* which were "Holland" type boats of American design, only capable of diving to 100 feet. *A 5 – A 13* were to an Admiralty design. They were credited at the time with a surface speed of 16 knots but it seems likely that the speed of 11.5 knots was more realistic.

This photograph shows a pair of "A" class boats running on the surface through the Solent with a large schooner, probably the *Cicely,* racing in the background. The short periscopes, standard compass outside the hull, and canvas "bridge" are prominent features. Photographs of submarines of the time show many of the crew on the hull or conning tower for air, as there was little space or oxygen in those crowded interiors.

Most British submarines have been manned by volunteers and the men who manned these early submarines were amongst the bravest of seamen.

St Vincent

BRITISH STATIONARY TRAINING SHIP FOR BOYS 1815 *Plate 134*

Built	Royal Naval dockyard, Plymouth
Completed	1815
Armament	120 guns

The *St Vincent* was completed at Plymouth dockyard in 1815 as a 120-gun first rate ship of the line. Similar ships were the *Nelson* (1814), *Howe* (1815) and *Britannia* (1820). The *St Vincent* saw little action in a British Navy at peace during the nineteenth century and she spent much time laid up. In 1862 she became a training ship, moored in Portsmouth harbour with a complement of instructors and boys under training as seamen. Similar ships were stationed at Devonport and Portland and although old wooden vessels were readily available and therefore cheap to initiate the service, they were really unsuitable for their purpose, though the atmosphere of masts and yards, painted ports and low deckheads was thought to instil respect for the traditions of the service and was better than the barrack atmosphere of shore establishments used in many countries at the time.

The old *St Vincent* lay off Gosport until 1906. She was later broken up.